The Devil's Brigade

The Devil's Brigade

by Robert H. Adleman
and Colonel
George Walton

NAVAL INSTITUTE PRESS
ANNAPOLIS, MARYLAND

Naval Institute Press
291 Wood Road
Annapolis, MD 21402

First Naval Institute Press paperback edition, 2004

Library of Congress Cataloging-in-Publication Data
Adleman, Robert H., 1919–
        The Devil's Brigade / by Robert H. Adleman and George Walton.–
1st Naval Institute Press pbk. ed.
        p. cm.
        Originally published: Philadelphia : Chilton, 1966.
        ISBN 1-59114-004-8 (alk. paper)
        1. First Special Service Force. 2. World War, 1939–1945–Regimental
histories–United States. 3. World War, 1939–1945–Regimental histories–
Canada. 4. World War, 1939–1945–Campaigns, Italy. I. Walton, George H.
II. Title.
        D769.295.S6A7 2004
        940.54'1273–dc22

                                                        2003044271

Printed in the United States of America on acid-free paper ∞
11 10 09 08 07 06 05 04   9 8 7 6 5 4 3 2 1

Reasonable efforts were made to contact the heirs of Col. George Walton.
Any heirs are encouraged to contact the Naval Institute Press.

For our two redheads

Preface

This dialogue occurred during a conference between Mr. Davis, a representative of the Operations Division, War Department General Staff, Mr. Geoffrey Pyke, and a British officer, Brigadier Duncan, on May 26, 1942, at the Munitions Building, Washington, D.C.

DAVIS: I think these are sacrifice troops. We can't keep them supplied. How will you get them out? They obviously have to get out before the snow comes. I never for one moment carried the thought in my mind that we would succor these troops that are dropped down there.

DUNCAN: Give them food for one month and gas for two hundred fifty miles and when the snow goes, bring them off by sea.

DAVIS: I don't think there will be such a thing. I'd put them
            down as lost troops and willing to pay for it—if they
            accomplish this.

DUNCAN: It's a desperate adventure, all right.

This is a book about a handful of men at war, the idea that
banded them together in combat, and their accomplishments. And,
although a large part of it describes the progress of the First Special
Service Force during the World War II campaign for Italy, it is not
a detailed history of that campaign. It is, instead, an account of what
it was like to conceive the Force, to organize, to lead and to fight for
it on a daily basis.

This is not to say that the exploits of the First Special Service
Force—or, as the Germans dubbed them, "The Devil's Brigade"—
are not worthy of careful, foot-by-foot documentation. Their accomplishments were fantastic considering their numbers were so few. But
that documentation has already been written. Lieutenant Colonel Robert D. Burhans, the man who served as the organization's chief Intelligence officer throughout its brief life, produced a definitive military
chronicle entitled *The First Special Service Force: A War History of
the North Americans, 1942–1944.* The authors of this book are deeply
in his debt because his text has been their indispensable guide.

We were fortunate enough to accumulate an abundance of first-
hand recollections and source material. Thousands of questionnaires

were mailed out and answered by surviving Forcemen or their families. For two years Colonel and Mrs. Walton traveled throughout North America interviewing Forcemen and other individuals whose lives had touched or centered upon Force activities. Countless trips were made to archives which contained information pertinent to this story.

An early determination was made to ignore completely the protective catch phrase, ". . . any resemblance to persons living or dead," etc. Every word here is factual. Every name is that of a living or dead person. Every incident happened in the form in which it is presented.

Our final decision on concept was shaped by one of the letters received in response to the questionnaires. Written by Lieutenant Colonel Robert M. Stuart, it read, in part:

> I'm glad someone is doing a book about the Force. I've always thought there was a lot to be told. What will be hard will be to get the flavor of the Force so that it will come through—for it had its own spice and taste and aroma. I've been in a lot of outfits since—Rangers during the Korean affair, airborne outfits in the States, and on a lot of oddball assignments as a covert intelligence man in Europe and have been mixed up in the Vietnam affair. None of these outfits have had the flair or the spirit or the capability, man for man, of the Force.
>
> We had our screwballs—maybe more than our share. They were at every level in the Force. Screwballs they may have been, but they were damn good screwballs and fighting

screwballs. Frederick had the spark to catch our imaginations and to turn that screwball oddity into what I think was probably as good a fighting outfit, man for man, as any ever produced in the U. S. Army or any other.

I was proud to be a part of the Thugs. We had our share of the selfish and self-seeking, too—but this share was small. And I think we had our share of the cowardly, too—but we had our own ways of taking care of these, ways that the people above the company level usually didn't know or ever find out about, as far as I know. And I might add that I knew of no selfish self-seekers among the enlisted men, either U. S. or Canadian—and this isn't anti-officer bias talking, for I was an officer and have been commissioned ever since. The enlisted men were superb, every damn one of them!

Here, then, is the story of the First Special Service Force, a military unit also known as "The Thugs," "Freddy's Freighters," "The Braves," and, most durably, "The Devil's Brigade." It is told, as nearly as possible, if not in the actual words, at least in the spirit of the men who were there.

It should be repeated again that there is not one undocumented sentence in this book. If it reads as if it were wildly implausible, so was the Devil's Brigade.

The Authors

Philadelphia, Pa. 1966

Acknowledgments

There are many who helped in the preparation of this book. Chief among these are the hundreds of ex-Forcemen who filled out our questionnaires and submitted to our interviews. The listing of their names elsewhere in this volume is our only way of thanking them for their patience and co-operation.

Some individuals, however, must be singled out for the exceptional part they played in the creation of this work.

Tom Allen, our former editor, saw the possibilities in the rough idea which we outlined to him and lost no time in accepting the book for publication by his firm. His understanding, enthusiasm and encouragement places us deeply in his debt.

Bob Burhans, chief Intelligence officer for the Force from its inception to its dissolution, and Orval J. Baldwin, the Force's G-1, have been generous sources of expertise.

Bill Mauldin, correspondent, cartoonist and gentleman made his wonderful cartoons available for our use with only a bow to the needs of copyright. Further, his drawings do more to capture the spirit of the Force than most of the hundreds of thousands of words filed by more conventional correspondents.

Lois C. Aldridge, of the World War II Record Division, National Archives (Alexandria, Va.), has been an indispensable guide during our search through the records.

Igor Weiss, chief librarian at the United States Military Academy at West Point, N.Y., and Miss Katherine Howell, chief librarian at the Wilmington, N.C., Public Library, have been co-operative and helpful far beyond official requirements.

And, finally, our patient and productive secretary, Amy Tressler, deserves our formal appreciation. In addition to doing a first-class job, she also agonized over every word with us.

The list appearing below is that of members of the Force who were either interviewed by the authors or contributed material. Their invaluable help is gratefully acknowledged.

Paul D. Adams
R. B. Aitken
Jack Akehurst
Bernhard K. Alvastad
Orval James Baldwin
Frank M. Barber
Jesse J. Bazemore
R. W. Beckett
William R. Bennett
Lynn A. Bish
John G. Bourne
Jean K. Bricker
A. J. Burdett
Robert D. Burhans
Angus M. Bush
Herbert W. Calvey
L. A. Camber
Salvador L. Canchola
Edward Cannon
Anthony Caprio
James F. Carroll
James E. Chenoweth
Albert G. Christian
Charles P. Cole
John F. Conway
E. C. Cooke
Charles F. Cooke
Percy M. Crichlow
Roy N. Cuff
W. G. Curran
Arnold E. Davis
John R. Dawson
Charles W. Deigman
Anthony V. Deltuva
Dale W. Dilley
Arthur E. Duebner

Robert B. Engle
Emil P. Eschenburg
Rev. Robert Essig
Dr. George Evashwick
Kenneth Fisher
Vincent T. Flynn
Lester F. Forrest
George B. G. Foster
Robert T. Frederick
Frank A. Fryza
Richard B. Fuller
Miss Mary Furiga
Chester Galvas
Mrs. James Garrett
Jacob Gartner
Eugene G. Goetz
Donald Goings
M. H. Goodwin
Walter J. Grabiec
Ben C. Gray
Albert H. Green
Donald J. Green
Ben C. Grey
Charles L. Ham-
  mond, Jr.
Charles M. Hammond
T. H. Harrison
S. T. Hayman
Cleatul L. Heath
Gus Heilman
Richard Hindle
Harry C. Hoffman
Eugene R. Hoppe
J. H. Van Houten
Floyd B. Hunsaker
John A. Izatt

J. G. Jacobson
J. T. Jamieson
Allan H. Jamison
Raymond H. Johnson
F. Johnston
Harold B. Jordan
Charles L. Kennedy
Raymond J. Kirk
Carl Klandl
Howard B. Knox
W. C. Knutson
Louis A. Kubler
John Kures
Merrill J. Kurtzhal
Ralph E. Lacy
Kenneth B. Lavery
Douglas B. Layton
Marcus G. Lee
Conrad Legault
Dan Lemaire
Aurele Levesque
D. W. Libby
Rev. Oliver E. Ligitt
Lewis M. Lindsay
Charles Locke
William Lucci
Fred D. Lyons
Robert R. Mackin
Don MacKinnon
William J. Mahoney
W. Winston Mair
William A. Maki
Edwin T. McCalligan
Eugene V. McCormick
John McKay
H. Keith McLellan

James R. Metzger
Vernon Meyer
Julius S. Milak
Robert G. Millikan
R. S. Minto
J. D. Mitchell
Leo Mitchell
Leo Moffet
Frederick Molson
Rafael P. Montone
L. W. Mountford
D. H. Munro
Jospeh D. Murphy
Robert L. Neal
Arthur C. Neeseman
Graham Neilson
John J. O'Malley
D. M. "Pat" O'Neill
Arvest Ouderkirk
A. W. Ovenden
Getty Page
Bernard J. Panhaskie
William A. Peacock
K. Peevers
Eugene Pelletier

Jasper R. Pennington
Mitchell Peronneali
William A. Pharis
Frederick J. Pike
Francis M. Pope
William A. Pratt
Roger N. Raaen
William T. Rachui
Ralph W. Randall
Dante Raponi
Keith W. Raymond
Major S. Reed
Roger J. Reindl
Finn Roll
Roy G. Rowley
James Ryan
George Sabine
Clarence M. Sample
Howard Schafer
William G. Sheldon
James Shimek
Dr. John Simms
Anthony J. Skomski
Anthony P. Skripac
William E. Slawson

Sheldon C. Sommers
William Squire
Alfred Steffensen
Kendan J. Stone
L. A. Storey
William S. Story
Lewis L. Stuart
Robert M. Stuart
Edward H. Thomas
J. T. Tullock
Adna H. Underhill
Arthur E. Vautour
Stanley C. Waters
Joe C. Walker
Wilson K. Wheatley
Kenneth Wickham
Russell R. Williams
James L. Wines
James S. Wines
Frank S. Wojiechowski
Casimir Yakevitski
Thomas Zabski
Harold Ziegler

Contents

The Devil's Brigade

1

Pyke

April 21, 1942
The civilian concerned is a very odd-looking individual, but talks well and may have an important contribution to make.
—GEORGE C. MARSHALL
Chief of Staff

One of the most original, if unrecognized, figures of the present century.
—THE TIMES OF LONDON
(February, 1948)

The following memorandum was circulated among his key staff members by General George C. Marshall, the head of the American armies:

April 21, 1942

Memorandum for the Deputy Chief of Staff,
A.C. of S. Operations
A.C. of S.

In London, Vice Admiral Lord Louis Mountbatten, the Chief of the newly organized Commando Forces, brought to me personally a man who is deeply interested in the development of a motorsled.

The idea is, with which Mountbatten is warmly in accord, that a considerable area in Europe, especially in Norway and certain Passes out of Italy into Germany are covered with snow for considerable periods of the year varying from 60 days up to 250.

If a snow vehicle, armored, carrying adequate guns and a small crew can be developed, it is possible that it may be used to considerable effect against critical points. They have in mind establishing a glacier base from the air in Norway, from which they could operate against the critical hydroelectric plants on which Germany depends to get out valuable ores. They have in mind the use of these vehicles in sudden raids so as to force German troop concentrations in a wasteful manner in rear of coastal garrisons.

The civilian concerned is to come to this country in the near future, and I would like arrangements to be made for taking him in charge and giving him an opportunity to explain his views and go into the matter of their possible development. He will probably be accompanied by one other civilian. Their feeling is that the development of these vehicles must be carried out in this country because of the inability of industry to manage such a matter hurriedly in England. The sleds should be available next fall. The numbers involved will be determined later but would not exceed 2,000 and probably not more than 500 or 600 as a beginning—which should not mean a serious complication of priorities.

The civilian concerned is a great admirer of Stefansson.* It might be that Stefansson could take him in tow, but it is necessary that some particular officer of ours be designated to go into the matter.

The civilian concerned is a very odd-looking individual, but talks well and may have an important contribution to make.

George C. Marshall
Chief of Staff

* The famous Polar explorer, Vilhjalmur Stefansson, who was at this time working on Arctic warfare for the U. S. Government.

The name of the man whom Lord Louis Mountbatten brought to General Marshall was Geoffrey Nathaniel Pyke.

Mountbatten, a man with a deep respect for creative thinking, had assembled in his London-based headquarters for Combined Operations a coterie of eminent civilian theoreticians. When answers were needed for particularly abstract questions, he figuratively jiggled this brain-pool, and a solution was returned to him. In an amazing number of instances he received productive answers. Sometimes he received answers before he was aware of the existence of a problem.

Pyke was a heartily disliked member of the group. Brilliant but contentious, productive but so personally difficult that he would have taxed the patience of a mummy, this gawky, wild-eyed eccentric drove everyone from him with a continuing cannonade of ideas, impatient criticisms and observations. The fact that so many of Pyke's ideas later became the basis for important advances in education, finance, engineering, and several other wildly disparate fields was of little moment during the frequent periods when the dislike of his fellows flared into loathing.

His associates couldn't stand him . . . not only because of the continuing onslaught on their mental processes, but also because, physically, he was noticeably less than pleasant. He rarely bathed, shaved or cut his hair. He wore spats to eliminate the need for wearing socks. He was jealous, suspicious, and dedicated to the supposition that the rest of mankind was banded against him.

He was also an important man. The *Times* of London later described him as "one of the most original, if unrecognized, figures of the present century." J. D. Bernal, himself considered among the most brilliant men on the faculty of London University, regarded Pyke as "one of the greatest geniuses of his time." In a two-column obituary devoted to him, *Time* magazine referred to Pyke as "Everybody's conscience."

Intensely literate and almost stultifyingly vocal, Pyke's powers of persuasion approached the hypnotic. On one prewar radio broadcast to the British population, he pegged the theme, "The Dynamics of Innovation," into an urgent plea that his fellow Englishmen offer less resistance to new ideas. He gave his audience a series of suggestions illustrating how a currently existing power shortage could be solved by the more intelligent use of human muscles, and the next day the British Broadcasting Company was swamped by volunteers from every part of the country. Just one broadcast in his oddly melodic voice turned this potentially pedestrian subject into a trumpet call.

Pyke was the preposterously unlikely sire of that group of unemotional cutthroats, The Devil's Brigade. His paternity was officially recognized in a letter from Mountbatten dated October 2, 1943, which said, in part:

> You must feel proud to think that the force, the creation of which you originally suggested to me in March 1942, has become such a vital necessity in the coming stage of the war that General Eisenhower and the C-in-C of the Middle East are vying between them to try and obtain the services of this Force, probably the most bold and imaginative scheme of this war, and owing its inception to you. It is still too secret to refer to it in a letter of this nature, but one day I feel that you will be able to look with pride on this child of your imagination." *

Geoffrey Pyke, at one time or another, was a foreign correspondent, the hero of a thrilling wartime escape from a German prison camp, an advertising agent, a financier, an experimental educationalist, a propagandist, a free-lance journalist, an organizer of charities, a statistician, a military tactician, an inventor, an economist, a broadcaster—and, as part of all of these things, a philosopher. He was unknown to the general public primarily because he devoted so much energy to the promotion of his ideas that he gave little thought to any promotion of himself.

Since Pyke's participation in this book ends shortly after his introduction of "Project Plough" to Lieutenant Colonel Robert T. Frederick and the American staff, it is necessary to explain that Pyke died by his own hand shortly after the

* David Lampe, *Pyke: The Unkown Genius* (London: Evans Bros., 1959).

*   4

end of World War II. At the time, he was attempting to rationalize problems which dealt with the basic laws of the Universe. He considered it his duty to establish a set of radical rules to govern certain concepts of time and space. He was agonized by the conviction that no study or survey which rested upon the principles of time could be accurate without an understanding of time itself. Without further detail, it must be noted that no human being, not even Albert Einstein, has been able to reduce these matters to an equation. Some learned persons who were privy to Pyke's preoccupation with this problem have inferred that his death was the result of his exasperated impatience with the infinite.

Geoffrey Nathaniel Pyke was born in 1894. His father was Lionel Edward Pyke, a descendant of Dutch Jews who had settled in England several centuries before. His mother was a strong-minded woman who, after the death of Lionel Pyke at the age of forty-four, surprisingly announced that Geoffrey would be sent to Wellington . . . a place where most of the boys were the sons of professional military officers, and which specialized in sending its graduates to Sandhurst, Britain's West Point.

A tall, gangling, painfully shy boy, his arrival struck an unpleasantly exotic note to the rest of the student body. Dressed in relics from his father's closet, and introduced to those around by his noticeably erratic mother, there was no more possibility of his being accepted and assimilated at this school than there would be later by the planners at the Pentagon. His ungainly appearance coupled with the news of his mother's catalogue of instructions to the authorities were all that his schoolmates needed to convince them that here was fair game for ruthless hazing. They made Pyke's life at Wellington pure hell . . . a condition that prevailed for two years before he withdrew and entered Pembroke College at Cambridge in order to read law.

When the First World War erupted, Pyke, who felt that he had had enough of the military mentality at Wellington to last him for his lifetime, decided to become a newspaper correspondent. He began as the Copenhagen-based correspondent for Reuters, but was promptly dismissed when the German ambassador protested that his presence constituted a breach of Danish neutrality. And, besides, his reports on military movements in the area were infinitely too precise.

He returned to London and began canvassing the editorial offices on Fleet Street announcing to all who would listen that he was among the world's greatest reporters and that any journal which employed him would enjoy a commanding lead over its competitors. As proof, he cited the German ambassador's unease at his accurate Danish observations.

Finally, at the *Daily Chronicle,* he found a young editor who showed signs of being impressed by his theme that the best news reports could be originated directly from the enemy capital.

"Suppose you get to Berlin, Mr. Pyke," asked the editor, "how will you get your dispatches back to us?"

Pyke, without the slightest idea of how he might accomplish this, smiled so condescendingly that the editor was impressed into abandoning this line of questioning. He put Pyke on, adding that he would not be responsible for anything but Pyke's expenses, a statement which included a blanket disclaimer of responsibility for Pyke's safety.

So Pyke, taking the preliminary precaution of buying a forged American passport to facilitate his entry through Sweden, went to Germany. He was captured by the police six days after reaching Berlin because of his airy unconcern with the need to hide the purpose of his visit. The Germans obviously didn't know what to make of this strange young man who persisted in lecturing his warders on military tactics, so he spent the next four months in solitary confinement.

Pyke made the most of his time. Denied writing materials, he devoted his days to mentally solving mathematical problems and to sharpening his powers of deductive reasoning . . . a skill which later became the basis for his entire existence.

Finally, in 1915, he was taken to Ruhleben, an immense civilian internment camp, where, with 300 other men, he shared a stable.

That winter was a grueling physical one for Pyke. He contracted blood poisoning and, on several occasions, food poisoning. He almost died after a bout with double pneumonia. Medical attention was withheld from him during all these sicknesses. But he pulled through. Although the physical privations left him gaunt and wasted, his mind was sharper than ever.

He began to think of escape.

His first step was to recruit a German-speaking fellow prisoner named Edward Falk. He told Falk that he had made a detailed study of the prison-camp schedule and had evolved the perfect escape plan. Since, invariably, all breakouts were attempted at night, he and Falk would simply stroll away in the bright sunlight, walk the 140 miles to the seacoast, there get a boat and row to safety.

Falk's first reaction was that he was insane, but he was no more immune to Pyke's powers of persuasion than any of the businessmen, high governmental officials and generals who later came under his spell.

So, one day, Pyke and Falk, walked through the compound engaged in a conversation which was apparently so absorbing that they took no notice of the desultorily growled commands by the guards that they get back to their own quarters. Walking and talking with deep animation, the very tall Pyke and the very short Falk reached the barbed wire fence which enclosed the camp grounds. They continued the conversation until satisfied that the guards were taking no further notice of them. In a flash, they fell to the ground and squeezed under the wire to the outside.

After their escape, they put the next phase of Pyke's plan into operation. Just as he had reasoned that little attention would be paid to anyone who might have the effrontery to break out of jail in the daytime, so he had also reasoned that no one ever pays attention to a peasant. The two men stole a cow, some rough clothing and proceeded to drive their animal toward safety.

And no one noticed anything alien about them.

Of the seventy-two escape attempts from Ruhleben throughout the war, only three were successful. Pyke later admitted, "Ours was the dullest . . . but it was the most scientific!"

The postwar years of Geoffrey Pyke were marked by marriage, the birth of a son, an entry upon the career of stockbroker, and, finally, the creation of a school for young people based upon principles so radically advanced that it attracted international attention.

But none of these events brought success or contentment. His marriage became a stormy and broken affair and he was reduced to receiving only infrequent visits from the son he had come to adore. His career as a financier ended abruptly when he persisted in siphoning off all the profits in order to support the school.

Without a source of funds, the school closed its doors. Despite the efforts of many of Britain's leading educators to save it by a general public appeal, Pyke's essay into the production of improved childhood behavior patterns was abandoned. But it is worth noting that the conclusions he secured during this brief period are the basis for many of today's commonly accepted educational theories.

Pyke was thrown into bankruptcy. His physical condition, never good since his experiences in the German prison camp, deteriorated rapidly. Emotionally, he was a complete wreck. He left his wife and took a small cottage in the country and withdrew from the society he felt had rejected him.

For the next five years he lived alone, subsisting on the small sums he managed to earn writing advertisements for Shell Petroleum, which, at that time, had a policy of helping needy intellectuals.

Finally, he began to write and to read again. He sent a stream of pieces to the newspapers—all of which were rejected because of length and sometimes because the editors found it impossible to discover the point he was making.

Pyke remembered everything that he read. Keeping as many as sixty books by his bedside at one time, his mind began to regain the flashing speed which had always characterized it. New ideas crowded into his head so rapidly that no one project ever reached maturity before it was supplanted by another. His notes from this period show that his ideas were characterized more by incoherence than by practicability.

Slowly, the paranoid mood began to loosen its grip on him. Friends began occasionally to drop in on him, and an increasing number of London-based intellectuals, educators and scientists wrote to request permission to visit him . . . a request that was generally refused.

During these five years he settled on a mode of dress which was later to cause such dismayed incredulity in the Pentagon. He wore a badly-soiled grey homburg, no necktie, a stained and crumpled suit, thick crepe-soled shoes and grew a scraggly Van Dyke beard. Also, he wore spats. This was sufficient as far as Pyke was concerned. The garb kept him warm and he asked nothing more of his wardrobe.

He began to pick up even more steam. Ideas poured from him in torrents, many of them based upon original concepts which captured the imagination of the limited group of men and women with access to his presence. A few of these intimates spread his ideas throughout the country. Alarmed by the dangers presented by the rise of Naziism, he was instrumental in creating a world-wide propaganda group whose purpose it was to combat the pseudoscientific bases that the Germans were using to defend their destructive policies.

The civil war began in Spain and he saw in the plight of the Loyalists a cause worth aiding. Forming a committee of eminent British statesmen, industrialists and trades-union officials under the banner of "Voluntary Industrial Aid for Spain," he evolved a plan which mushroomed into massive public support for the legal government of that battle-torn country. British workers enthusiastically adopted Pyke's plan of voluntary aid.

Another plan which roused wide public interest was his vivid concept of the terrible damage that bombing would do to English cities. He suggested that the huge chalk deposits located in southern England be excavated in order to provide shelter for great masses of people. It is the opinion of many responsible men today that if his idea had been accepted, thousands would have been saved from death during the World War II air raids.

In the summer of 1940 he turned his attention to the preparation of a new set of memorandums designed to clarify the issues which had begun to engulf the world. In the first essay, he tried to define the true aims of World War II. In it, he prophesied a Europe divided between East and West, and he showed that a shattered Germany would benefit from the division. He indicated his belief that Europe would ultimately be dominated by the East.

Another of the plans contained the first seed of what later grew into the First Special Service Force. It is to be found in a memorandum which Pyke sent to the British Cabinet. In it, he advanced the use of a new military strategy . . . one in which a small but tough British force might be able to attack successfully an infinitely larger number of Germans if provided with the type of machinery which would give them versatility and speed.

Leo Amery, a member of the British Cabinet who had become Pyke's disciple and friend, supported this plan, but was totally unable to convince the members of Britain's military establishment of its merits. The generals remained unimpressed by Amery's vigorous efforts to sell them on the validity of Pyke's thinking. In desperation, Amery decided to submit it to the newly formed Combined Operations (Commando) Headquarters, but that body, after displaying mild interest, also rejected the scheme.

Pyke, however, had now acquired a powerful ally. Amery's sponsorship initiated a chain of events which finally brought Pyke to semiofficial eminence. For the first time since his decline, events began to move Pyke's way. Of course, not even Pyke could foresee that the shortly-to-be-announced appointment of Lord Louis Mountbatten to the Office of Chief of Combined Operations would also have the effect of bringing to Geoffrey Pyke the title of "Civilian Director of Programmes of Combined Operations." This position eventually secured him the respectful attention of Prime Minister Winston Churchill, President Franklin Delano Roosevelt and General George C. Marshall.

Under Mountbatten, the Combined Operations Headquarters rapidly became the only military department in

Whitehall that concerned itself with purely offensive actions against the enemy. This combination of dynamic action and the towering character of Mountbatten, who was an intelligent, responsive and daring man, soon began to attract a circle of thinkers and doers without parallel in any other military establishment in the world. The balance wheel for these thinkers was a hard core of seasoned military men capable of providing workable details for any plan which Lord Louis might pluck from his coterie of original minds. Desks were given to zoologists, ex-commandos and marines. A young American film actor named Douglas Fairbanks, Jr., was put in charge of devices designed to confuse the enemy. And, finally, there was the addition of Pyke.

Leo Amery sent a personal letter to Mountbatten about the man who had conceived the plan which had been rejected many months earlier by Mountbatten's predecessor. He suggested that even if the plan were not feasible, Geoffrey Pyke was obviously the possessor of exactly the type of mind that would interest Mountbatten. Pyke was asked to visit Combined Operations Headquarters for the purpose of being interviewed as a potential staff member. His first meeting with Lord Louis was characterized by surprise on both sides. The immaculate Chief of Combined Operations required every bit of his famed poise to hide his reaction to a tall painfully thin man, whose beard sadly needed trimming, whose distinctly dirty collar possessed no tie, and whose trousers not only had never known a pressing iron but also failed to meet the spats-swathed, crepe-soled shoes by at least six inches.

On the other hand, Pyke was mildly shocked to learn of the meagerness of Mountbatten's salary. He received this information after opening the conversation by blandly asking for a salary which, Lord Louis explained, was far in excess of his own. Pyke shrugged and then brushed the matter of money aside.

"I've got something more important to discuss," he announced. "I've got a plan here whereby a thousand British soldiers can tie down a force of a half a million Germans."

This was the kind of explosive preamble that could excite Mountbatten. The two men bent over the 54-page memo that Pyke had brought with him. The first few paragraphs were enough to convince the chief that here was a soundly based scheme that demanded serious attention. Pyke had conditioned his entire plan on the invention of a new vehicle that would travel over snow at new rates of speed and with certainty of performance. He had few practical suggestions for the creation of the machine contemplated, but he was certain that its development presented no more problems than the development of the tank in the previous World War.

This vehicle, Pyke said, would be a vital instrument in controlling the progress of winter warfare. Since almost 70 per cent of Europe lay under snow for approximately five months out of the year, a small group of trained winter-fighters, who had intelligently selected their targets, could be reasonably expected to attract and tie down the efforts of an infinitely larger enemy force. And, he added, probably beat them, because the time and the choice of engagement would be under the control of the attackers.

Norway, in Pyke's opinion, would be the ideal locale for this offensive action. Where France, Belgium or Holland might be difficult because of openness of terrain, Norway with its long dark nights, its mountains, and its sparse population, would be most difficult for the Germans to defend. Pyke brought in the hardy character of the Norwegian people. He pointed out that although the Germans had conquered the country, they had not "occupied" it in the full military sense. They had fortified their conquest, but, so far, had not sent a large military force to guard it since, by any definition, it would have been a more rigorous target for the Allies to retake than almost any other.

He went on to explain that if a force of well-trained and desperate men were to be parachuted into the country and provided with machines that could travel fast *over,* and not through, the snow, they could destroy bridges, tunnels, trains, tracks, hydroelectric stations and other targets of opportunity in quick succession. The German could not afford this dagger at their throats. They would be forced to send large armies into the area in order to contain these guerrillas. The obvious and immediate benefit, Pyke said, would be to severely lessen

German military strength in other areas. Further, loss of the strategic advantages of the Norwegian occupation would be a major setback to the German military master plan.

The remainder of Pyke's memorandum was devoted to a discussion of the development of the proposed snow machine. He produced page after page of research which described every machine which had ever been considered for this type of work. He summed up the theoretical weaknesses and strengths of each entry and then went on to list the additional features that would have to be evolved before the machine could deliver the flexibility and dependability demanded by the operation he was suggesting. His confidence was contagious, even though it was based on only the sketchiest elements of practicality.

It was an exciting concept. Mountbatten, caught up both by the daring and by the infinite details of the plan, peppered Pyke with questions. In answering them, Pyke exhibited what appeared to be an intimate knowledge of the engineering problems that would have to be met as well as the standards to be set by the firm designated to produce the machine. Pyke had not contented himself with listing the basic engineering and military concepts. He went on into the realm of detailed strategy and calculated the capabilities of the force in light of known enemy strengths.

Amazed at the depth and soundness of the proposal, Mountbatten spent the rest of the day discussing the points of the memo with its creator. Pyke had an answer for every question, and a solution for every problem or objection voiced by Mountbatten.

Lord Louis was tremendously impressed. Here was a minutely detailed plan, worked out by Pyke at a time when he had absolutely no access to military intelligence material, and yet he had exhaustively and accurately discussed every aspect of Norway's defense, its terrain and its strategic importance. In order to arrive at these conclusions, Pyke had used no other resources than the material available in the newspapers, the libraries and the prodigious capabilities of his own mind. The net effect of Pyke's plan was to suggest and document an entirely new concept of warfare. While

Pyke continued to bend excitedly over his documents, Mountbatten saw in the abrasive man before him an additional dimension of value. This man, he reasoned, could yield more than extraordinary creativity, he could also shock and irritate other staff members into greater productivity. The conventional staff would dislike Pyke, but this dislike, combined with the respect that would be undoubtedly produced by an exhibit of his soaring intellect at work, might force them into an almost full realization of their own potential.

This may appear to be a form of cynical manipulation on Mountbatten's part, but it must be remembered that he was totally obsessed by the need to win a war. Ordinary men might have shrunk from introducing such potential turmoil into their headquarters but not even his detractors describe Mountbatten as belonging in this category.

Pyke was quickly installed in Combined Operations Headquarters and given the title "Director of Programmes," a vague enough label to allow him sufficient freedom to poke into any operational movement which excited his attention. His Norwegian plan was given the code name of "Operation Plough" and a series of high-level conferences for its consideration were immediately initiated.

As any of Pyke's earlier friends might have predicted, his appointment signaled the beginning of Mountbatten's being deluged with a flood of ideas, suggestions and concepts. As had been envisioned, the presence of Pyke in Combined Operations Headquarters soon became a major source of irritation to the other staff members. They complained that some of his thoughts were so wild that they weren't sure that a joke wasn't being played upon them. They said that he persisted in approaching problems with the naiveté of a five-year-old, but they did not take into consideration that the basis for all of Pyke's rationalizations was that he must never take anything for granted . . . thus freeing his mind from rigid preconceptions.

There was grumbling that Pyke was undisciplined, and that he refused to quit meddling in an idea after it had been sent to the staff for implementation. They failed to realize that this actually represented the strictest form of self-discipline, for Pyke always forced himself to keep thinking through any given problem until it was firmly in the hands of some-one with a thorough understanding of the issues.

In the meantime, Lord Louis was progressing with the development of "Project Plough." He included it on the agenda at a special meeting called by Prime Minister Winston Churchill on April 11, 1942, to discuss the general strategic question of an invasion of the Continent. At the meeting President Roosevelt was represented by Harry Hopkins and General George C. Marshall.

When Mountbatten introduced a short digest of the Norway invasion plan, Churchill was extremely impressed. The Prime Minister noted in the minutes of the meeting, "Never in the history of human conflict will so few immobilize so many."

There is reason to believe that Mountbatten knew he was on safe grounds when broaching the subject of Norway to the Prime Minister. Churchill's enthusiasm for a Norwegian landing had become "a recurrent nightmare" to his staff.*

At this conference, a decision to implement the plan was reached. It was agreed that the United States would develop and manufacture the necessary "armoured fighting snow vehicles" and that Mr. Pyke should go to the United States as soon as possible after General Marshall's return and work under his general direction.

There was a further authorization to the Chief of Combined Operations that he invite the Norwegian, Canadian and Russian authorities to send officers experienced in snow operations to work with Mr. Pyke under General Marshall's direction.

Within two weeks, Pyke was flown to America, where he

* "Why he [Churchill] wanted to go back and what he was going to do there . . . we never found out. The only reason he ever gave was that Hitler had unrolled the map of Europe starting with Norway and he would start rolling it up again with Norway. It had no strategic prospects of any kind and yet he insisted on returning to it. Heaven knows what we should have done in Norway had we landed there!" Sir Arthur Bryant, *The Turn of the Tide—A History of the War Years,* based on the diaries of Field Marshal Lord Alanbrooke (New York, Doubleday & Co., 1957).

met with Marshall's deputy chief of staff, Lieutenant General Joseph T. McNarney, and other high-ranking staff officers.

The meeting was an unproductive one because the Americans evidently considered Pyke as an oddity whose high sponsorship forced them to extend only the courtesy of a hearing. When he began a detailed explanation of his ideas, they were amazed both by the complexities inherent in the development of his snow machine and by his insistence that the vehicle must be ready for combat within nine months.

Pyke completed the solidification of their resistance by ending his presentation with the offhand statement that of course the Americans realized that before they undertook the job, they would have to make a comprehensive investigation into the physical nature of *snow*. When they pressed him for specific details, Pyke became angrily abusive. He inferred that since he had given them the plan, it was now their job to implement it.

Recent consideration of the War Department files concerning this meeting indicates that Pyke's impression that it had accomplished nothing was entirely correct. Although the American officers assured him they would bring his plans to fruition, they were apparently unanimous in private opinion that the idea was worthless and should be abandoned at the first opportunity.

The next few weeks produced nothing to change Pyke's feeling. He became convinced that if the Americans did offer plans for the production of the snow vehicle, it would be along conventional lines and utilizing whatever designs existing facilities made easiest to produce.

In turn, the Americans became irritated at Pyke's repeated insinuations of their lack of enthusiasm and they began to deal directly with the military officers whom Mountbatten had sent along as aides for Pyke. On many occasions, Pyke was actually excluded from their meetings with the British officers on grounds of military security.

Pyke fought back with a barrage of cables to Mountbatten telling him that he was being "sold short," but the latter, assuming that Pyke was simply displaying his usual impatience with the military mind, sent back answers that were designed primarily as soothing agents. In a rage, Pyke fired off a 3,000-word telegram which announced his firm determination to resign, a decision that was promptly rescinded when both Mountbatten and J. D. Bernal, a fellow scientist on the staff, sent letters which in effect said, "Don't be an ass, we need you."

In June, a need to consider invasion plans brought Mountbatten to Washington, where he then had the opportunity to confer with Pyke in person. After discussion with Pyke and the British officers who had accompanied Pyke to America, Mountbatten decided that Project Plough was, indeed, being sidetracked.

To obtain corrective action, Mountbatten took Pyke to see Marshall's Assistant Chief of Staff, an officer so little known at the time that he was referred to in British memorandums, as "Eisenhauer." Eisenhower's reaction was a reassuring one. He pointed out the difficulties inherent in the situation and then promised that Pyke would henceforth be kept fully informed of all developments.

Mountbatten was impressed by Eisenhower, but being the kind of man who reinforced hopes with hard facts, he next went to President Roosevelt to remind him of Churchill's very strong interest in the project. Roosevelt immediately proposed a meeting between Pyke and Harry Hopkins for the unstated reason that if, in the future, the military attempted to close doors to Pyke, the resourceful "assistant President" would forcefully re-open them.

As a result of this high-level intercession, a series of moves apparently designed to implement the project were brought into being. Pyke, satisfied that at last Project Plough was approaching reality, returned his energies to the consideration of the creation of a workable snow machine, pausing only to infuriate Dr. Vannevar Bush, the Director of the American Office of Scientific Research and Development, with the observation that until Bush and his staff learned something about the nature of snow, their contributions to the project could only be minimal.

The appointment of a young American Army officer, Lieutenant Colonel Robert T. Frederick, to recruit the fighting men for the project was further evidence to Pyke of the genuine interest the Americans finally were taking in his project.

He did not know that Frederick was the author of an earlier secret Pentagon memorandum which, in effect, stated that Project Plough should be abandoned or redirected at the earliest opportunity.

II

Frederick

If we had a dozen men like him, we would have smashed Hitler in 1942. He's the greatest fighting general of all time.
          —WINSTON CHURCHILL, on receiving,
          from General Eisenhower, the news
          of the Force's success at Monte
          la Difensa.

Robert Tryon Frederick and Geoffrey Pyke were both the sons of strong-minded mothers. Both men traveled paths that were remote from normal patterns. Pyke was so often occupied with questioning existing concepts that his accuracy was generally cited by his fellows as just another example of his general obnoxiousness.

Frederick's bravery and dash went so far beyond the normal definitions of those terms that quite a few of his brother generals habitually referred to him as "that crazy son of a bitch." A normal man does not keep fighting after he has been wounded nine times. Nor does he jeopardize the safety of his entire command by personally risking capture while ranging far behind enemy lines.

Separately and in other, quieter times, it might have been possible to dismiss Pyke and Frederick as eccentrics. But given the perfect coincidence of their life lines intersecting during the creation of a war machine, their combined march toward some sort of greatness was inevitable.

It took a rare brain like Pyke's to conceive of the Force. It took Frederick's genius for command to assemble, lead and prove the Force in battle.

Inevitably, the two men came to detest each other. Naturally antipathetic personalities, the pressures and frustrations of wartime were enough to evolve each one into an irritant and nuisance in the other's eyes. It is doubtful that Pyke ever knew that Frederick was the author of the negative memorandum which was being used in the early days of 1942 by conservative forces in the Pentagon as the basis for an attempt to destroy his idea. And Frederick probably never fully realized the extent of Pyke's genius. After he had finally received the responsibility of bringing the Force into being, he sought to have Pyke sent back to England as a meddling nuisance.

We have seen why Pyke was Pyke. Now, who was Robert T. Frederick?

To begin with, he was, and is, an exceptionally attractive man. Slender, tall and vigorously youthful, he impressed his enlisted men and fellow officers by his dynamic impatience and incisive mind. He was a combat general of rare magnetism. In attempting to describe him, one of his men said, "He had a special sort of a quality . . . a movie idol type."

Frederick had the ability to attract and retain almost fanatical loyalty. Long after the war was over, the news that he had suffered a serious accident at his walnut grove in California spread to surviving veterans of the Force in America and Canada. The newspaper wire services were besieged with requests for information as to his condition until, as one editor put it, "It seemed as if something was happening to the Pope himself."

He gave this loyalty as unstintingly as he received it. A Canadian Forceman named Foster reports, "After the war he went to no end of trouble to clear up a matter for me where everyone else failed. He did this while recovering from the severe injuries he had suffered in an accident. As always, he was unselfish and devoted."

He was an inspiring leader, a man of epic bravery who stole off on innumerable patrols behind enemy lines—a general leading a handful of enlisted men. The men worshiped him and he returned their love. But he led them or sent them into danger on every possible opportunity. He was a man who was always surrounded by the smell of death and to be placed under his direction meant that chances of survival were almost nil.

And yet, when he said good-bye to the Force to assume a larger command, almost everyone of these murderous Canadian and American veterans had tears in his eyes. Understand, this is not rhetoric . . . these cold-blooded professionals literally idolized this man, even knowing that the exigencies of warfare had impressed him into the role of a Judas goat. They did this because he gave this group of individualists and outcasts something that no one else in the world had the power to bestow. He gave them his respect and their own, for being probably the best fighting force this continent ever produced.

Although Frederick loved good talk as another man might enjoy food and drink, he struck many as emotionless. But once in Italy a patrol of his men discovered him on his knees praying at the side of a fatally-wounded soldier when no chaplain was near by. They saw him tenderly hold the man's hand until he died.

His physical endurance was legendary. Compact but slight in appearance he could, in the words of Bill Rachui, a Texan in the Third Regiment, "last longer in battle without sleep than any man I know."

Frederick was whipcord tough. After the war, he was having a drink in a barroom in a small West Coast city. A policeman walked in and couldn't believe that the young man who looked as if he were barely in his thirties was entitled to wear the two stars of a major general, so he demanded to see Frederick's identification card. Frederick obliged him.

21   *

The policeman, still feeling that something was wrong, studied it and then dropped it to the floor. Frederick told him to pick it up. When the burly cop refused, Frederick knocked him out with one punch.

Stories about Robert Frederick approach the status of legends. Many of them cannot be documented; participants and eyewitnesses, still under the spell of the fanatical loyalty that the man generated, refuse to discuss anything that might be considered even faintly detrimental to him.

On a recent trip made through the United States and Canada for the purpose of interviewing ex-Forcemen, the same question was asked at every meeting: "Can you ever recall anything derogatory being said about General Frederick?" Only one man was able to recall a negative. "Once," he said, "after General Frederick took over the command of the 36th Division, a Forceman was in a public lavatory in Italy. He heard two members of the division discussing their new commander. 'I hear we got a new CG,' observed one of them. The other answered, 'Yeah, I seen him and he looks like a skinny gigolo, so I guess he's not gonna do too much.' Without bothering to introduce himself, the Forceman punched the speaker in the mouth, sending him headlong into the urinal."

For example, mystery still clouds the circumstances under which he left the service of the United States at an age so young that he was scarcely approaching the peak of his potential contributions to this country. Even now he avoids the inevitable questions on the matter, remaining quietly at home in Palo Alto, California. He is seemingly content to read the papers, and answer, in desultory fashion, the correspondence that streams in from fellow ex-Forcemen. Occasionally he interests himself in the affairs of veterans' organizations. The only stimulus that moves him to action is a request for help from anyone with whom he shared the World War II days of youth and glory.

There are, of course, many rumors surrounding his retirement. The most insistent one is that when he was sent as part of the military mission to Greece right after the war, he became the object of a high-ranking minister's dislike. To appease the influential politician, American authorities re-called Frederick. The politician wasn't satisfied. So Frederick was given the option of retiring or being fired. Whether or not the politician had threatened to use his very high position as a means of moving Greece further to the left isn't known. All that is known is that Frederick came home, took off his uniform, and, like a good soldier, kept his mouth shut. He has maintained this posture throughout, even when the ru-mors enlarged his supposed escapade to where it involved a member of the royal house.

The rumor may or may not be true. But the inescapable fact remains that the value of having a Robert Frederick in Korea or Vietnam fighting guerrillas would far outweigh any momentary political advantage accruing as a result of his sacrifice to the vanity of a Mediterranean politician, ally or not.

Strong men breed strong enemies, and Frederick has never been without a full complement.

Robert Frederick was born in San Francisco on March 14, 1907. His father, Dr. M. White Frederick, had studied in Europe until the age of thirty-four. Among the many degrees he received during that period was one in medicine; so, when called home by his family, he set up practice as an eye, ear, nose and throat specialist.

Dr. Frederick was a courteous, considerate and some-what lackadaisical man influenced by a strong sense of duty. This last trait proved rewarding when he responded promptly to an emergency call from a San Francisco hospital to attend a nurse stricken with typhoid. On arrival, he dis-covered that his patient, a sturdy pioneer type named Pauline McCurdy, was not only quite sick, she was also attractive. The doctor married his patient shortly after her recovery.

Mrs. Frederick, who died in 1964, remained a woman of immense gusto even when in her nineties. As often as she could persuade someone to act as an escort, she booked airline passage for Nevada where she indulged her appetite for ad-venture by taking a fling at the faro and roulette tables. General Frederick, always the dutiful son, obligingly waited each time at least twenty-four hours after his mother's absence had been discovered before setting out to bring her back.

Dr. Frederick's wife respected her husband's early membership in the urbane Continental world. It seemed to her to be superior even to the level of the San Francisco society in which they moved as man and wife. She resolved that her son would be as acceptably cosmopolitan as her husband. Perhaps she went too far. The restrictions she placed on childhood activity and violence combined with the bookish disposition inherited from his father provided her son with the outer façade of a gentle, studious boy. But it was only a façade. Inwardly, he dreamed of adventure. He proved this by materially exaggerating his true age of thirteen in order to be accepted as a private in the California National Guard. He spent every summer thereafter participating in the Citizen's Military Training Corps (he also enlisted in the Air Corps Reserve). At the age of sixteen, he was commissioned a 2nd lieutenant in the Cavalry Reserve.

A Senator, who was also a family friend, secured an Annapolis appointment for the boy, but a chance to vagabond down to the South Pacific intervened. When young Frederick showed up a year later at the legislator's office to inquire about the opportunity, he was told that the Annapolis vacancy had been filled. The Senator suggested, in its place, a remaining opening he had for West Point. The invitation was quickly accepted. At this time Frederick was seventeen.

To his surprise, Bob Frederick found the Point to be just as strictly governed by rules of deportment as the home which he had left. Instead of rebelling, he forced himself to resume the attitude of adaptability which was apparently as important in the military world as it had been in the limited circle which was San Francisco society in those days.

The Army rarely takes the trouble to go into a man's psyche to discover his true nature. Frederick was accepted by his classmates at the Point as only what he seemed to be . . . the studious and reserved son of a well-to-do San Francisco doctor. He was noted as a man who could be depended upon, one to deliver the solid organizational support required by the men of action who actually lead armies.

The description contained in his class book, *The Howitzer,* is proof enough that his classmates saw absolutely no traces in him of the fierce drive that later characterized his every move in combat:

ROBERT TRYON FREDERICK

The activities of every class are made stable by at least one guiding hand . . . the hand of one who has that essential common sense with the ability and will to use it. Thus, 1928 has its mainstay in Fred, the man who has made this book a success. He has given invaluable aid to the Dialectic Society in all of its many activities. Whether it be managing a year book, providing the Corps with Christmas Cards, decorating a ball room, arranging exhibits from outside firms—or convincing the Tactical Department that a change should be made—Fred has been asked to do it and has always done it well.

He has a natural and a modest personality that is bound to please. Both officers and cadets ask his advice on affairs of the Corps—knowing that they will get a practical and workable judgment.

When he graduated in 1928, Frederick's standing in his various courses was as undistinguished as the above description. His class position was 124th out of 250 graduates. The only mark that might have served as clue to his future stature was that he placed seventh in the class in Tactics.

A few hours after graduation, he traveled down to New York to marry Ruth Harloe, the daughter of a Brooklyn physician. Their marriage has resulted in two daughters and eight grandchildren, all of whom find it hard to believe that the now gentle and unassertive man, who reminds so many of their friends of a retired high-school principal, was actually the fire-breathing subject of the awards, citations, newspaper and magazine stories that are yellowing in a corner of the Frederick garage.

His early career as an officer was free of note. Assigned to the Coast Artillery, he served under the Harbor Defense Command and with an antiaircraft artillery unit at Fort Winfield Scott, in California.

After several tours of duty in the field he entered the Coast Artillery School at Fortress Monroe, Virginia, where he graduated in 1938 with a good enough record to merit an enrollment in the Command and General Staff School at Fort Leavenworth, Kansas.

Upon his graduation from Staff School in 1939, his demonstrated deductive ability earned him a posting to what was then the War Plans Division and which subsequently became known as the Operations Division of the War Department General Staff. This was in August 1941, a few months before the Japanese forces attacked Pearl Harbor.

Although his duties were never bluntly described, his chief function in the Pentagon was almost certainly to study plans referred to the General Staff by individuals too important to receive a summary negative, to dissect them, and then to construct a detailed and soundly-based military reason for rejection. This is a necessary function, despite its seeming sterility. Every day in the year, the Army receives suggestions, schemes and ideas from reputable and highly-placed citizens who feel that they have arrived at simple solutions to complex military problems.

Frederick's background indicated that he was an introspective staff officer ideal for the job. And there was nothing in the execution of his duties to indicate that the assignment was anything but an accurate assessment of his abilities. A steady stream of negative reports went from his desk to disappear into the maw of the military bureaucracy. He must have done his work well, because when General Marshall brought back from London a suggested project which had been enthusiastically endorsed by Winston Churchill and Lord Louis Mountbatten, the matter was promptly referred to Lieutenant Colonel Robert Frederick by General Crawford, the Deputy Assistant Chief of Staff.

On May 22, 1942, he was furnished a copy of the report which had been originally handed to General Marshall by Mountbatten with the explanation that it was a condensation of Geoffrey Pyke's exhaustively detailed concept of achieving great military gains in Europe through the initiation of strong diversionary tactics in Norway's snow fields. Frederick was told to make an evaluation of the operational aspects of the plan. He was given no other instructions. Nor were any required.

With typical thoroughness, Frederick spent twelve days investigating every facet and interviewing every authority he could find on the subject. A shortened version of the fourteen-page, single-spaced, closely reasoned negative report that he finally prepared for the signature of the recently appointed Chief of Operations Division, Major General Dwight D. Eisenhower, reads as follows:

BRIEF

MEMORANDUM FOR THE CHIEF OF STAFF
    Subject: Plough Project.

I. *Discussion.*

1. Mr. Geoffrey Pyke has proposed development of a motor vehicle capable of operating over snow with mobility and speed approximately equal to that of the normal military track vehicle. He suggests that this snow vehicle be employed in Norway and Rumania in operations to destroy installations providing essential materials for Germany, and on the southern slopes of the Alps to destroy Italian installations.

2. It is believed that a suitable vehicle for operation in snow can be developed within about two months. Tentative design of the vehicle indicates that it will be an amphibious, track-laying vehicle weighing about three thousand (3,000) pounds and capable of carrying a load of approximately twelve hundred (1,200) pounds. Pilot models are now being constructed. Suitable places for testing the vehicles during this summer are being examined.

3. Special methods of demolition are being investigated by the Engineer Board.

4. A careful study of Mr. Pyke's proposal, as it applies to Norway, has been made and indicates that the snow vehicle is not well adapted to the type of operation contemplated. It is believed that the same effect on the German war effort can be achieved by other means, the most promising of which is by subversive acts by native Norwegians. Norwegians selected and

trained in the United States, and furnished the equipment and information necessary to destroy vital installations in Norway, could assist the natives in the undertaking.

5. If the snow vehicles are to be ready for employment during the winter of 1942–43, they must be manufactured under the highest priority rating. This would interfere greatly with the manufacture of other equipment essential to the Bolero Plan.*

6. There is not sufficient time to adequately train the personnel required for the operations Mr. Pyke proposes for the coming winter.

7. The diversion of personnel, aircraft and shipping for the proposed operation would interfere with the Bolero Plan.

8. Consideration of possible employment of the snow vehicle indicates that it is not suitable for general employment as a combat vehicle due to its vulnerability and inability to carry adequate firepower. At this time there is no operation planned for the European Theater which could utilize this vehicle to any great extent. The snow vehicle appears to be particularly well suited for employment where patrols are maintained under extreme winter conditions.

II. *Action Recommended.*

It is recommended that:

1. The plan proposed by Mr. Geoffrey Pyke for United States operations in Norway to destroy the hydroelectric plants and other installations vital to Germany's war effort, not be undertaken as proposed.

2. The Assistant Chief of Staff G-4 arrange the production of the snow vehicle under a priority that will not interfere materially with the Bolero Plan, and that these vehicles when produced be furnished to the Mountain Division, Alaska Defense Command, Greenland Base Command, Iceland Base Command, and other forces that can utilize them in winter operations.

3. Tests be conducted with the snow vehicles, as they become available, to determine their capabilities, limitations, and application to operations under winter conditions.

4. Plans be developed for attacking the installations in Nor-

* The code name that then was used to describe the projected Continental invasion, or Second Front.

way that are vital to Germany's war effort, through the employment of subversive elements in Norway assisted by personnel
trained in the United States.

5. That plans for bombing attacks against important installations in Norway be prepared.

Glad that a complex project had come to an end, Frederick turned the document over to his superiors, and directed
his attention to the stack of paperwork which had pyramided
on his desk during this special assignment. He dismissed
Project Plough from his mind.

On June 3, 1942, General Eisenhower returned from
England and was handed the negative report prepared for his
signature. Instead of signing it, his famous temper exploded.

Did they, he asked his staff, conceive that they or he
could lightly dismiss a plan which had earned the enthusiasm
and loyalty of men like Churchill and Mountbatten? Further,
he wanted to know, what made the Pentagon planners so
blithely certain that they could quickly discover flaws in planning which were not apparent to these two seasoned veterans
of countless strategy sessions? The storm continued and there
was nothing that the staff members could do to ease it. Finally,
Eisenhower told them to bring him the reports and documents which had been produced by Frederick's investigation.
He also told them to bring Frederick.

Eisenhower was a professional. He attached no blame to
Frederick for the course of events, since he was aware that
Frederick's assignment had been completed in accordance
with tacit instructions from above.

Frederick recalls that Eisenhower said to him, "I can't
sign that report."

"Why not, General?"

"Because I told them in London that we were going
ahead full speed with this project."

Eisenhower then told Frederick to call the Army Ground
Force headquarters and get an officer designated to assume
command.

This meeting proved to be the most important event in
Frederick's life. Later that afternoon, when Eisenhower and

Mountbatten left for a conference at the Russian Embassy, they were accompanied by the young officer whose quietly precise confidence in himself had impressed the General during their brief meeting.

Project Plough was the subject of an animated discussion at the Embassy. The Russians were very much interested in the plan and were quite anxious to be assigned some of the vehicles envisioned in Pyke's memorandum. They felt that these would be of inestimable value on their own frozen front.

Next day, a high-level meeting was held by Eisenhower in his office. Attending was Lieutenant General Joseph Mc-Narney, who was General Marshall's Deputy, Lord Mountbatten, Pyke, Colonel Hull and Colonel Davis of the Operations Division and, to the surprise of his immediate superiors, Lieutenant Colonel Robert Frederick.

At this meeting, Mountbatten mildly criticized the War Department for its activities to date. Too astute a man to be misled by vague representations of progress, Mountbatten had been disturbed by the reception that Project Plough was getting in America. But, as always, he kept his own counsel. Now, he sensed, the plan was back on the rails. He had an immense respect for Eisenhower's honesty and ability, and when Eisenhower assured him, as he did in this meeting, that Project Plough would be prosecuted with all possible vigor, he was satisfied.

In order to mollify Pyke, who had been disgruntled even though he had no firm knowledge that his plan had been slated for extinction, General Eisenhower promised that he would appoint an officer to supervise all phases of the project, who would have no other duty but Project Plough, and who would work directly as a consultant with Pyke.

No reference was made to Frederick other than to introduce him as the man who had conducted that part of the investigation which dealt with American capabilities to produce Pyke's snow machine.

As a matter of fact, after the meeting Frederick asked General Crawford if he were now free of Project Plough. The specter of the ever-increasing pile of papers on his desk haunted him and he wanted desperately to get away from this time-consuming trip through the upper echelons. Crawford agreed that Frederick might go back to his work, but added, "Keep in touch . . . for the time being, anyway."

That afternoon, the Army Ground Forces designated Lieutenant Colonel H. R. Johnson as the officer to take charge of Project Plough. He was told that Frederick was familiar with all of the details of his new assignment and it was suggested that he lose no time in acquiring the reports and background materials that Frederick had compiled.

Frederick's sense of fairness kept him from clouding this information with the negative conclusions that had ended his original report. He simply apprised Johnson of the facts that he had uncovered and let the newcomer digest them in any way he preferred.

But the other leading characters were not so charitable. Two days later, on Monday, June 8, Johnson met with Pyke, who, of course, had not a shred of Frederick's tact, diplomacy and consideration for others.

The two men were at immediate cross purposes. Johnson advised Pyke of the manner in which he intended to carry out his assignment and inferred rather strongly that Pyke's suggestions and opinions would be most unwelcome. Having been exposed to this kind of blind antagonism all his life, Pyke instinctively recognized that Johnson would never provide the leadership that he felt Project Plough needed so desperately. He threw up his hands and went back to his hotel.

That night he got in touch with Mountbatten, who was away from Washington on a trip. Next day Mountbatten was back in the capital and immediately summoned Johnson and Frederick to his office.

Johnson spoke first. He told Mountbatten, in effect, that if this project was really going to amount to something he was willing to give it his co-operation . . . but if it was just another idea that might never become operative, he just wasn't too anxious to be involved. These remarks were an extension of the observations he had made earlier in the day to General Eisenhower, who had then promptly dismissed him from his office with the not too gentle reminder that Army officers generally did as they were told.

Mountbatten did not comment on Johnson's stipulations. He simply sat silently, and it soon became obvious to the others in the room that the Chief of Combined Operations had turned his thoughts into more absorbing channels. Finally, he appeared to have reached an inner decision which greatly satisfied him, and, returning his attention to Johnson, called the meeting to an end.

That night, Frederick received a telephone call from a British officer in the Secretariat of the Combined Chiefs of Staff. The officer told Frederick that he was the new officer in charge of Project Plough.

Frederick was stunned. Afterwards, he said, "I was shocked. It was beyond my comprehension that I should be the man picked. I had written this report in which I recommended that there be no Force and had been overruled and then I finally found out that I was to be the CO. I was amazed. But I was also terribly happy!"

There are many written descriptions of this incident, and many people are given or claim the credit for having made this perfectly pitched appointment.

There are some who maintain that the Government of Canada, as a condition precedent to supplying troops for the project, insisted that it be headed by Frederick, who had impressed them during the preliminary investigations he had made in Canada to ascertain the mobility of troops in a cold and snow-locked climate.

Lieutenant Colonel Robert D. Burhans, the staff Intelligence officer for the Brigade throughout its brief history, says in his excellent history of the group, that the choice was General Eisenhower's. After examining several candidates for the job, according to Burhans, Eisenhower sent for Frederick and said, "Frederick, you take this Project Plough. You've been over the whole thing. You're in charge now. Let me know what you need."

But to many other people who were on the scene during that period, including several presently high-ranking general officers in the American Army, the choice was inescapably Mountbatten's.

Mountbatten is on the record as an uncannily accurate

judge of men. It is quite proper to believe that where Frederick's classmates at West Point and the superior officers who had evaluated him up to this point in his career completely misread him, his capacity for leadership would have been evident to Mountbatten. Lord Louis had a demonstrated record of selecting the right man for the right place and he was too professionally involved with Project Plough to risk the assignment of another "unattuned" officer like Johnson.

Further, the act took a certain daring unorthodoxy, not normally typical of Eisenhower, a traditionalist noted for his devotion to the value of compromise and the preservation of existing values. It is highly unlikely that he would pick a man to command a force who had produced scores of reasons why it should not come into existence. But Mountbatten had the vision and, what's more, the humor to contemplate such a move. Further, he was so secure in his position among the Combined Chiefs that he could afford to suggest the assignment without feeling that he risked criticism should it prove an unwise election.

The appointment had to be Mountbatten's, but the responsibilities were now Frederick's. He spent the next day turning over his duties and jobs in progress to the rest of the officers in his section. Naturally, he took particular pleasure in sending out to others for adoption the no longer menacing mound of papers on his desk.

By evening, he was on his way to Canada with Mountbatten and Pyke in order to present the plan to the Canadian Army Chief of Staff, General Kenneth Stuart. Winston Churchill had felt that the inclusion of Canadian troops would enhance the value of the organization and had even suggested that it be named "The North American Force."

Upon their arrival, the trio was invited to lunch with the Earl of Athlone, Canada's Governor General, and Princess Alice, his wife. This was heady company for a man who just a few days before had been an obscure lieutenant colonel laboring in the Pentagon at a job that, in effect, carried the rating of a glorified chief clerk.

The highly satisfactory Canadian visit lasted for five days. Mountbatten's proposal brought enthusiastic affirmatives from the Canadian officials and, with the Canadians in the fold, Lord Louis departed. Pyke and Frederick stayed on. Among the subjects that received further discussion was the participation of the Norwegian Government in the plan and Pyke's continued insistence that the proposed Project Plough force be trained as small groups of guerrillas rather than in regular military formations.

The worth of Pyke's concept of this particular point is borne out by the fact that this is exactly descriptive of the training now being received by the modern descendants of the Brigade, the green-bereted Special Forces.

Frederick's contribution to these extended conversations was the stipulation that if Canada were willing to participate, Canada must send him its toughest and strongest soldiers. It was during this period that Frederick introduced his concept of American-Canadian solidarity which, for the life of the First Special Service Force, wiped out some of the boundary lines between the two countries.

Frederick made his point so well that Canada's subsequent contribution represented the elite of its armed forces. Under the direction of the Canadian General Staff, every volunteer for the Force was rigorously screened for strength, intelligence and ferocity.

This technique was at variance with the criteria later employed by American recruiters for the Force. As a matter of fact, many of the Yankee "volunteers" came from military stockades . . . places which a minimum of intelligence is needed to enter. The miracle that the Canadian volunteers and the American roughnecks worked so well together came to pass primarily because of the exposure given Frederick during this period to Canadian thinking and attitudes. When the Canadians came into the Force, he was ready to handle them properly.

Pyke was not so well received as Frederick. This was to be expected. Any meeting or series of meetings which combined both Pyke and the opportunity for extended conversation produced an inevitable reaction.

In this particular situation, the reaction took the form of a note passed to Frederick by the Canadian Major General

Murchie (Vice Chief of Staff) which the General had scribbled during one of Pyke's long-winded discourses.

When Frederick opened the note, he read the General's message, which was, "What the hell does he want?"

The two men looked at each other in silent communion. An instant understanding was born. Thereafter, Frederick always found it relatively easy to secure the co-operation of the Canadian military.

Next morning, Frederick went to the headquarters of the Canadian Army to be pleasantly surprised by the news that Canada was officially willing to extend quick co-operation to the project. The authorities agreed that the United States Army would carry out the planning and intelligence for the program and that Canada would furnish as many officers and enlisted men as would be required. They also offered the use of any training area in Canada that might be considered desirable for the project. And, finally, they offered the resources of the Canadian National Research Council to help develop the proposed snow vehicle.

This vehicle, which later came to be known as the "Weasel," plays an important part in the papers, diaries and records which document the early days of Project Plough and the First Special Service Force. Pyke had made it a matter of primary importance that a suitable machine be developed, and both Mountbatten and General Marshall had agreed that before the proposed Force could find any level of effectiveness at all, the Weasel must be designed, produced and ready to go.

As a result, Frederick and his staff were to spend a disproportionate share of the months ahead in discussions with engineers, in locating properly snow-encrusted terrain for testing purposes, and in arranging the endless priorities necessary to get the vehicle rolling off the assembly lines. This turned out to be a cruel waste of precious time because the Weasel actually played no part in the Force's subsequent history. When Norway later decided to discontinue its participation in Project Plough, the urgent need for mechanical mastery of the snow also disappeared.

Still in Ottawa, Lieutenant Colonel Frederick was beginning to question the proposition that a close and continued association with Geoffrey Pyke represented an unmixed blessing. Pyke had many personal peculiarities. Some of them proved highly irritating to Frederick, notably, Pyke's insistence that the door to their hotel room be bolted by the double-keyed lock generally found only in bank safe-deposit vaults.

Pyke and Frederick had one of the keys to this lock, and the hotel manager was given the other. As a result, entry or departure from their quarters took on the aspects of a troop movement. Pyke insisted that this security precaution was vitally necessary. He firmly believed that the world was peopled with individuals dedicated to the theft of his ideas.*

On the fifth day of their visit, Frederick, concluding that he had accomplished everything that he could reasonably hope for, told Pyke that he was going back to Washington. Pyke was annoyed. He insisted that Frederick stay on for a few more days. This placed Frederick in an ambiguous position. Although he had no technical obligation to accept Pyke's commands under the terms of Eisenhower's representations to Mountbatten, he felt that he should not offend the Englishman. Perhaps the quick conclusion of Colonel Johnson's participation in Project Plough after his arbitrary attitude with Pyke was still fresh in Frederick's mind. So he patiently explained to the Englishman that there was an incredible mass of details that had to receive attention before the project could go any further. He offered to stay in Canada if Pyke would help him with this drudgery.

This, of course, was perfectly calculated to produce an agreement that he leave. Pyke gave qualified assent on the condition that Frederick first write him a memorandum exactly describing his plans upon return. He considered this a

* In this particular case, his apprehension might have been justified. It later developed that Pyke was carrying with him the notes for "Pykerite," the system of transforming ice into a material as hard as metal and which was the basis for his idea of constructing a disposable naval super-vessel. This vessel, under the code name of "Habbakuk," was to become a major subject of scientific and military controversy in the waning days of the war.

great concession and told Frederick that if the memo were not completely satisfactory, the officer must stay on in Canada until an understanding was reached.

Frederick, choking ever so slightly, promptly sat down and listed every project he intended to put in motion as soon as he got back to Washington. Pyke received the document with a very judicious air. After reading it, he agreed to accept it provided also that Frederick, upon his return, would undertake an additional list of chores that *he* conceived necessary. Among them were getting Pyke a credit card for telephone and telegraph, getting dictaphone equipment for his hotel room, getting a set of offices with the understanding that should Pyke desire additional space, he would have the option of dispossessing occupants of adjacent rooms, arranging air priority for him whenever he might want to travel, having an assistant Librarian of Congress put at the disposal of Project Plough, and keeping him informed while he remained in Ottawa of everything going on in the project's organization.

Frederick, now both thoroughly impatient and thoroughly saturated with Pyke's repeated descriptions of his World War I escape from the prison camp, agreed to every stipulation, and promptly left for Washington. Upon his arrival, he found a message from General Eisenhower which told him to prepare a directive for Project Plough which would relieve him from every other duty and to describe the organization of the Force as he wanted it to be. The message also contained the news that he was to be officially appointed as commanding officer and, therefore, to include everything in the directive that Frederick conceived necessary to the successful accomplishment of the plan. Evidently Ike had received a full report of Frederick's success in Canada. It is rare that a blank check like this is issued to a comparatively junior officer.

Frederick spent the next day preparing the required draft which he sent that afternoon to General McNarney, who officially approved it and sent it on through channels. Frederick devoted the rest of the day to determining requirements for the initial headquarters of the project and selecting the officers he wanted for his basic staff. He also received several phone calls from Pyke in Ottawa which he later described as ". . . in a dictatorial manner, [he] issued orders and made demands, mostly ridiculous."

His planning preparations were interrupted only once more that day. He went with General Moses to General Mc-Narney in order to get an official clarification of Pyke's relation to the project. McNarney told the officers that Pyke was in America in the capacity of adviser and that he was not empowered by the War Department to give orders to U. S. personnel. He added that it was not necessary to comply with Pyke's requests or to consult with him except when such actions might be desirable for the project.

In spite of this authorization to rid himself of an irritant, Frederick continued to treat Pyke with courtesy and consideration. But, in private conversations, he indicated a more human reaction.

"The son of a bitch won't let me alone," Frederick reported. "I'm with him all day and he talks, talks, talks. Almost everything he says makes sense but after a while my ears close up. I stop listening because I get numb and although I'm sure that the things he is saying are brilliant, I just can't absorb them any more.

"And then," he sadly continued, "I get away from him. But I'm afraid to go home. As soon as I do, the phone will ring and it's Pyke again . . . talking, talking, talking!"

But, as evidence that Frederick was far from being the meek and long-suffering listener he painted himself, this letter was sent shortly after Pyke had arrived in America in order to acquaint himself with the progress of Project Plough:

July 1, 1942

Mr. Geoffrey Pyke
Director of Programmes for Combined Operations
Lee Sheraton Hotel
Washington, D.C.

Dear Mr. Pyke:

It has come to my attention that you have been discussing the project on which we are engaged with persons who should not have knowledge of it.

I am sure that it is not necessary to tell you that the success of the project depends greatly on the secrecy with which the planning, training, and other preparations are carried out. To disclose the fact that such an operation is contemplated, or even being investigated, may cause its failure.

The War Department cannot devote to the project the personnel, equipment, training facilities, time, and money that it requires, if there is likelihood that the success of the project is being jeopardized by indiscreet disclosures of its nature. You must agree that information reaches the enemy certainly and rapidly, and that any knowledge of a contemplated operation will serve him well in preparing to meet it. To attempt an operation of the type we contemplate against a fore-warned enemy would result only in the loss of all that we are putting into it— including the annihilation of a valuable force of carefully selected and highly trained men.

I must ask you not to discuss the project with anyone who has not been specifically approved by the United States War Department to receive information of this project, and I also request that all papers and documents pertaining to this project be left in the secure place provided for your use in this office, or with local British military authorities who have facilities for safeguarding them.

Sincerely yours,

ROBERT T. FREDERICK

In answer, Pyke protested with what amounted to wide-eyed innocence. He assured Frederick that he had been the very soul of caution and, further, he would undergo any hardship in order to avoid hampering the progress of his brain child.

Frederick exhibited additional evidence of his tactfulness when, at a meeting with Pyke, he suggested that he act as Pyke's intermediary by conveying all of Pyke's suggestions and instructions to the American agencies concerned. He promised to keep Pyke fully informed of all phases, invite him to every vital meeting and staff discussion, and comply with all proper requests. This attempt to shield Pyke from the antagonism and rudeness his conduct invariably generated was obvious as an act of consideration to all but the Englishman, who accepted the proffered services as no more than his due.

On June 27, Frederick sent Pyke a letter which clearly exceeded the minimum respect for the man that his superior officers had suggested. Among other matters, it contained these considerate words:

> You may rest assured that in every way we shall devote ourselves to the fulfillment and accomplishment of the plan you conceived. We shall probably call upon you frequently for assistance and advice, and we shall keep you informed of our plans and progress.
>
> I am sure that we shall be able to labor harmoniously for the ultimate achievement of this important piece of work and I hope that we have, and will continue to have, your faith and confidence.

Pyke responded to this consideration with a totally uncharacteristic display of mildness and appreciation:

July 1st, 1942

Dear Colonel Frederick,

Many thanks for your weekly report which I am studying with care.

Meanwhile, I send you a rather hasty note to say that whenever there is anything that you or your officers wish to see me about, you have only to call me.

Whenever you want to use me as a sounding board, as it were, to talk to me to help get clear the many difficult problems which face you, I will cancel any appointment that is not with so to speak one of our "seniors," such as one of the President's friends, to be at your disposal. We can talk freely in my room here over a meal. You have to eat sometime . . . and somewhere, and you need never hesitate to ask yourself.

Should I be out when you come, Colonel Wedderburn and my secretary, who will probably know my engagements, have instructions to arrange accordingly.

Could I please have a copy of the information collected and the conclusions arrived at as a result of the snow experiments

made by Mr. Putnam and Mr. James on the Columbia Ice-
field?

Yours sincerely,
/s/ Geoffrey Pyke
Director of Programmes
(Combined Operations)

Colonel R. T. Frederick
General Staff
U. S. Army
Washington, D.C.

Pyke's letter to Frederick is testimony that the Englishman had finally realized that every echelon at the Pentagon
was united in opposition to him. Official antagonism was, of
course, nothing new to Pyke, but here in America he had no
prospect of beating it. His only ally was Mountbatten, and
Lord Louis was too involved in matters of larger concern to
devote anything but sporadic attention to his assistant's difficulties with another country's bureaucracy.

The resistance to Pyke's attempt to retain a semblance of
control over Project Plough seems to have been led by General McNarney, who had conceived a ferocious dislike for the
Englishman. Frederick, in the beginning days of the schism,
tried not to take sides. Uneasily aware that the memorandum
he had originally written to torpedo Project Plough was still
being produced by the Pentagon as evidence of the unworka-
bility of the scheme, he was devoting every bit of his energies
to bringing the Force into being before a major showdown
could jeopardize his finally realized dream of a major combat
command.

Pyke was aware of the dislike he had generated, but, happily, did not realize the full extent of the machinations of the
considerable number of generals, engineers, automotive de-
signers, meteorologists and staff members who were now involved in both the project and in the determination to send
him back to England. War Department files still bristle with
letters, reports of telephone conversations, and memorandums of meetings all devoted to this latter group's vehemently
expressed desire to rid themselves of a man who, they felt,

was a meddler and, at best, only a pseudo-scientist with few professional credentials.

This was an old Pyke difficulty in a new locale. The officers at Combined Operations Headquarters had voiced exactly the same complaint to Lord Louis: "Pyke couldn't keep from interfering with the staff operations necessary to bring one of his ideas into fruition."

Finally, Pyke gave his ill-wishers the opportunity for which they had been searching. He mounted an attack on the Norwegian meteorologist, Colonel S. Petterssen, who had been assigned to the project in order to supply the planners with expert advice as to the probable effect Scandinavian weather conditions might have on the snow fighters of Project Plough. Pyke accused Petterssen of attempting to sabotage him and then issued an ill-advised threat to use his influence with President Roosevelt to have everyone fired who disagreed with him. His actual words were, "I'll get a big broom that's going to sweep things clean around here!"

The controversy erupted into a matter of such proportions that the White House finally commissioned Harry Hopkins to conduct an investigation into the causes and the accuracy of the charges being made by both sides—that is, Pyke against everyone, including some members of his own staff who joined the Americans in the attempt to end his participation in the project.

Frederick, by this time, was thoroughly disgusted with the machinations and the backbiting involved in the situation. He was particularly annoyed with Pyke's consistently difficult personal attitude. Although, intellectually, he was far more able than the ordinary military man to appreciate the Englishman's capacity for original thought, he had become so emotionally caught up in the necessity to bring Project Plough into being that he no longer had the patience (or the desire) to protect the man from the consequences of his eccentric behavior. Besides, as a realist, he now set great store on Colonel Petterssen's contributions to the planning, and had serious doubts that Pyke had anything left to give to the project. Pyke's value, he felt, was confined to the original concept. Any further participation would become simply uninformed tinkering.

A few days after Harry Hopkins and his staff had concluded their investigation into *l'affaire Pyke*, Frederick was asked to comment on his findings. His reply included a professionally precise evaluation of the situation:

As the entire Project Plough, and its development so far, evolve around Mr. Geoffrey Pyke and his basic concept, it seems that comments on Mr. Pyke may properly be a part of this note. Mr. Pyke is an eccentric and unusual individual. He has an imaginative and intellectual mind but is wholly lacking in technical knowledge and is not at all practical. His approach to a problem is the scientific approach requiring long investigation, research and consideration of all available, or procurable, data. Such an approach is not to be condemned and in many cases is proper. For this Project, however, the time element is so vital that we must progress in that manner which will give us the desired results, as, after all, it is only the results that count. Although Mr. Pyke has given more than two and one-half years to the study of this Project, he still answers questions and requests for assistance with the statement "All I have done is to formulate a problem for other people to solve." Due to his unusual manner of living Mr. Pyke is somewhat difficult to work with. His normal working day is from noon until after midnight. He is apparently interested in a number of things other than this Project, and in spite of the fact that he desires to be kept fully informed of progress, plans, and developments, he has, on several occasions, not attended important meetings where the Project was discussed due to "appointments with high officials." He is completely lacking in appreciation of the many phases of preparation that must be undertaken along with the development of the snow vehicle. He has no knowledge of the methods or requirements for training personnel. He does not appreciate the ramifications and administrative details of creating a special military organization. He appears to have an aversion to organization and orderliness.

Shortly afterwards, Frederick received a copy of a memorandum addressed to General Marshall from Harry Hopkins asking for information which could be used to reply to a cablegram from the Prime Minister who had evidently heard the rumbling concerning the status of Project Plough. Frederick was directed to prepare the reply for Marshall's signature. He complied, saying only, in effect, that the work was proceeding with all the energy and resources of the War Department and that it was confidently believed that they would be ready to undertake the Project during the coming winter.

Both General Handy, Chief of the Operations Division, and the chief assistant to Harry Hopkins approved his letter, but General McNarney, on being shown a copy of the draft, rewrote it to include a stinging criticism of Pyke and sent it on over his signature.

McNarney's version reads as follows:

July 9, 1942

Dear Harry:

In your memorandum of July 7, you asked if there is anything you can tell the Prime Minister in reply to his cable asking what the prospects are of carrying out the Mountbatten Plough scheme this winter.

The War Department is energetically pushing the project. Basic units of the force have been activated at Fort William Henry Harrison, Helena, Montana, and will consist of 133 officers and 1,688 men. Special weapons, equipment, and methods are being investigated and developed at a promising rate.

The principal handicap to the project has been Mr. Pyke. His proclivity to discuss details of the scheme with more people than is necessary is jeopardizing the security. His unwillingness to work within the organizational framework which has been set up has resulted in conflicting orders which have caused more confusion.

I am fully confident, however, that we shall be ready to undertake this project this winter.

Sincerely,
/s/ Joseph T. McNarney
JOSEPH T. MCNARNEY
Lieut. General, U. S. Army
Deputy Chief of Staff

The Honorable Harry L. Hopkins
The White House
Washington, D.C.

[Original dispatched from Office
Chief of Staff, July 9, 1942]

This letter evidently had the effect of terminating Pyke's influence in America. Shortly thereafter, he returned to England where the news of his rebuff delighted his many ill-wishers. Even Mountbatten appears to have been affected by the storm of criticism that Pyke had generated in America. When a later project of Pyke's, "The Habbakuk Ice Boat" scheme began to receive serious consideration in both countries, Pyke was precluded from participation in the planning. He received the disappointing news from a general who told him that Lord Louis had just sent a telegram which said:

> Dean Mackenzie has just sent me a message to say that it is his considered opinion that if Pyke comes out it would have a disastrous effect on American participation in this scheme, and he would have to advise his government accordingly. In the light of this uncompromising attitude I am afraid Pyke will have to stand down for the good of his own scheme. Consulted Bernal who entirely agrees. We are both so sorry.*

Pyke never forgot his treatment in America. Rightly or wrongly, he remained convinced that the entire affair was an example of the dedicated thickheadedness of most military planners. This conviction as to the severe limitations of the military mind remained with him until the day in February 1948 when he killed himself with an overdose of sleeping pills. Yet, even in death, the enmity he inspired did not cease. A Norwegian officer, hearing of the event, said, "It's the only sensible thing that Pyke ever did." †

* *Pyke: The Unknown Genius,* ibid.

† Writing in the *Atlantic Monthly,* March 1965, in an article headed "Churchill and the Scientists," Dr. Vannevar Bush illustrated the continuing ill will the scientists felt toward Pyke by saying: "There was a pseudo-scientist named Pike [*sic*]. He has since committed suicide and cannot reply, so I will not be hard on him. He was short on physics, especially short on engineering judgment, but he had lots of ideas, some of them superficially brilliant and intriguing. He had not the slightest concept of what organization and operating in channels meant. Many have not. But he was a consummate salesman of a sort. On one of his schemes, the ramifications of which are too complex to relate, he apparently sold Lord Mountbatten, and, from all

Throughout this sequence of events, Frederick, never, for a moment, had abandoned the relentless pace he considered necessary to bring Project Plough into existence by the following winter.

He envisioned the Force which would implement Project Plough as being lesser in size than a division. This dictated that it be given the military description of "Brigade." The unit was to be composed of three regiments, a headquarters company, and a service battalion whose duty it would be to relieve combat troops from all housekeeping and most maintenance functions.

His key staff members began to arrive on the scene. On June 19, Major Orval J. Baldwin, a graying engineer who had been connected with the National Resources Planning Board, reported for duty as G-4, the staff officer concerned with logistics and supply.

Major Baldwin was accompanied by Captain Robert D. Burhans, the son of a Michigan State college professor, who had been trained in winter warfare before being detailed to the Army Intelligence Section in Washington. Burhans became G-2, or Intelligence officer.

Baldwin, a precise and conservative man, provided a perfect complement to Frederick's newly revealed impatience with detail. In the months ahead, Baldwin was a source of calm strength. While Frederick ranged all over the United States, and made periodic flying trips to Canada and England in order to iron out the problems presented by the creation

appearances, through him the Prime Minister. Pike and Mountbatten visited the Secretary of War and the President and then appeared in my office. Pike told me the program was approved and going ahead, and asked what I was going to do.

"I replied, courteously, I trust in Mountbatten's presence, that I took orders from the President and no one else, and that no project went forward in my shop without adequate review and recommendation by our own group. That was that. The President never mentioned this particular project to me. There was confusion and real damage was barely avoided. But the scheme never reached its objective, which is indeed fortunate, for putting it into effect would certainly have cost lives." [The scheme referred to, is, of course, Project Plough. Authors.]

of a binational force, Baldwin steadily attended to the thousand vexations which accompanied the setting up of housekeeping.

Other key staff members arrived on the scene. Major John Shinberger, the wild and improbable paratrooper, came in to supervise training activities as G-3, and Lieutenant Finn Roll, the blond, bland-faced Norwegian who later provided many of the memorable highlights of the training period at Helena, joined the group as Captain Burhan's assistant Intelligence officer.

Major Kenneth G. Wickham, a former companion of Frederick in Hawaii and an uncannily efficient acquirer and manipulator of personnel, completed the staff positions by being named G-1.

Robert Tryon Frederick, relieved of Pyke, was in business. Project Plough had begun its metamorphosis into the Devils' Brigade.

Frederick and his staff, products of the ultra-paternalistic Army system, which spells out almost every detail of every day through a combination of training manuals, operations manuals, tradition, and directives from above, now found themselves adrift in completely uncharted waters.

There were no precedents available that summer for the formation of the First Special Service Force. Requests for guidance from higher or lateral echelons were met with puzzled shrugs and, quite often, a solid lack of co-operation. No one wanted to stick his neck out. The feeling was, obviously, that association with an oddball outfit such as this could boomerang as soon as its inevitable collapse took place. There was little sympathy in the Army bureaucracy of those days for doing things differently. Department heads had generally achieved their positions by unwavering conformity, and, as a result, were understandably hostile to any short-cutting of the system that had rewarded them so well. They saw no reason to divert their men or material to an organization so totally lacking in precedent as the handful of men under Frederick's banner.

He began his own intelligence system with the purchase of subscriptions to several newspapers, and dealt directly with the several foreign governments involved in the planning. He sent Shinberger and a few others flying around the country to find an unused National Guard camp where he could get on with the training of his men.

Baldwin initiated the job of describing the uniforms and supplies required by the Force, while Wickham took on the laborious task of translating Frederick's concept of battle readiness into the preliminary terms of the exact sort of men they would need.

Wickham found that he could expect little or no co-operation from the various Army personnel offices. So, instead of requesting men, he described positions. Army psychologists were asked to list the qualities desirable in fighters who would be assigned to the suicidal missions contemplated for the Force, and then Frederick and his personnel chief, using the lists as guides, drew up the standards for the officers and enlisted men they were about to recruit.

For the senior officers, they set an arbitrary age limit of thirty-five, demanded that they be in excellent physical condition and be willing to undergo parachute training. They placed special stress on men who had had experience living in subzero temperatures in mountainous or arctic regions, and who had previously commanded units of at least company size in the field. Branch of service was immaterial.

The junior officers, Frederick felt, should not have been previously conditioned by other commanders. He had a well-defined feeling that he wanted to train his own, so he searched the graduating classes in the various officer candidate schools throughout the country. Almost 90 per cent of his lieutenants came from this source.

As for enlisted men, he asked only that they be rough, tough and unafraid of anything. The only restriction was an educational one. Frederick stipulated that they should have had no less than three years of grammar school.

The recruiting notices that were sent to be tacked on Army post bulletin boards stated that preference would be given to men who had previously been "Lumberjacks, Forest Rangers, Hunters, Northwoodsmen, Game Wardens, Prospectors and Explorers."

As a practical matter, many post commanders seized this

opportunity to empty their stockades and rid themselves of hard-case troublemakers in all categories. Prisoners frequently were given the option of continuing their sentences or "volunteering" for Frederick's Force.

There are, of course, indignant official rejections of this description of how the Force was formed. But there are also numerous carefully documented rebuttals to these in existence. Among them is a typewritten memorandum from Frederick (corrected and amended in his own handwriting) which reads:

> So that you will better understand the "volunteer" system, I am going to read two messages I received when I was forming the unit. From one post I received a telegram that said: *"All volunteers for your command have departed this date. Direct the officer in charge and armed guards to return to this station as soon as practicable."*
>
> From another post I received this message: *"All personnel transferred to your command are en route except 42 men AWOL, 26 men sick not in line of duty and requiring further treatment, and 14 men in confinement awaiting final action on remission of sentences. These volunteers for your command will be transferred as soon as available."* I never quite got the whole story because almost all the messages were received in code, and as we had no deciphering equipment we could not read them. My adjutant had a large desk drawer full of coded messages but by the time we received the codes and deciphering devices, I had too many other problems to worry about old messages.
>
> And that is just about the way the "volunteer" system worked. [italics, authors]

Another example of the type of men being recruited for the unit is supplied by Major Shinberger's efforts to enroll a previously known man who had all the qualities of an ideal Forceman. There was only one hitch. The man was serving a sentence for murder. Shinberger tried valiantly to get him, but to no avail, since the sentence was being carried out in a state prison. Shinberger later said, "I'd of gotten him if it had been a Federal pen!"

Many of the Forcemen, of course, were not felons. There were also ex-college men, teachers, farmers, and the former bodyguards of movie stars and political bosses. But it would be difficult for an observer to separate the two categories on the basis of their subsequent combat records. The ex-Sunday school teachers and ex-choir singers like the Canadian, Bill Story, proved just as tough in battle as the most hardened ex-con. This was not a coincidence. Frederick deliberately set out to assemble a group of men who shared the common denominator of past, present or potential hardness. He accepted no others.

This qualification extended even to the men for the subsidiary services, such as flying the planes to drop the men into combat. In an August telephone conversation with Baldwin concerning the caliber of six pilots recently assigned to the Force, the following dialogue took place:

MAJOR BALDWIN: Do you have a bush flier in one of those six?
COLONEL FREDERICK: No.
BALDWIN: Well, damn it, one of those were supposed to be a good bush flier. I'll have to check up on that.
FREDERICK: I don't know. If he is, I don't know who it is.
BALDWIN: What are their ranks?
FREDERICK: They are all second lieutenants and one first lieutenant. They are all people who have been in trouble with the Air Corps for violating flying regulations, or one thing and another.
BALDWIN: That's fine, then they are not afraid to fly.

As the Force began to pick up size, weight, and speed, no addition was more strikingly colorful than the blond Norwegian hell-raiser who served as Burhan's assistant Intelligence officer, Lieutenant Finn Roll.

Roll was the possessor of dual citizenship. During the 1920s, his father had been appointed to the staff of the American Consulate in Hamburg where he had earned the considerable gratitude of the American Red Cross for his help in feeding the needy victims of the runaway inflation then convulsing the country. As a result, his son inherited an option, to be exercised on his twenty-first birthday, of choosing citizenship in either Norway or America.

Prior to Finn's time for election, the Germans invaded Norway and his father became an active member of the underground. The Germans, who had compiled a thick dossier on the activities of the Roll family, contacted Finn and demanded he inform them of his choice of nationality.

He answered that he would make his declaration within a few days. That night, he and a friend commandeered a twenty-foot sailboat and headed for England. In London, he went to the United States Embassy and made his request for American citizenship. After securing a letter of introduction from a friendly Embassy attaché to an Arkansas Senator, he left for Washington.

Roll, who spoke five languages, had no difficulty in securing a commission in Army Intelligence. Because of his fluency in Norwegian, he was assigned to the Force during the period that the invasion of his homeland was still considered as its primary target.

Burhans recalls his first meeting with Roll: "Shinberger and I were in the Canteen behind the Munitions Building one day, when we noticed this big and obviously new lieutenant who had just joined our outfit. He ate nothing and looked quite peculiar, but since he seemed rather withdrawn, we didn't make any comment.

"Later that afternoon, I got talking to him and asked him what was wrong. He answered that he had been commissioned for thirty days but had received no pay and so he hadn't eaten for several days. I gave him $10 and sent him out for a meal thinking that I had finally seen the ultimate in naive reticence!"

In training, Roll became a "jump master" for recruits who were being taught parachute tactics. In combat, Roll, actuated by the hatred he felt for the Germans, proved to be an abusive and aggressive interrogator. One German prisoner confessed to a guard, "I think that big man was ready to kill me if I didn't answer."

Another stranger to normal patterns of conduct was the Operations and Training officer, Major John Baird Shinberger, who came to Frederick by way of a parachute regiment. Shinberger, a man of great drive, left almost every Army associate with the impression that if his energy had been directed by less erratic judgment, he would have reached a ranking position in the military hierarchy.

Frederick saw this quality of initiative and felt he could harness it for the good of the Force. The proof of the accuracy of Frederick's hunch is that the rigorous training which honed the Brigade into a superb fighting unit is generally considered to be a direct result of Shinberger's concepts. However, the following September, when Frederick appointed another of his old companions, Colonel Paul D. Adams, as his executive officer, the early exit of Shinberger from the Force was ordained. Shinberger was recklessly flamboyant, and Adams (who is now a four-star general) is a relentlessly logical man possessed by certain concepts of conduct and discipline who never lets down the barriers of rank. They were natural opposites.

But while Shinberger was with them in the early days, he added to the Force a wild and woolly dimension which never disappeared thereafter. Short, stocky and enjoying a high degree of muscular co-ordination, he was thoroughly masculine in appearance. He was born in the Navy town of Norfolk, Virginia. He spent his early years preparing himself for Annapolis but he was never able to get the coveted appointment. Disappointed, Shinberger turned to the Army and was nominated to West Point. It took him five years to graduate, with a standing that left him third from the very bottom of his class. As a matter of fact, until the very night before graduation, he wasn't sure that he would be commissioned.

Burhans recommended John Shinberger to Frederick, after recalling his bravado in an infantry battalion in which both men had served in 1938. The battalion had been commanded by an officer who had incurred Shinberger's violent dislike during an earlier investigation that the two men had made of CCC camps. The commanding officer, aware of Shinberger's poorly concealed feelings, decided to make life as unpleasant as possible for him. He ordered Shinberger to accompany him on another inspection tour.

Shinberger asked to be relieved of the assignment but permission was not only refused, he was also sharply told to be at the CO's quarters next morning, with a car checked out for the trip. The next morning came, but Shinberger did not. Pleased with the prospect of having caught his antagonistic aide in disobedience of a direct order, the CO called the Duty Officer and told him to place Shinberger under arrest. He was told that Shinberger was in the hospital with a broken leg. The commanding officer could never prove it, but the whole post happily buzzed with the story of how Shinberger had jumped out of a second-floor window in order to avoid the duty.

Before his marriage, his prowess as a bachelor was the subject of much admiring comment at Army camps throughout the country. This activity stopped abruptly with his wedding vows. Thereafter he spent most of his spare time in reading the Bible, an occupation which caused much speculation at the Force's first headquarters in Helena, because he customarily did his reading on a cot under which he kept a foot-locker full of live rattlesnakes.

These snakes are very well fixed in the memories of the survivors of those days. A majority of the former Forcemen claim to have participated in the off-duty pursuit of rattle-snake trapping. The rattlers were presented to Shinberger, who collected them on the theory that the best way of ridding himself of an aversion to reptiles was to keep a clutch of them near by. He felt that familiarity would eventually breed contempt, a goal which was materially slowed by certain Forcemen's habit of sliding a long pole underneath the tent and banging it against the snake-filled locker, while Shinberger was absorbed in the Scriptures. This practice, of course, not only delayed the rapport between Shinberger and his snakes, it also materially diluted the proper meekness of spirit which he sought through Bible study.

In 1941, as a paratrooper captain charged with the responsibility of forming the first U. S. Army airborne artillery,

Shinberger began making his reputation as a man who got things done. When his telegraph request for certain weapons was not filled within forty-eight hours, he composed a second wire and signed it with the name of Brigadier General Brehon Somervell, War Dept. Supply and Procurement chief. The guns made their appearance on the following day.

On one occasion, the supply section at Helena informed Shinberger that they had been equipped with only three of the large sewing machine needles that were needed to sew torn straps back on parachutes, and that two of them were already broken. He fired off a telegram to the Service Command requesting 10,000 more needles, quieting the doubts of his supply sergeant with the comment, "Well, we'll never run out of them again."

Shinberger loved to write letters and to use the telephone. While at Helena he incurred monthly telephone charges which, in size and cost, would have done credit to almost any complete department in the Army hierarchy. Very few of these calls had any relation to Force activities. One day, the chaplain casually told Shinberger that he had just received a letter from his wife in Panama in which she mentioned that she had not been feeling well. Shinberger promptly picked up the phone and called her. After an introductory conversation, he tossed the phone over to the amazed chaplain, remarking reassuringly, "She says she's feeling better."

Frederick, owning the strong convictions about wastefulness which sometimes characterize the children of families who have had money for a long time, was quite annoyed by this addiction to toll calls. Even though Shinberger outranked Wickham, Frederick ordered that "The Prussian," as Shinberger had been nicknamed by the enlisted men, could make no long-distance calls that were not first approved by the Personnel officer. This contributed to Shinberger's growing discontent with the aura of rigid discipline which Colonel Adams was attempting to introduce into life at Helena. He and Adams, throughout this period, never exchanged a civil word. Finally, he went to Frederick and requested a transfer. The request did not surprise Frederick nor did it meet with his disapproval. He had made up his mind to get rid of Shinberger just a few days prior when, at lunch, their meal had been interrupted by a junior officer's saying, "Colonel Shinberger, do you know that your rattlesnakes are running around loose?"

Frederick recalls, "Shinberger excused himself and left the mess tent. He came back in a little while and reported that he had killed them all. Then he went on with his meal as if nothing had happened.

"That did it for me. I was convinced that Shinberger was *too* irrational."

Like Pyke at a comparable stage in the Force's development, Shinberger had made his contribution. And Frederick showed no more reluctance in getting rid of him than he had earlier in demanding Pyke be returned to England.

Shinberger was posted to the London headquarters of General Jacob Devers, who assigned him to the reading of every piece of paper produced by the rest of the staff. "If Shinny can understand it," remarked Devers, "then it can be safely given to the lowest private."

His conduct during the subsequent invasion of the Continent was heroic in the extreme. He was provost marshal at Omaha Beach, and afterward, while commanding an engineer battalion in Belgium, he took on an enemy tank singlehandedly, receiving from the incident a number of serious wounds as well as the Distinguished Service Cross.

Shinberger later told Burhans that, as he lay in the ditch where the tank had left him to die, "I made a pact with God. If He would spare me, I would devote the rest of my life to the Church."

He kept his promise. After he had been given a medical discharge following recovery from his wounds, he entered the Episcopal Theological Seminary in Alexandria, Virginia. Ordained a priest, he was assigned to a series of rural churches. He was an impressive figure in these pulpits, because he wore his medals on his surplice. His body healed, but his mind never quite recovered from the traumatic experiences of his wartime career. He suffered several nervous breakdowns and finally, in 1959, was admitted to the Virginia State Hospital as a hopeless mental case. There he killed himself.

In later years, General Frederick gave Shinberger credit for instilling in the men of the Force the concept that they were the finest soldiers who ever existed. "The Prussian" set almost impossibly high training standards, and when the men attained them, their belief in their own abilities became boundless.

Frederick was not free from frustrations while he was assembling the Force. He encountered a series of obstructions, most of them originating with the Army Ground Forces Command, which would have thoroughly discouraged anyone less convinced that the formation of the Brigade represented a military dream that might never again recur. Relief finally came on a highly symbolic date. On July 4, 1942, Frederick received a call from a friend in AGF (Army Ground Forces) Headquarters, who unofficially notified him that orders were being cut transferring the force directly to the jurisdiction of the War Department. The same document would include the official activation order of the unit, a detail which, so far, had apparently been overlooked by the individuals most intimately concerned with its creation. This was Saturday.

On the next day, the order was received and the Force officially came into being. Frederick, having previously decided that Fort William Henry Harrison in Helena, Montana, offered the best opportunities to train his men to fight in the way he envisioned, promptly sent Shinberger off to begin reshaping the facilities of the base into maximum operational efficiency. Two days later, Robert Frederick was promoted to the rank of full colonel. Project Plough had finally shifted into high gear.

Frederick had made no mistake in sending Shinberger as his advance man to Helena. He received a telegram from the stocky major on July 7 which contained an enthusiastic endorsement of the fitness of the locale as a training base. This was not the only time that day that Frederick was to be made aware of Shinberger's existence.

Throughout the afternoon, his telephone switchboard was jammed with incoming calls from the division engineer, the Chief of Engineers, representatives of the 9th Corps commander in whose bailiwick Helena was situated, members of the Services of Supply and many others. Each caller demanded to know what in the hell all the commotion was about. They had been barraged that morning with messages and directives from Shinberger on the scene insisting that they get promptly to work in Helena.

Most of Frederick's callers hadn't the slightest knowledge of the Force's existence, let alone being aware of the need for the remodeling plans which Shinberger was insisting that they produce for Fort Harrison. Frederick explained the urgency of the situation to each caller in turn and, to a man, they promised their co-operation.

Next morning, Shinberger returned from Helena ablaze with plans and ideas. He spent the morning explaining construction goals to the engineers assigned to the project and then, in highly dramatic terms, described the eager co-operation that the Force could expect from the people of Helena. He told Frederick that most of the city's businessmen were amazed and overjoyed by the award of an active and entirely unsolicited army camp to their area. And, as Shinberger observed, these people were Westereners . . . people with big hearts who could be expected to adopt the Force as their own. Not one member of the Force who was ever based at Fort Harrison found any reason to quarrel with Shinberger's estimate of their new neighbors.

The name, "First Special Service Forces," was officially adopted by Frederick during this period. He was besieged with titles by the Army's public relations experts who came up with a lurid group of selections, each evidently chosen to frighten the enemy to death, in the event the Force proved unable to physically perform this job.

Frederick didn't want any name that was overly descriptive of the firepower or projected activities of his Brigade. "First Special Service Force" sounded innocently close enough to the Special Services (the name given to the Army's entertainment branch) to camouflage the true purpose of his outfit. This was the name that was entered on Army records. Of course, this misleading label gave rise to a series of misconceptions. Whenever an outsider later questioned the name and the significance of the red, white, and blue braided cord that Forcemen proudly looped over their shoulders, they were usually informed that the men who bore this name and wore the crossed arrows and spearhead insignia were, in fact, members of a company of master barbers whose mission was to insure the neatness of our troops overseas.

The problems presented by the participation of Canadian troops were not so easily solved. Although it was determined to divide staff and command positions equally between representatives of the two countries, two matters with serious morale implications came into focus during this organizational period.

1. The pay scale of the Americans was much higher than that of their Canadian counterparts. If the Canadians were to be paid American rates, it would be considered unfair preferment. Ii the Canadians were paid less than the Americans in the Force, there might soon be a quite logical aura of dissatisfaction radiating from anyone who was getting less money for doing the same job as the man who slept in the next bunk.

2. There was a further question concerning loyalties. Could a Canadian be forced to accept an American order? Could an American's refusal to obey a direct command from a Canadian superior be considered a punishable military offense?

These potentially ugly questions were resolved by common sense. The Canadians never did achieve parity in pay scales with the Americans. But since the Americans were paid once a month and were generally broke a few days thereafter, while the Canadians got their monthly pay in two installments, it became a matter of only academic importance. Both sides graciously borrowed money from the other.

As for accepting commands, the organization quickly matured into an outfit where only those who could command respect would issue orders. Promotions were solely on merit and the few grumblers at the system were generally those who couldn't measure up . . . and Frederick got rid of them in short order.

The time had come to move the Force's headquarters to Helena. On July 19, Colonel Frederick, the newly-promoted Lieutenant Colonel Shinberger, Major Burhans, and two lieutenants flew to Montana.

III

That Summer of 1942

I got a list of 200 in today from the West and Northwest, and there are some likely looking prospects in it—some that are not so good, too. I think that what we are probably going to have to do, Colonel, is just take them as they come in. You give them a quick look-over and if you see somebody that you don't like the looks of, or that has some obvious defects, bounce him ...... right now all we have is their names, serial numbers, and one or two words on their background—like lumberjack, or trapper, or farmer or something of the kind.

—Major Baldwin to Colonel Frederick,
in telephone report, August 5, 1942.

They came from all over and the first few weeks in Fort Harrison were chaos. Trains and trucks brought in shipments of men with the regularity of an escalator belt. Carpenters, plumbers and electricians were in everyone's way . . . moving the headquarters building, tearing down old structures, cutting and grading streets and attending to all the details which, normally, would have been completed long before the base was opened for occupancy.

Frederick and his small staff seemed to be in dozens of places at once. Their tension, however, only barely covered the happiness they felt at seeing their project come alive.

The arriving men were bewildered. The vague secrecy which had cloaked their new assignment was in no way dispelled by the sight of scores of different uniforms and insignias and the sounds of frantic building activity thundering all about them.

Especially the Canadians. Told little by their government except that they had been detailed to serve in an elite force where toughness and a willingness to ignore the heavy odds against survival were only starting points, these picked men were astonished by the strange and apparently totally uncoordinated scene that confronted them. A Canadian, William C. Knutson recalls that when the Force recruiting party first came to his station, "there were approximately eighty-five of us who signed up, but after taking medical and IQ tests there were only twenty-six left. Then Colonel Williams talked to us and advised anyone that was married to drop out as the Force was likely to have a short but lively life. I believe we ended up with sixteen men who went to Helena for training."

William Story, who had sung in a Winnipeg choir, graphically re-created the events which transformed him from a Canadian soldier into a Forceman: "Around the end of June 1942, as I recall, word flashed through the Sergeants' Mess that a call had gone out for men to volunteer as paratroops for a new unit being formed. The First Canadian Parachute Battalion had recently been put together, with many of its men taking their first training at Fort Benning. Most of us assumed initially that we would be joining this group. There were five or six of us from the Winnipeg Light Infantry who volunteered, including Major Jack Sector, formerly of the Royal Winnipeg Rifles, Sergeant W. J. Robinson, Sergeant Jim Playford (both with me in Fifth Company), Sergeant Blackie Blackburn, and Corporal Sam Boroditsky. Interesting . . . two Jews, two Catholics, and two Protestants if memory serves me correctly. Blackie just squeezed under the weight limit, Sam just made the minimum height.

"In any event, we were accepted and off we went to

Currie Barracks in Calgary. Part of the attraction for the paratroops, I recall now, was the jump pay—plus the promise we would keep our rank. Another part, for me, was the basic question—could I pluck up enough courage to jump? Very basic.

"We arrived at Currie Barracks and the sergeant NCO's and warrant officers got their first shock. The traditional and hallowed Sergeants' Mess was out—we would mess with the other ranks. After bitching a bit we discovered this was because we would be going to an American Army camp where there were no Sergeants' Messes.

"I recall there were a number of things that had to be done. We signed a statement indicating our willingness to obey orders when given by a U. S. Army officer. We also took an IQ test and it was my understanding that NCO's had to pass with at least the minimum requirement for officers in regular units, and that privates had to have the NCO level. Officers were set higher than the norm for commissioned ranks. I seem to recall also that we were asked if we would be willing to undertake hazardous duty.

"We found at Currie Barracks men from virtually every unit of the Canadian Army in the West. We were told that men from Eastern units were being assembled in Ottawa.

"Finally we boarded trains for Helena. It was about this time that we were able to establish firmly our actual destination. Prior to then, there had been many rumors, including Helena, Benning, etc. We were in our Canadian summer uniforms—uniform jackets with brass buttons, shirts, ties, and long khaki trousers. The buttons had to be kept shined, unlike the American type. Some also wore Bermuda shorts and short-sleeved shirts open at the neck—this was regular summer issue for training purposes. Worn with this uniform were puttees.

"Because of the many units we were drawn from, there were many different cap badges. Men from the Highland units, like the Queen's Own Cameron Highlanders of Winnipeg, wore the large Scottish tam. The few 'Tankers' wore the black beret made famous later by Monty [Field-Marshal Montgomery].

"It was a hot and tired crew that finally pulled into the siding at Fort Harrison that August day. And what they saw didn't serve to lessen the heat. The camp was a cloud of dust. Bulldozers were hard at work leveling the area where the huts would go. Gangs of workmen were laying down pyramidal tent bottoms; others were erecting tents in streets. The big parachute drying towers were under construction; the mock-up area, with the harness rigs, was not yet finished. Actually, nothing was finished; and much had barely begun. The PX consisted of a small brick building which confined itself to selling soft drinks, candy, and a few essentials. For Canadians from Vernon, also a relatively new camp, this was no real hardship, although the dust and heat were worse. For Americans from well-established U. S. Army camps, this was for the birds. Many came, many went, a few stayed, undaunted by the facilities, because they liked the people they were with, or because what they had before had been worse, in one way or another.

"Two by two we were assigned to tents in a company street. In each tent we found an American pair. We found, too, that some people had arrived before us and were in command positions. Thus, our company commander, fresh from Fort Belvoir, I think, occupied that position by being there first. We had one Canadian platoon commander, Bill Bennett, and two Americans. Our company sergeant major was a Canadian; the rest of us sergeants scattered ourselves around in platoon positions as best we could find. I can recall jockeying for the position of section leader with several sergeants in the platoon during that first week. I finally won out—they had all left by the first train available. By then, I had longevity.

"In the tent with me was Stoney Wines, a buck sergeant from the U.S. 7th Cavalry and former Golden Gloves fighter. With him was 'Jonas' Bush, also a buck. Just who the other Canadian was I have forgotten. We had some hot arguments at first about each other's Army.

"Both Stoney and Jonas had to learn we didn't take kindly to jokes about the King and Queen; nor did we enjoy being told Canadians were fools for continuing to be colonists and paying taxes to England. It took a day or so of discussion to educate our American tentmates in British history following 1776.

"Men of both armies were attracted by the uniforms of the other. So we swapped, and after a few days, it was impossible to tell on the streets of Helena which were the Americans and which were the Canadians. The Americans gave up this business first, however. They found the attractive brass buttons down the front of the Canadian uniform had to be polished to keep their shine. This was beyond most of them. The Canadians liked the U. S. uniform because it looked like a Canadian officer's uniform. Also, they didn't have to polish the buttons.

"As we became accustomed to Helena, we found we could buy bits of uniforms downtown. I bought a hat, a garrison cap, and promptly adorned it with my cap badge—a large maple leaf wreath in the center of which was a beaver. This was tastefully backed by a piece of red felt. Looked fine on the garrison hat, but it left the post MP's more than somewhat confused. I wore it for months; even wore it home on our first leave sometime in December or late November.

"We eventually were issued American OD blouses and trousers. But the Canadians struggled to keep their identity. So much of the camp was U. S. Army it was hard to remain obviously Canadian. Lots of us did by putting up our Canadian NCO stripes on the U. S. uniform. This also proved confusing to the MP's. Gradually, however, this practice disappeared, especially when promotions came through. We were gradually feeling pride of unit, rather than of Army."

There was one soldier in Canadian uniform who, immediately upon detraining asked to be brought to the commanding officer. He was directed to where Major Wickham was standing and told that whatever he wanted to know, Wickham could tell him.

The soldier walked over to Wickham, saluted, stood at attention, and didn't go on because he obviously didn't know how the information he was going to deliver would be received.

Wickham waited patiently in silence.

Finally, the soldier blurted out his story. He wasn't a Canadian. He was a deserter from the American Army who had gone up north to enlist in the Canadian Army. When he saw the notice posted for the Force, he had immediately volunteered without thinking of the possible entangling consequences.

Wickham, continuing his silence for a few moments, studied the soldier before him. He finally asked, "Why did you desert from one Army to get into another?"

"I thought I'd get into the fighting faster," the deserter answered.

Wickham remembers saying, "If that's all that's been bothering you, I think we're finally going to make you happy. You're going to get as much fighting as you can handle."

Wickham tidied up the whole matter by having the Canadian Army issue the man a discharge. He then reduced the American charges against the man from desertion to AWOL, and permitted him to remain in the Force.

Jack Akehurst of Ontario, the son of an Anglican clergyman, who became a regimental commanding officer with the Force, remembers that his first reaction was "the extreme youthfulness, even of the senior officers. I felt old at thirty-four, and was told that I should have been rejected at that age except for my experience in cold climate. I was, and had been for years, connected with mining in Southern Ontario before joining the Army in 1940. In fact, I was asked how tall, how heavy, how old, and to each I was a reject. But when asked where did I come from, I said 'Kirkland Lake, Ontario,' and I was in. It certainly made me curious and I felt the Force was not formed for any tropical venture."

There were others. Frederick Pike had been a welterweight boxing champion in the Merchant Marine. Robert Hiscox had been a safe blower, a profession which he apparently did not abandon while in the Force and to which he subsequently returned. After the war he became the leading (and only) member of what the Toronto papers referred to as "The Polka Dot Gang." When he was finally caught in the middle of a job, he blew himself to pieces with a bottle of nitroglycerine rather than be taken by the police.

On the other hand, cocky Conrad Legault, another man who became an outstanding combat fighter, said "When they interviewed me for the Force, they took me, even though I had no jail record!"

It took very little time for the Americans to establish a kinship with the Canadians. On both sides the men were lean, mean and tough. One leveling agent in a potentially explosive situation was found at the station platform where they were immediately subjected to a scrutiny of their genitals for evidence of venereal disease . . . a rite known to the Army as a "short arm inspection." Tough men often laugh at the same things. When a Canadian private named Poirier was assigned to hitherto exclusively U. S. Army barracks, the curious stares that followed him as he slung his gear on the cot were broken only when a tall and rangy Texan came over to him and said, "Ah'm Sergeant Baar in charge heah. Wheah you-all from?"

The answer came, "Ah'm from Canada, wheah you-all from?"

A one-time Indiana farm boy named John Dawson mentioned the impact produced by the Dominion soldiers: "Fresh out of basic training, and in the Quartermaster at that, I was very impressed with the men flooding in from other depots, cavalrymen, infantry, artillery, engineers, mainly old Army men with years of service, and colorful Canadians in brief shorts, usually sporting berets with the colors of Highland regiments, many of them from overseas divisions, and a few who had been at Dunkirk. In a word, I had an inferiority complex that took months of training and eventually combat to overcome."

"Of course," said a 2nd Regiment man, "the Canadians had some funny ways. When you passed them some food in the Mess Hall, they would let you hold the platter or bowl while they helped themselves. The only way we broke this habit up was to just let the dish drop in their laps. It worked."

A Service Battalion man said, "They were new to us. And especially to the Texans. Have seen some pretty good rough and tumble fights. But it didn't take them long to see that we were all about the same type of people."

The American contingent represented backgrounds as

wide and varied as their country could produce. When recruiting officers asked for volunteers, sometimes describing the Force as "a place where there's going to be a short and exciting life," the opportunity proved irresistible to precisely the type of man that Frederick was looking for.

For example, Harold Schaeffer was born on a Minnesota farm. At 21, he left home for Montana, California and, just before he enlisted, the railroad freight yards in Alaska.

Bill Pharis was a roustabout in the Texas oil fields. W. B. Shelton, now a faculty member and a Ph.D. at the University of Massachusetts, participated as a Yale graduate student in zoological expeditions to the China-Tibet border before he became a member in good standing of the Force's 2nd Regiment. Anthony Skomski was raised in a rough and tumble Detroit neighborhood where most of his friends were factory hands of Polish descent.

Another man who became an outstanding fighter was John Kures, whom the Forcemen called, "The Mad Russian." He was drafted in 1942 from Cleveland, Ohio, and sent to Fort Ord, California, where he volunteered for Airborne training at Fort Benning. Late in 1942 he was detached from Benning and sent with thirteen others to Palo Alto Air Base to drop supplies to the 87th Mountain Infantry Battalion, which was lost in the mountains along the Pacific Coast. Returning to Benning, Kures went AWOL. After being caught by the military police, he was put in the stockade at Indiantown Gap. It was from here that Kures volunteered, was accepted by the First Special Service Force, and sent to Helena.

Colonel William J. Mahoney, one of the first regimental commanders, describes his own introduction to the Force:

"When I reported in at Helena, Montana, I was taken to General (then Colonel) Frederick. After a few moments he asked me if I was ready to start jump training—parachute training, that is. I thought he was kidding. 'Did the screening board tell you that by volunteering to join this outfit you agreed to train in parachuting?' 'Hell, no,' I told him.

"I felt that it was important not to make Frederick mad, but I had no desire to start jumping out of airplanes. Besides all I saw on my way to the camp was a wide expanse of plains and hills, and a few shacks. There were no jump towers, no airplanes—nothing. Frederick then told me to find a place to bunk down for the night and then check back with him in the morning. I got my gear out of the car and moved into a spare shack for the night. Sometime during the night I went out to look for a latrine, and found these guys all out sleeping on the ground, and a big huskie Eskimo dog keeping a watch. It was then I realized I was mixed up with no ordinary outfit, and these fellows were not just the run of the ordinary G.I. I knew at Camp Robert. I had a feeling there was something very different about these fellows, and that this was not just going to be an ordinary organization.

"Needless to say, the next day I told Frederick that I was prepared to start jump training and anything else he wanted me to do. So he told me I could stay with them for a while and sorta try out for the team."

Not all of the new arrivals relished the company that was being assembled. A Service Battalion clerk remembers that as his train neared Helena, "All kinds of disquieting rumors about the Force were reaching my ears . . . that the Force was composed of jailbirds, thieves, murderers, whose sole form of entertainment was tearing apart towns and committing wholsale mayhem. Frankly, since I am not of a particularly pugnacious temperament, I was becoming thoroughly alarmed!"

The Red Cross representative in the Force, Getty Page, stated, "I know that many of the Force people had several wives. I also was told about a Texas rustler and the border patrolman who had been searching for him. Both men were of the adventurous sort, so when they had the opportunity to join a hot outfit, they both volunteered. One of the men had been rustling cattle across the border and the other was the border lawman who had been searching to arrest him. They came on to one another in the First Special Force, and the law officer said, "OK, we'll forget it for the time being. But when this is all over, I'm going to take you in!"

This matter of criminality is still one of the most controversial facets of the question, "Where did they come from?"

It is beyond dispute that many of the Forcemen had no prison records prior to or following their period of service. But while researching the material for these pages, a few letters like the following one from the Jefferson County (Ohio) Jail were received:

> I was in the Force from the beginning to the end. I was also in the Korean War. I am in jail for assault and battery. When I finish here, I will be taken to Erie, Pa., about an automobile accident. So two wars and twenty years later, this is how I end up. Sorry I can't help you more. Good luck with your book. I hope I have the opportunity to read it.
>
> Sincerely yours,
>
> F—— J——

Fort Harrison began to take shape. By July 19, 1942, two-thirds of the tent frames, adequate mess halls, latrines, and other buildings needed for the rapidly swelling ranks of the men were ready for use. Goaded by Frederick's staff, the contractors threw up new buildings overnight and moved existing buildings to new locations in an afternoon. By mid-August, the majority of the Force was on hand and undergoing the training and welding process that transformed hellions and roughnecks into superb, professional soldiers.

In the meantime, as Shinberger had prophesied, the open-hearted Westerners of Helena adopted the Force as their own. A small town itself, it recognized most of the Forcemen as sons of other small towns. The rapport that was immediately established was also based on the fact that a majority of the city's population were descendants of miners, trappers and guides. The character of the Forcemen was not an alien quality in Helena. The townspeople took the Forcemen to their homes for Sunday suppers, and, despite gasoline rationing, waited in line in their cars outside the camp's gates on weekends to act as voluntary chauffeurs.

Most of the people of Helena were as proud of the Forcemen as they were of their own sons. To this day, many Americans and Canadians in all parts of the world still correspond with the friends they made in Helena.

When the Force was scheduled for a jump, scores of Helenans drove out to watch. Their interest warmed the hearts of most of the men; though, as one of them once observed, "Maybe they're waiting for the chute that won't open." There were other factors which contributed to this relationship. The Force contained a relatively small number of men. Had it been a division instead of a brigade, it could have swamped the city, thus arousing the feeling of resentment which often followed the initial patriotic frenzy that gripped other towns situated near Army posts.

Colonel R. W. Beckett, now chief general counsel and vice president of the Canadian International Paper Company, still visualizes his first day in Helena. American uniforms had not been issued yet to the Canadians; so, on his trip to town, he was decked out in plaid kilts, sporran, bare knees, and bright white spats. As he paced down the street with the typical Highlander stride, he heard one woman call to her friend, "Maysie, Maysie, look quick!" Two lolling cowboys wearing wide hats, levis, and high-heeled boots, brought the cigarettes dangling from their lips to attention. "Jim, for Christ's sake," one said, "what was that?"

The Canadians took a while to accept Helena. Some of them expected that the townspeople would be wearing six-guns slung low and were quite surprised to find a high order of civic accomplishment. But, within a few days of arrival, they felt as much at home in the town as did the Americans. In fact, the townspeople stretched their friendship for the Force to a point that might easily strain the belief of anyone stationed in other Army towns during those days.

The Forcemen, overenthused by their demolition training, often either blew up targets not on the training schedule or used twice as much dynamite as was required. These habits frequently had the unhappy result of blowing out many of the town's plate-glass windows. But the mayor suggested to his constituents that no charge be made for the damage. Broken windows were considered one of Helena's contributions to the war effort. And, when the boys practiced newly learned principles of unarmed combat in night spots like The Gold Bar, The Corner, or the Log Cabin Night Club, the bartenders simply got as many breakables as they could out of the way until the fight subsided. The bartenders of Helena, according to all reports, were an especially noble breed. At any time, any Forceman could borrow at least $5, using his paratrooper's wings as security. On the memorable Saturday nights when the Forcemen came to town, the copings on the upper floors around the town's leading hotel provided an irresistible challenge. Drunken Forcemen staggered along the foot-wide ledge which surrounded the walls of the hotel's fourth and fifth floors. This route was more popular than hallways when they went from room to room.

One of the few occasions when the property owners actively complained to the authorities was recalled by Conrad Legault. A friend of his brought a young woman up to his hotel room. He told her to wait while he ran some water for his bath. Emptying his pocket, he threw a dynamite cap on the bureau. A few minutes later, he was horrified to see his girl pick up the cap and pull the fuse lighter. He grabbed it and rushed to the window, but he could not throw it out because there were too many people in the street. He finally tossed it in the bathtub and shut the door. The explosion blew the tub into small pieces, as well as the bathroom, the adjoining room, and the one below. The soldier quickly dressed and disappeared, taking his girl friend with him. Colonel Frederick received a letter from the manager but nothing was ever done about the incident.

Two Canadians named Leo Moffet and Arvest Ouderkirk still think of the night that initiated the actual welding of the two national groups into one homogeneous unit.

When the Canadians received their first pay they went to The Gold Bar. Some wore kilts and others British summer uniforms—shorts and knee socks. As the evening wore on, some miners mumbled insulting remarks about the Canadians, who, frequently lectured on the fact that they were guests of the U. S., glumly swallowed the insults. But American Forcemen in the bar were under no such restraint and went after the miners. When the MP's arrived and learned the cause of the brawl, they refused to interfere. The Ameri·

can soldiers continued to throw the miners out of the bar until it became quiet.

This fight did much to bring the two nationalities in the Force solidly together and from then on there was a fine feeling between the two groups. Shortly afterwards American uniforms were issued to the whole Force and everyone forgot who was Canadian and who was American.

The military police were not always as co-operative. The Forcemen considered them as natural targets, and whenever and wherever they came in contact with the MP's, they regarded the meeting as an invitation to practice unarmed combat.

Once, in a neighboring city, an MP tried to enforce a corps headquarters directive against bloused pants legs on the person of a visiting Forceman named McGinty.

"Pull those pants outa yer boots," he directed.

"Where I come from, that's the uniform," replied McGinty; "so why don't you try pulling them outa my boots yourself?"

The MP moved in, club raised at the ready position, and suddenly found himself on his backside on the street, clutching at his vital parts and moaning. Four more MP's arrived, three of whom joined the first one in the gutter. The fourth raced away, shouting for reinforcements. When they arrived, McGinty had disappeared. A military police lieutenant turned up next day at Fort William Henry Harrison demanding that the man who had nearly murdered four of his men be found and punished. He was bluntly told, "There's a war on, Lieutenant. We don't have time."

This belief in direct action seemed to mark the conduct of almost every member of the Force. Colonel Wickham once told the story of a Mexican-American who, just before the Brigade's first Christmas together planned to go home on furlough to see his father. Somehow the soldier heard that the sergeant major was not going to give him leave. He went back to his tent to get his gun so he could kill the sergeant. He was overcome before he carried out his plan and brought to Wickham. The latter gave him quite a lecture, ending in the boy's breaking down in tears. When Wickham had finished he asked the Mexican what he was going to do now, expecting that he would offer his apologies. Instead, the soldier said, "I'm now going to kill the sergeant."

There were other results of this combination of beans-filled young soldiers and an appreciative town. Approximately 200 marriages between members of the Force and the girls of Helena took place during the period of the Brigade's residence there. These marriages were almost equally distributed between the United States and Canadian personnel and included both officers and enlisted men.

The chaplains of all the faiths represented in the Force tried to stem the rush of bookings for the post chapel, between whose two steeples the Force's training planes, one wing delicately lifted for clear passage, often flew. They pointed out, as diplomatically as possible, the uncertain future that lay before such unions, but their advice was enthusiastically ignored.

Many of these marriages endured. A veteran named Arthur Vantour notes:

"To me the town of Helena was a wonder with all its neon lights. I could walk up and down the street at night just to be under the lights and think how the boys back home would envy me if they could see me now. I was the USO's best customer too, for their late-evening coffee and doughnuts.

"One night while there I saw a young little girl jitterbugging, as we called it in the olden days, with one of my fellow Canadian soldiers. I started doing the same and have been dancing with her ever since."

Of course, not all unions were as idyllic. Here are the comments of a farm-bred cynic:

"I liked Helena and its people, and all Montanans; though I didn't fall head over heels the way some did, vowing to return and settle after the war, mainly because I didn't see how you could put weight on cattle on that thin a stand of grass, and I didn't know what to look for in mining.

"My acquaintance with her daughters was scant, unless you counted the ones in Ida's Rooms, etc. Helena was not the largest of cities, even with only the Force boys to absorb, so the belles could afford to be choosy. Besides, as a man on the station platform had told us, a Yank's only hope for a date was if there should be more girls than Canadians. When a few cursory strolls bore this out, I gave up hope, and got on with the war, keeping sex strictly at the animal (or supermarket) level.

"There was one big, uncouth, bone-headed man from Service Co., who married one of the 'working girls,' Jackie, a free enterpriser who had a nice house (or apartment) a couple of blocks from the regular 'chancre alley.' Some of us were patrons in her premarital days, and only learned of her nuptials to 'Colgate' (the groom had about four front teeth missing) when we went as customers. The husband was having beer with the boys in the parlor, while Jackie finished her evening's work, and Cal remarked later that 'back home they said that being married to a schoolteacher was as good as having a dozen milk cows, and probably a wife like this one should be worth fifty.' "

Contacts as close as these had the inevitable effect of uniting town and camp into a consolidated rumor mill.

The men had never been informed of their ultimate destination. Colonel Frederick and his staff kept their knowledge of Project Plough's mission to themselves . . . an attitude that was stiffly maintained even when inquisitive state and Federal legislators appeared on the scene. But, of course, the rumors flew. One which enjoyed a healthy vogue was that the Force was being trained to raid Hitler's mountain retreat. Other speculations included Poland, the Rumanian oil fields, and sabotage on the Russian front.

Then, slowly, an accurate estimate began to take shape. These men were tough, but few of them were fools. Snow training and the presence of Norwegian ski instructors zeroed the projected locale into Norway. The intensive schooling in demolition made the nature of their mission clear. Qualification tests as parachutists pointed the way to a mass drop. The targets in Norway became a matter of common knowledge, simply because that country's network of hydroelectric stations was the chief prize of the German occupation.

So, the men knew. In short order, they communicated this knowledge to their girl friends in town who then shared the intelligence with their families. The people of Helena had the objectivity to attach an additional dimension to this information. Since they weren't the ones who were to do the jumping . . . they correctly saw the mission as suicidal.

And they felt closer than ever to the men of the Force.

IV

The Gate
Swings Both Ways

In short, if the Force said do something, we did it because we really wanted to stay in the Force.

—TONY SKOMSKI

By the last of August, almost all of the men in the combat echelon had already made their initial parachute jump from the C-47s assigned to the Force. This speed-up program winnowed out the fainthearted in addition to being an invaluable preparation for training. It quickly became known that all you had to do to achieve separation from the Force was to refuse to jump. In Helena during those days, there was a saying: "The gate swings both ways."

Since Frederick, Baldwin and Wickham immediately transferred out any soldier who didn't measure up to the standards that they had set, the recruiting tempo was stepped up to the point where the gate kept swinging so violently that it began to resemble a revolving door.

Part of a Telephone Conversation Between Colonel
Frederick and Major Burhans as Recorded by a War
Department Stenographer, August 1, 1942.

COLONEL FREDERICK: We jumped everybody today here.

MAJOR BURHANS: I understand you had some pretty good luck.

COLONEL FREDERICK: Yes. Everybody jumped, that is some of them are going to jump in a few minutes now, and so far only one broken leg.

MAJOR BURHANS: Only one?

COLONEL FREDERICK: Yes, out of thirty-four.

MAJOR BURHANS: Well, that's pretty good work.

COLONEL FREDERICK: P—— he got up to jump but couldn't take it.

MAJOR BURHANS: Oh, P—— didn't—he refused?

COLONEL FREDERICK: So I think Wickham asked Baldwin to get [transfer] orders on him, I believe.

MAJOR BURHANS: Yes.

COLONEL FREDERICK: All right, well, I have nothing else here.

MAJOR BURHANS: All right, sir.

COLONEL FREDERICK: You might tell Baldwin that those parachute boots that he was getting out here for me by special delivery airmail a couple of weeks ago have not yet arrived and I had to jump in a pair of bedroom slippers.

MAJOR BURHANS: You did?

COLONEL FREDERICK: Yes.

MAJOR BURHANS: Oh, you jumped too?

COLONEL FREDERICK: Oh, sure—what the hell?

MAJOR BURHANS: How'd it go?

COLONEL FREDERICK: Fine.

The combat units were now being conformed to the group's Table of Organization . . . that military holy of holies without which no army is comfortable, since it prescribes not only the number of men, but also what food they should eat, what clothes they may wear, and to what promotions they may aspire. There are few graver sins that a commander can commit than to exceed his Table of Organization. Frederick, realizing this, had drawn himself a unique T.O.

His three regiments had no duties except to prepare for fighting and then fight. His Service Battalion was designed to act as the housekeeping unit for the troops and, in a pinch, help them fight. And the headquarters group were trained to lead. And fight. Additionally, he had prudently obtained consent to a 30 per cent overstrength, until the Force had achieved permanent form.

Using late December as a target day, the Force began the most rigorous training schedule ever undertaken by an American Army unit. The entire program was based on attaining and maintaining peak physical fitness. The troops got up at 4:45 A.M. and by 6:30 had breakfasted, cleaned quarters and were bending and twisting through an involved series of calisthenics. By 8 o'clock the combat units had gone through a mile and a quarter obstacle course on the run. This pace was maintained throughout the day. Four nights a week, training lectures from 7 to 9 were held for all troops. Regular army cadence was 120 steps to the minute. The Force marched at 140. Punctuality at all formations was made into a cardinal virtue, and those who couldn't keep up with the pace were dismissed from the Brigade . . . a fate which these fiercely independent men began to regard with dread.

The differences between Canadian and American drill commands were an initial problem, but Frederick resolved it by choosing the best of each. When the Americans questioned swinging their arms high in the British tradition, they were told that it would help them in ski training. The Canadians, unused to the "To the rear, march" commands, were almost run over by sharply pivoting Americans. Though they soon learned the maneuver, they never quite lost the conviction that the sharply barked American marching orders sounded more like a fox hunt than a drill.

Shinberger boiled the normal three-month parachute training time down to six days. Many men jumped with far less preparation. Frederick, for example, submitted to a ten-minute description of how to twist in the harness and roll so as to absorb the shock of landing before he impatiently swung a parachute on his back and said, "That's enough. Let's go."

Most Forcemen found as much zest in jumping as they did in fighting. One Forceman dove out of the plane on each of his two qualifying flights and, as a result, came down entangled in his chute both times. Normally, this would have meant being automatically washed out. But he wangled a third chance, got some of the best parachutists to go with him on the next try and, with their advice, executed "a lovely jump."

One of the most remarkable instructors in camp during this period was the much-traveled Irishman, Dermot ("Pat") O'Neill, a civilian expert whom Frederick imported to teach hand-to-hand fighting.

Before 1941, Pat had been a detective, a member of a riot squad, and an officer of the far-famed Shanghai International Police. His reputation for a brand of fighting in which he mixed jujitsu, karate, and several other methods of barehandedly crippling an antagonist, had brought him to the attention of Colonel William ("Wild Bill") Donovan, who made him a member of the super-spy organization he was then forming, the O.S.S.*

Through his Intelligence connections, Burhans had heard of O'Neill and recommended him to Frederick. Frederick, overlooking the minor detail that O'Neill was not an American citizen, said, "Get him for the Force. We're going to be able to use him." This was an eminently accurate statement. O'Neill proved so effective a teacher that later, in combat, a Forceman offhandedly reported, "I killed the Kraut with an O'Neill in the nuts."

O'Neill recollects the effect of his teaching in the early days: "I recall hearing of clashes between the miners and our men which showed, at least in the early days, that a gang of miners were more than a match for the untrained Commandos; however, this quickly changed as the hand-to-hand training got under way. Some of the incidents that resulted were serious enough to prompt Colonel Adams to bring this

---

* Donovan later attempted to remove O'Neill and get him back in the O.S.S., but Frederick had by this time secured a U. S. commission for his instructor and kept him in the Force.

to the attention of the officers, especially when officials of neighboring towns complained about the severe way their law enforcement officers were handled."

For their demolition training, the Forcemen were assigned an apparently unlimited supply of the latest explosives, and they cheerfully set out to blow up everything in sight.

A number of abandoned mines in the area had been given to the Force as targets. The owners were glad to have them blown apart since the machinery in them had value only as scrap iron. But the Forcemen used so much explosives that they pulverized the machinery beyond reclamation as scrap iron. Occasionally they would blow up the wrong mine or even the wrong house. Once they loaded an old bridge with so much dynamite that they knocked over most of the chimneys in a nearby town.

The First Special Service Force had an affinity for explosives, guns, and the excitement that went with them. After they arrived, the men often "borrowed" the Weasels for unauthorized hunting trips. One of the pilots and his passenger was killed when they used the plane for a coyote hunting safari which took place after a particularly salubrious party. Even Chaplain Leggitt, in recalling the training that he undertook during this period, said tersely, "My training was selective, but I tried to be on hand during all schedules. Qualified with carbine and Tommy gun."

This infatuation with detonation didn't stop when the sun went down. A favorite off-duty trick was to put rounds of live ammunition on the top of a hot stove and then watch friends dive for cover. Dynamite caps were often thrown in the stoves. One night a blasting cap blew a chunk of iron into one boy's head and skewered another with metal splinters. They spent the night having pieces dug out of them and then made the morning drill formation. Other nights were punctuated with the sounds of exploding garbage cans.

The same spirit prevailed on many of the long and grueling marches that were scheduled to build up physical endurance. At one time the Mad Russian, John Kures, in revenge for a fancied wrong, stuffed his platoon lieutenant's pack with rocks just before they set out on a forced 50-mile march. These marches were important. If a man fell out, it generally meant instant dismissal from the Force. It was not uncommon to see men, after one of these grueling hikes, wring blood out of their socks.

"I recall many soldiers who ended up with blisters worn away to raw meat," says Sergeant Fuller.

"We did not want any 'quitters' in our outfit," said Tony Skomski. "If you were exhausted on a hike, or from running with a full pack after hiking six hours, it was acceptable to pass out. But if you just plain quit, we didn't want the man in the outfit."

It was assumed that those that passed out had stayed up too late at night chasing girls or were drinking too much. They were gotten in shape by being made to run after supper while carrying a .30-cal. machine gun on their shoulder.

It is worthwhile, at this point, to focus on two men whose exploits occupy a prominent place in the folklore of the First Special Service Force. Sergeant Jacob Walkmeister, a burly 1st Regiment medical corpsman, was often whispered about as "a former big-shot racketeer from Chicago." The other man, Lieutenant Graham Heilman, was known to have been a football player at the University of Virginia, where he had added to his income by the operation of a prosperous off-campus bar. Both were eminently worthy of notice. Walkmeister, for example, later became a favorite for correspondent Bill Mauldin's cartoons of the Italian campaign. In a recent conversation, an ex-Forceman, who has since become a high official of the Department of the Interior, had tears in his eyes as he described Walkmeister's death in battle.

It is a matter of many recollections that Sergeant Jake had curly hair, a flowing handlebar mustache, called every officer "Lieutenant," and was followed by a covey of girl friends to every Force training base in the States.

Lieutenant Heilman later achieved fame throughout Italy when he became the mayor and principal citizen of a village located in the middle of no man's land. He had received the nickname, "Gus" after his athletic labors at the university created such a personal thirst he decided to eliminate the middleman by opening his own bar and grill in the town of Charlottesville. Obviously, "Graham" was much too formal a name for the proprietor of a public house. This was his first recorded display of community spirit. His tavern, the "Cavalier Bar & Grill" proved so popular with his fellow students that the college authorities were almost saddened when he received his draft notice in 1941. Almost.

Gus, after evaluating the situation, decided that his contribution to the morale of the home front (he sold very good beer at reasonable prices) outweighed whatever marginal value his services might have for the military establishment. He assured the draft board that the fact that he was making a pile of money at the Cavalier had nothing to do with his re-luctance to don a uniform. The draft board was composed of men of small vision who were inclined to take their chances with the community's morale, and they insisted that he put on a uniform at his earliest convenience.

Gus, refusing to be hurt by the indifference of these uninspired men, pulled every political string that he or his customers knew of, in order to stay out of the Army. Nothing worked. And, in spite of the assurances of friends in high office, he was not stationed near Charlottesville as they had promised, but, as he later inelegantly though accurately phrased it, "They shipped my ass to Jefferson Barracks, Missouri." He remained there for five days and then was sent further west to an air base in Utah.

By now, visions of the lost profits of the Cavalier were driving him frantic. So he volunteered for the Infantry Officer Candidate School which had the virtue of being situated in nearby Georgia. Contrary to his hopes, the training at the Infantry School was so sustained that he had no opportunity for weekend supervisory trips to the Cavalier Bar & Grill. In short order, he became known as one of the most complete foul-ups who ever wangled his way into officer training. His record was so bad that it became quite evident that no power on earth would ever convince the school commandant to recommend him for a commission. The alternative had the effect of depressing Gus even more than the prospect of losing the Cavalier: men who were dropped out of the school were sent as replacements to overseas-bound infantry organizations.

Therefore, when a recruiting party from the First Special Service Force, led by Colonel Shinberger, came through in a search for potential junior officers, Gus Heilman was among the first eager volunteers. He lied like a trooper to the interviewers. They asked him if he could ski and he swore that his skiing was of Olympic caliber. He had never been on skis in his life. They asked him how tough he thought he was and he told them about the Cavalier. Only, instead of describing his duties at the cash register, he told them that he had been the bouncer, and had thrown dozens of unruly drunks out of the place in the course of a single night.

Brawny and convincing, Gus Heilman was among the twenty Fort Benning men accepted for the Force. He was commissioned on the spot, issued the gold bars of a second lieutenant, and told to return to his quarters, pack, and get back on the double, as the Force was in immediate need of junior officers.

He had the grace to hide his bars when he returned to his barracks, because he was uneasily aware that if any of his comrades were to see him wearing them, he would be immediately reported for impersonating an officer. On their part, his friends saw nothing strange in Gus's packing and getting ready to go. They had been expecting him to be thrown out of the school from the day of his arrival.

Because of his football conditioning, Gus did not find the training at Helena overly difficult. His attitude was consistently one of stubborn meanness, a position that he felt was justified in light of the fact that his patriotism in volunteering for this isolated outfit had finally forced him to sell the Cavalier Bar & Grill at a considerable loss. Big, tough, mean and resentful . . . Heilman, in spite of himself, was the ideal Forceman.

He and Roy Woolhiser used the weekends for hunting trips in the mountains of Montana. By displaying the same initiative that had led him to acquire a taproom while at college, he had now acquired the only shotgun at Fort Harrison and once fetched back 110 prairie chickens from a solo safari in nearby Gallatin Canyon. He became one of Pat

O'Neill's most enthusiastic students and his resultant skill at vicious unarmed combat would have made him the undisputed boss of his platoon, even if he hadn't already been provided with the bars of a shavetail. He also became adept at catching the rattlesnakes which were so dutifully presented to Colonel Shinberger.

He never surrendered his somewhat jaundiced views on proper behavior. One stinging cold morning, Woolhiser asked him for a cup of coffee. Heilman straightfacedly ladeled a mugful of the dishwater that was being kept warm atop the potbellied stove in the middle of their tent and gave it to his friend who drank it gratefully. When Heilman later pointed out Woolhiser's lack of palate, the battle that ensued became the subject of much admiring comment throughout the camp.

Throughout the rest of his training in the States, Heilman continued an audible barrage of criticism directed against his fellow officers, the soldiers under him, the type of training they were all receiving, and, on every occasion, disappeared for unauthorized absences. In spite of all this, Heilman was one of the best-liked men in the Force. His men consistently found humor in everything he did. Later, in combat, Gus never lacked for volunteers to accompany him on patrols.

Ski training, even to the tall and angular Texans who called their skis "Torture Boards," presented a further opportunity for the men to turn their bodies into superbly conditioned, instantly-reacting instruments of combat. John Bourne, of the 3rd Regiment, describes it vividly:

> One of the best parts of our training at Helena, Montana, was the ski instruction given to us by twelve Norwegian ski instructors. Most of these men had escaped from Norway and had been in the Norwegian forces at some time or other. The training started before the snow fell when we went for short cross-country runs (about five miles) equipped with ski poles. Besides the cross-country running, we used to run up and down the hill that was named "Muscle Mountain" pretending we were on skis, running straight up and zigzagging on the way down.
>
> When the snow fell, arrangements were made with one of

the railways to establish a camp made up of boxcars which were normally used for work crews. This camp was located at a place called Blossburg on the Continental Divide. Each regiment was sent there for two periods of three weeks and a number of officers were chosen as assistant instructors. At the end of the second three-week period, all men in the Special Service Force were able to go on a 30-mile cross-country ski trip in one day, carrying a loaded rucksack and a rifle. This in itself was quite a feat as there were over 300 men in the Force who had never seen snow before, a number of whom came from Texas and other Southern states.

The iron hand of Colonel Adams was felt in this phase of our training, as he would not permit us to use the arctic equipment that had been issued to the Force, and instructions were given that our noonday meal throughout this period of training would consist of one Spam sandwich, one chocolate bar and an apple. Considering the amount of energy being used each day this meal was not really enough to go on. However, it taught us to get along with lean rations in very severe winter conditions.

After this phase of the training, we carried out several overnight exercises using the Weasels and our skis where we all learned how to look after ourselves at subzero temperatures without shelter or the use of fire. Again, this part of the training was of great value to us when we got into the mountains in Italy during the winter of 1943–44.

The difficult and intense training regime produced a strong sense of pride. It was evident that only the most superior human beings could endure it. It went beyond boast and talk. You either stood the gaff or your records were stamped with the three initials that the men came to dread, "RTU" . . . Return To Unit.

In their raw stages, the Forcemen may have been malcontents or social rejects. Here they became members of a superbly seasoned elite. Each had the option to leave at any time, but no one ever willingly accepted it once the initial weeding-out process had been accomplished. The men looked about them and thought, "I'm as good as anyone here. I'm better than any soldier anywhere else." This was a rare identity to have earned. They regarded with perhaps subconscious gratitude the leaders who had given them this opportunity. Their officers proved themselves in the same crucible. The weak ones had been shaken out. There were few whom the men would not have followed anywhere, because they had earned their right to lead.

This spirit was a living and almost tangible thing. New recruits who joined gaped at what they saw. A former first sergeant in another branch of the service commented, "I was amazed at the closeness of the enlisted men and officers. They all acted as if they were a select military fraternity, and although I heard some belly-aching in the barracks, the way that everyone closed in on any outsider who made a detrimental crack about the Force was fantastic. There was nothing like it anywhere else in the Army. I can't tell you how badly I wanted to be accepted as a member of this outfit."

Colonel Frederick never attained really full dimensions to the Force during this period. He would appear at a training session, or might suddenly show up at a supply tent or visit the motor pool to learn to drive a Weasel and drink a cup of coffee with the sergeant in charge, but these were only interludes. He considered that his function was to remain on the move . . . rounding up additional men and supplies from all parts of the country.

As the training program moved forward, Frederick's headquarters at the Munitions Building in Washington had been investigating the feasibility of additional targets for the Force. Raids on the Ploesti oil fields were being considered, since this was one of the richest prizes and worthy of a group of trained saboteurs. Italy was considered a good secondary goal because of the concentration of heavy machine industry in its north.

Still, the Force Intelligence staff worked long hours accumulating further information on Norway . . . information which would have to be precise if the Forcemen were to have any prospect of escaping with their lives after accomplishing their objective. To resolve some of the questions inherent in these possibilities, Frederick left for London to consult with Mountbatten and other members of the British military establishment and to establish further contact with General Eisenhower, who was now based in the United Kingdom.

It was mid-September when Frederick informed Eisenhower of the status of the project's training and its future plans. The Commanding General showed interest, but gave no indication that he felt he had any further control over Frederick or Project Plough. This interview left Frederick with a curious feeling of unease. He made an appointment the following day to see Mountbatten about the aircraft required by his operational planning.

The meeting with the Chief of Combined Operations did nothing to dispel Frederick's feeling that his Force no longer held the interest of these men. Mountbatten told Frederick that it had been his impression that the Americans would completely equip and supply the Force and that he had serious doubts that Frederick's requisition for British bombers would be met. He suggested that Frederick make the request directly to the Air Marshal. The silence of the Air Vice-Marshal who was also present at the meeting was particularly disquieting to Frederick.

Next day, Frederick was informed that he should review his plans at a meeting of the Chiefs of Staff. He informed Eisenhower of this invitation who, again sparing with his words, simply said, "Go ahead and state your case."

This meeting was a frustrating experience. The Chiefs, although pleasant in manner, were obviously antagonistic to the project's proposed use of British aircraft. The session concluded with a request by the Chief of Air Staff that Frederick submit a detailed account of his plans. He added that he would study the memorandum in an attempt to determine whether or not it represented a justifiable diversion of British resources.

At another meeting the Norwegians displayed an entirely unexpected lack of enthusiasm for the prospect of using their homeland as the initial site of the project's activities. Their formally stated reasons for wishing to leave a project in which they had originally entered with enthusiasm took many forms, but from the perspective that time and distance provides, it seems obvious now that Project Plough had begun to take on an aspect of such efficiency that they had become convinced that its employment would result in the almost total industrial destruction of their country.

Thoroughly disheartened, Frederick left England to return home. He was convinced that Project Plough had lost its support in high places. And, without such support, he felt defenseless against the massed weight of the American high command . . . a group which had never shown any friendliness to the First Special Service Force.

His plane took off on September 20, but was grounded in Ireland because of bad weather. For the next four days, Frederick sat in a damp hotel room in Adare and considered the collapse of the world he had been building in Helena.

Frederick was far from an impractical man. He realized that those with whom he had been consulting were reacting to the realities of a changing situation. Through their eyes, he could see that the Force would offer no deterrent to the German war machine then rolling steadily toward Moscow . . . that the needs of war now indicated that the main Allied effort be directed to North Africa and, as a result, the snow-trained men of Project Plough could not, on paper, be considered a preferred asset in that campaign. He also understood the deep anguish which prompted the withdrawal from the project by the Norwegians.

He felt that under these circumstances it was morally wrong to carry the training of the Force any further. By now, his involvement with the men of the Brigade was a deep and emotional thing, far beyond the normal parent's love with which many commanding officers regard their troops. He had passed the point of infatuation with an extension of his own image . . . his feelings were that of sincere respect for an entity which had earned the right to fair treatment. He owed the men of the Force an accurate summary of the situation.

Instead of continuing toward home when the weather broke, he returned to London and Mountbatten. The two men spoke openly to each other. Mountbatten told him that upward-spiraling pressures were being brought to diminish Combined Operation's influence in Whitehall, the British War Department's headquarters.

These pressures, Lord Louis said, made it difficult for him to fight for a project which was unacceptable to the Norwegian Government and which, under present conditions, no longer represented a sound reason for the diversion of material and men.

On his part, Frederick admitted that he had no answer to the problem of aircraft. Neither his background as a professionally-trained planner nor his innate honesty would permit him to offer specious arguments of tactical urgency.

The meeting ended with an agreement to let Project Plough die.

Frederick lost no time in regrets. After leaving Lord Louis, he sent a cable to his office in Washington's Munitions Building. It read: "Suspend current planning."

When Frederick returned to Washington at the end of September, he made a detailed report to the General Staff informing them of the decision reached in London. The Canadian Government, advised of the cancellation of Project Plough, decided to terminate their participation in the First Special Service Force. However, an unexpected ally, General George C. Marshall, persuaded the Canadians to rescind this decision on the ground that such a move would have a very bad effect on what had been a highly successful experiment in teamwork by the two countries. This action relit the spark of Frederick's competitive nature. Project Plough might be dying, but he decided he'd be damned if he'd admit the Force was a corpse until the final death sentence was administered by Washington.

Frederick met with his staff and told them what had happened. Allowing disappointment no time to sap their energies, he set them to changing the Tables of Organization and list of equipment. This transformed the Brigade from a one-purpose force into a versatile organization capable of meeting almost any combat situation. Total dependence on the Weasel was eliminated. The combat elements were given submachine guns, Browning light machine guns, and the recently developed bazooka rocket launcher. Shortly afterwards, all platoons received flame throwers, 60-mm. mortars and the new Johnson light machine gun, which proved to be an overwhelming favorite in battle.

Baldwin seemed to have a sixth sense which alerted him to every new development in Washington. He swapped the Marines out of a large number of "Johnny guns," wangled the latest in radio equipment and clothing, and talked the Ordnance Department into supplying substantial amounts of a sensational new explosive, "RS." He even had contacts with the National Inventors Council. One day he came in with a New York doctor's plans for a poison dart which gave every evidence of practicality. However, it developed that this idea was specifically forbidden by the Hague Convention, and the Force went into combat without blowguns.

Although Norway had withdrawn its country as an arena, the Norwegian officers honored their commitment to supply training in snow tactics. Most of the ski instructors at the Force's first headquarters in Montana were Norwegian. The majority of the Forcemen used this appearance as a basis to float the rumor that their first destination would be the Scandinavian peninsula.

It was now November. Frederick had become a more shadowy figure than ever to the Forcemen . . . a commanding officer who was forever going off on unexplained trips to undisclosed places. He had turned into a man searching for a mission.

Friends in high places had secured permission for him to continue the Force's training, but none of his frequent trips to Washington yielded anything in the form of a target for his extraordinary assault force. General Marshall told him to prepare a study of possible Special Service Force operations in the Caucasus Mountains, a task Frederick completed in two weeks. His study disclosed that the Russians had twenty-eight divisions in the path of the German troops. He felt this was probably enough to halt or stall any advance through the easily defended pass to the Transcaucasus valleys. Frederick's professional integrity resulted in a report which indicated little need for the employment of his men.

In late November he was told by the General Staff to take his Force to New Guinea. The wild scramble for maps and tropical combat information was abruptly halted next day when another call came into the Munitions Building which said, in effect, "Forget New Guinea. Kiska is set for an invasion next spring. You'll go there."

That night another call came in from Operations saying that it was premature to begin making up troop lists for Kiska. The Force was still unemployed. Worse yet, every man on the staff realized that, like the effect on an overtrained prize fighter, there was always the danger of leaving the fight in the dressing room, and that the Force was now in this very position. This was a real cause for concern. Although Frederick and his staff officers carefully kept the uncertainty of the Force's destination away from them, he knew that if the Forcemen ever felt that their utilization was in doubt, the self-confidence, which made them into a superb company of mentally and physically trained professionals would be gone.

The training continued. The individual soldiers were resourceful, tough and had developed a thirst for combat which was almost unquenchable. By late December, they had begun to approach their peak. It became obvious that more of the same would result in diminishing returns. So Frederick granted everyone a ten-day Christmas leave.

The men went home, strutted and flexed their muscles before the folks, and then eagerly returned to camp to be among their own kind. The trips yielded huge dividends in morale. When the men looked at the world outside Helena, the realization of just how good they had become suddenly came over them. These men . . . these erstwhile undisciplined brawlers and malcontents, these formerly undistinguished farm boys, teachers and choir singers . . . returned to Helena with an almost mystical new regard for their organization. They had been conditioned to look upon the Force as their home, the Forcemen as their only peers, and the conditioning was successful. The Christmas furlough proved it.

In February, the Norwegian ski specialists reported that in two weeks of training, 99 per cent of the Force had become competent skiers, even by Norwegian Army standards. Armed with this report, Frederick received permission to visit Lt. General Simon B. Buckner in the Alaskan Department. Buckner, his department pauperized by the continued diversion of his men to other commands (while he was preparing for the oncoming invasions of Adak, Amchitka, Attu and Kiska), was excited by Frederick's description of his men and their capacity to fight in frigid temperatures. He sent a wire to Washington urging that the First Special Service Force be attached to his command.

Coincidentally, General Eisenhower, who had been planning for the invasion of Sicily, recalled the impression Frederick had made on him and requested of the War Department that the Force be given him for "Operation Husky," the code name for the Italian invasion.

Frederick and his Force had finally become popular. His confidence in the capability of an elite striking group was justified. But before a decision on either destination could be reached one last bit of versatility was required. For schooling in amphibious landing tactics, the Force was ordered to Camp Bradford, the Naval Operations Base in Norfolk, Virginia.

The news that the Force was to leave swept over Helena like an unwelcome storm, leaving a train of hasty marriages and choked farewells in its wake. To bid a proper good-bye, on Army Day, April 6, the 2,300 men of the Force gathered themselves in full array and paraded through Helena, where they were reviewed by the Governor of Montana. The Helenans, who lined the streets, looked as if they were watching their own sons march away.

Warmth, however, was conspicuously absent when the Force reached Norfolk. Generations of navy men had worn away the novelty of a uniform in Norfolk, which warily considered soldiers, sailors, and marines as leading, but irksome, local consumers. The Brigade, however, was especially under suspicion. The townspeople and the shore patrol had been hearing strange rumors about this odd group of men, which bore the unfamiliar title of the First Special Service Force.

The Force quickly sensed dislike and a generally skeptical attitude. So they showed everybody. To the amazement of the Amphibious School staff, the Forcemen went up and down the practice riggings wearing full packs in faster time than it had ever been done before. Army inspection teams, in an almost unparalleled move, declared the Force had completed its training a full week before the already-accelerated course was formally finished.

Some of the highlights of the Norfolk stay are most graphically described by survivors of the Force. Percy Mc-Donald Crichlow, a former schoolmaster in the West Indies who became part of the Canadian contingent to the Brigade, had this to say about Norfolk:

> Only one thing annoyed me here. The Captain told me that he wanted me to go as section leader in number 3 Platoon. That platoon didn't have a good name because one part of the platoon had tried to kill the other half in a live-round training exercise at Helena. I told the Captain flatly that I just didn't want the job, even if it did carry promotion to staff sergeant. But he and the Lieutenant talked me into it and I went over there feeling like a lamb going into a lion's den.

Robert K. Shafer, a 1st Regiment NCO, had what could have been a highly embarrassing experience:

> While on a maneuvers at Bradford, we were on the boats heading for shore in mock attack. One of the men along side of me said, "Well, how do you like it?" It was raining and cold. I says, "Not worth a damn; I'd like to have Frederick out here with us and see how he likes it; and, lo and behold, it was *him*. Man, when we got to shore and hit it, I took off and lost myself quick!

Having had their fill of practicing Pat O'Neill's methods of infighting on the miners of Helena and on each other, the Forcemen enthusiastically welcomed the suspicion and dislike with which they were regarded by the shore patrol and ma-rines. It promised them a new set of sparring partners. On one trip to town, a Forceman indicated his doubt of the Marine Corps' reputation for toughness by betting a leatherneck $5 that he could take away the marine's bayonet from him with his bare hands. He won his bet. Other Forcemen soon made a practice of disarming marines whenever they met them in town.

The Coast Artillery Commanding General, who commanded the training post, told Frederick that if these activities were not stopped, he would "sic" his police detachment on the Forcemen. He also intimated to Frederick that he thought that the Force's reputation badly needed deflating. Unimpressed, Frederick bet the General $10 that not only were his Forcemen as good as they thought they were, but they could prove it by thwarting every security precaution that the General's guards had built into their camp.

The two men agreed to meet next morning to settle the wager. After breakfast, Frederick took the General on a tour of his own post. He pointed out that his Forcemen had stealthily infiltrated the camp during the night and placed simulated explosives under every barracks, building, and gun installation in the area. He also showed the General where a charge of simulated dynamite had been hidden under his own bed. Frederick cheerfully pocketed the General's $10. The General expressed no more doubts about the Force's capabilities.

Shortly afterwards, the Force left Norfolk to practice simulated landings and night loadings along the shores of the Chesapeake. Of this exercise, an awed naval ensign reported:

> The best Army Division averages about one minute per platoon load from the first man over to the time the boat pulled away. The Marines did it in fifty-two seconds, which was the best we had seen till then. But these guys did it *in thirty-five seconds,* with absolute silence, a minimum of commands, and carrying full combat loads.

The legend was forming . . .

In late May, the Force moved to Fort Ethan Allen in Burlington, Vermont, for its final staging ground in America. Here the training was continued, but the goal now was the thin edge of perfection. And, as before, their reputation preceded them.

Jim Kurtzhal indicated the difficulty that this presented:

93 *

"The story had been circulated that we were a bunch of ex-cons, and they wouldn't let their daughters out on the streets. It took about two weeks to convince people in town that we were gentlemen. Of course, we had to throw the Air Force out of town before we got along.

Another obstacle to the town's acceptance of the Force as "gentlemen" was the blowing of the safe at the office of a local dry cleaning plant. It might have gone unnoticed except that the safe of the Planters Peanut Company near Norfolk had also been similarly blown while the Force had been stationed *there*. Questions were raised in some quarters. However, everyone, including Private Hiscox (as before noted, later discovered to be the only member of Canada's "Polka Dot" gang) went about their affairs in so businesslike a manner that suspicion never became evidence. It is a matter only of historical interest to mention that, thereafter, whenever Hiscox and the Force were stationed anywhere near a town possessing a safe which looked as if it had valuable contents, that safe was blown.

Lieutenant Colonel Stuart reported the treatment the Force received as having been caused by "the rumor around town that we were a bunch of criminals that had been pardoned to join the outfit—and General Frederick's frequent reference to us as his 'thugs' * didn't help that situation at all. My land-lady would not take a check for the rent—even a check on the local bank. When my wife arrived (we were married in Helena), I had difficulty getting a hotel room reservation at first because I didn't have a marriage license with me to show the room clerk."

As a result of this slowness of the atmosphere to thaw, the Forcemen took to spending their weekend leaves in Montreal. However, their exuberant leisure-time activities soon dampened that city's appreciation. As a token of their disdain for this lack of understanding, it became a tradition for Forcemen

---

* It is only fair to mention that General Frederick disputes this remark: "I can't recall ever having referred to my men as 'thugs.' There were other adjectives I might have used, but not thugs."

to let loose a few live chickens in the passenger station before going home.

Colonel Bourne was personally embarrassed by the Forcemen's conviction that they could thumb their noses at the world. Driving to Montreal, he noticed one of his enlisted men standing by the road in an effort to hitch his way to Canada. Naturally, he stopped and took the man with him as a passenger. When the Colonel returned to Force Headquarters on Sunday night, he found that the man had not only been AWOL, he also had the gall to use his commanding officer to abet his illegal absence.

The most memorable event which occurred during Burlington training was the appearance of one Lieutenant Colonel Edwin A. Walker, as a Force regimental commander.

"He impressed us very much," says one of the men who served with him in the 3rd Regiment. "Coming from the Artillery, he wasn't in the best of shape. When he came on a 25-mile route march with us and he had to hobble back. But he got there and back, alright."

Walker was strongly attached to his mother, who spent quite some time visiting him at Fort Ethan Allen. This caused some comment since the Forcemen were not particularly noted for responding to a mother's influence.

Informed by the Operations Division in Washington that his organization was destined for the United Kingdom, where they would engage in commandolike raids across the English Channel into France, Frederick prepared for a July 25th embarkation date. That date was never met. General Marshall, because of both military and political pressures, had decided that the Japanese should be expelled from the Aleutian Islands, their only foothold in North America. General Buckner, hearing this news, lost no time in requesting that the First Special Service Force be attached to his command. The request was granted. For the first time since Project Plough, the Forcemen had a mission they would actually fulfill.

On June 15, 1943, the long-awaited overseas inspection team arrived in camp. The inspectors found out that the standard criteria used to evaluate military units were absolutely inadequate when applied to Frederick's Brigade. Normally, a grade of 75 per cent was sufficient to pass an organization through tests on maintenance, map reading, physical fitness and other military requirements. 100 per cent was, of course, considered perfect. Force units averaged 125 per cent, and on several occasions achieved *200 per cent!*

"Amazement" is the only adequate description of the inspectors' reactions as they saw the loads and quantities of ammunition that these men carried quickly, silently and with no apparent loss of breath. They told Frederick they felt that his Brigade showed all of the co-ordination and teamwork of a champion professional ball club. That night the inspectors filed their reports for the Army Ground Force Headquarters. The First Special Service Force was ready for any job that had to be done. Any job.

Pvt. Hoffman spoke for everyone when he observed, "We all felt time was wasting and we wanted combat before the war ended."

V

The Dry Run

We've ferried a lot of troops on a lot of invasions, and, mostly, the night before they write letters home or talk to the chaplains. But not these crazy bastards. Why, their officers had to go in and bust up their crap games when it came time to go ashore for the fight.

> —A Chief Petty Officer aboard one of the invasion ships which carried the First Special Service Force to Kiska.

The rumors were wrong.

For the past month, all the talk had been of the European Theater and a confrontation with the Germans. This feeling persisted even after the men boarded the hot and dirty day coaches which took them to Angel Island, the embarkation point in San Francisco Bay.

Lieutenant Percy Crichlow described the trip: "The railway journey out of Burlington fooled us at first. We felt sure we were going south to New York. Then the doubts started when we turned west. Later we just sat back and enjoyed the scenery, especially Colorado."

"The train was a stinking mess of vomit and stale whiskey and cigarettes, the whole Force was on a drunk from the time we boarded the train until we got on the ferry for the Island," remembers another and less aesthetic Forceman.

After a week's stay on Angel Island the destination of the Force was no longer a secret. The arctic gear that was being issued pointed unmistakably to the Aleutians.

On the evening of July 9, the men, under the supervision of Colonel Frederick and Major Baldwin, loaded into the two Liberty ships that were to take them northward. The strength of the Brigade at that moment was 169 officers and 2,283 enlisted men. Approximately 75 per cent of these were combat troops. This was the total number of troops slated as the first invasion wave against an estimated 12,000 heavily armed, well-dug-in Japanese defenders. Force mission would be to hold the beachhead while the main landing force went ashore.

Some of the original Helena contingent of officers had been replaced. The Canadian executive officer of the Brigade, Lieutenant Colonel John McQueen, had broken a leg in a parachute jump and had been replaced by Colonel Paul Adams who, by this time, was variously known as "Chew Chew," "Iron Ass," and "Smiling Jack." Colonel Shinberger, whose dash had withered before Adams' steady stare, was followed in the Operations post by Major Emil Eschenberg. Lieutenant Colonel Alfred C. Marshall, a handsome West Pointer who had been rescued by Frederick from a Quartermaster Corps assignment, remained in command of the 1st Regiment. Lieutenant Colonel D. D. Williamson, a Canadian who bore the nickname "Windy Willy," commanded the 2nd Regiment. The 3rd Regiment was under the iron supervision of the polo-playing Texan, Lieutenant Colonel Edwin A. Walker.

The Service Battalion, which had progressed from a military experiment into a highly valuable adjunct by freeing the fighters to do nothing but fight, was commanded by a former Kansas City clothing merchant, Lieutenant Colonel Gerald Rodehayer.

After the Force put out to sea, two bits of information

were received which had special significance for the men. The first, the news of the Allied landings in Sicily, did not receive as much attention as the announcement by the Navy Department that the light cruiser U.S.S. *Helena* had been sunk in the Pacific. The men interrupted their poker and crap games long enough to chip in $5,500 which was later sent to Helena for a monument to commemorate the stay of the First Special Service Force.

One of the Force's most cherished legends was born of the gambling during this voyage. "Sugar" Kane, who was later killed in Italy, was supposed to have won an amount variously reported as $1,000 to $10,000. After landing at Amchitka, he buried it in a corner of his tent. Then, he couldn't find it. Frederick later heard that this had happened and asked the man if he wanted to go back and get his forgotten wealth. Kane stated that no amount of money was worth returning to Amchitka. To this day, certain Forcemen annually make halfhearted resolutions to "go up there and look around, next Summer."

Gambling did not become general until the fifth or sixth day at sea. Up till then, there had been a general submission to the violent seasickness caused by the pitching and tossing of the old, half-filled ships in the rough waters.

Sgt. Chenoweth describes the aftermath of one particular meal: "The menu consisted of sauerkraut and franks. Everybody got sick. The kraut clogged up the urinals and as the ship listed, the water would run off on the floor and as a mixture of kraut, franks and etc., was ankle deep. Crawling on hands and knees was in order as one couldn't stand up in the slick, slimy mess. I observed all of this as I braced myself between the pipes in one corner of the head. As sick as I was, I had to chuckle as some of my buddies came sliding in on all fours and trying to hit a toilet bowl or urinal."

Once the ships had ploughed into smoother waters, part of each day began to be devoted to training for the job ahead. All units were given a complete map of the Aleutians and a portfolio of information concerning Kiska and other targets. They were drilled in this information until each man could draw a map of the island from memory. The training continued until the boats put into the Alaskan harbor of Adak Island.

That night, the two ships were visited by Frederick, who had flown up before them. He told the men that as a result of his planning sessions with the campaign's commander, Rear Admiral Thomas C. Kinkaid, they would proceed to Amchitka Island and make camp.

Frederick had spent most of the preceding week familiarizing himself with the bivouac and training area assigned to his troops, as well as meeting the commanders of the other units who would participate in the invasion. He had also whiled away the time until his troops came by flying a bombing mission over Kiska. Since this represented his combat baptism, his personal diary entry for the day may be quoted:

> Due to engine trouble, the plane I was in was delayed in take-off and took off at 12:30, half an hour behind the others. I hoped to have a look at Amchitka in passing, but it was completely blanketed by fog. We passed the other bombers returning from Kiska and arrived there alone to receive the full benefit of antiaircraft fire from North Head and other guns in the Kiska Harbor area.
>
> The bombs were dropped on Little Kiska from an altitude of about 9,000 feet while the plane was under heavy AA fire, and the pilot promptly dived to about 3,000 feet after the bombs were released. As the bombsight was broken, it was necessary for the pilot to maintain straight and level flight for much longer than is normally necessary.
>
> I was pleased to find that the close AA fire which upset most of the plane's crew and almost unnerved some of them did not frighten or bother me.
>
> After circling beyond Little Kiska we flew off to the west to fly along the northeast shore of Kiska for reconnaissance. We saw the force of cruisers steaming in for the attack and then flew from the northwest to southeast over Kiska, receiving heavy AA fire from a battery the pilot did not know was there. After diving away from this fire and circling to the north just beyond the battleship force consisting of two battleships and a heavy cruiser,

we watched the naval bombardment which started on the dot of 1500. It was an impressive sight to see these naval ships sailing formation and firing rapidly. After watching the naval firing for a little more than half an hour we flew back to Adak.

At Amchitka, the Force turned its attention to the other units who would be making the fight with them. They liked the sight of the Alaska Scouts, because, in these rugged ex-trappers and guides, they could recognize kindred souls. The other Army and Navy units were only subjects for speculation as to how well they would hold up their end of the job. The fact that some of these other units bore ferocious names, such as "The Widow-makers," and "Corlett's Long Knives (a group named after the senior Army general on the scene)," struck the Forcemen as an adolescent gesture.

This attitude was always a source of despair to the military heraldry and public relations men. When the Force flag had been designed, space had been left blank against the day when some Forceman would utter an imperishable slogan. But the space remained empty throughout the life of the Brigade since the comment that came closest to immortality (and printability) was "ah, screw them krauts."

Percy Crichlow furnishes a setting of scene: "Amchitka was certainly different, covered with muskeg or tundra or whatever you chose to call it. Roads raised above the flat surface, tents in excavated squares with drains to keep the water from filling the hole. The whole thing seemed like one vast sponge. Attempted guard duty near the coast was just a farce: I couldn't recognize one hummock from another, when I left the Guard tent I couldn't find my way back and sometimes I couldn't find a sentry when I took out the relief detail. Most men got shoe paks and rubber suits: there were no shoe paks for me as my feet were small, so I just had to make do with my jump boots. There was training in the landing craft on kelp-lined shores.

"Once we heard a broadcast on a radio that said we were surrounded and cut off on Amchitka and should surrender when the successful Japanese attack came. Obviously nobody knew who was surrounding whom. Then came a week of fog;

one of the lads in my tent brought back the news that the Air Force boys after days of inactivity had been over Kiska and felt that some definite change had taken place. He waited for some official word, but it soon became obvious that we were going in as planned. There was a lot of propaganda about Corlett's Long Knives and Widow-makers, etc., but I think most of the men looked on that as kid's stuff. They were old soldiers who preferred to be in an outfit where the pay and food was good and where there were going to be few weak links when the showdown came. Nobody believed that we were hero-type except perhaps the boys up in HQ who were known, of course, as the 'chairborne troops.' "

After a great deal of intramural bickering between the Army and the Navy, plans for the invasion began to take shape. Many disputes were on childish levels, such as whether or not the Navy had the right to assign new sector names to areas on maps already printed by the Army. This had a distasteful effect on Frederick. Although conditioned by his training to the pettiness with which some military minds will approach almost any new project, he could not bring himself to accept it where the lives of his men were concerned. This willingness to fight higher echelons for what he conceived to be the welfare of his command was a frequent source of irritation to his superiors throughout his career.

On the face of available evidence, there was little reason for the oncoming invasion. The Japanese could only have viewed their tenuous hold on the Aleutians as an embarrassment. By this time the tempo of the American war effort had quickened to where Japanese use of the area as a base from which to mount an attack on America was highly unlikely. Probably the most important source of urgency for the action which brought the Force to Alaska was the American elections. A substantial bonus of public approval accrued to the Administration as soon as the last invader was expelled from the soil of North America.

Frederick was too intelligent a man, too seasoned a planner, not to have realized that there was no military reason for the invasion. Further, the invasion plans that were being presented to him by the staffs of Admiral Kinkaid and Major

General Charles H. Corlett unmistakably indicated that his entire command would probably be eradicated within 24 hours of H-hour.

The profound depths of his feeling for his men combined with the apparent dishonesty of the target choice made Frederick only reluctantly patient with the displays of jealousy being evidenced by each of the headquarters above him. He was repelled by incidents such as the one where Major Baldwin was kept from presenting an urgent request for supplies until a Navy captain had completed feeding the pack of dogs he had brought with him from the States. However, he was a trained soldier. A job had been given him to do, and so he began making visits to each staff in order to bring the planning to completion. Entries in his personal diary at this time throw light on the difficulties he faced.

July 30, 1943
There is a great lack of concerted thought and interest by the several headquarters involved, and a certain amount of jealously and clashes of personality pervade.
July 31, 1943
I am beginning to wonder if the clothing and equipment will hold up until the operation is started. . . . Reports about enemy and friendly activities are at least four or five days old when they reach us, and so far we have been unable to get any photographs. All photographs of Kiska, even those taken by the Army Air Forces during the bombing missions, must be turned into the Navy for review and release; and the Navy releases only those that they approve. I have sent several radios [wireless messages] to Adak requesting information about the maps shipped here for us, but so far have received no word. For our type of work and the training methods we have employed, this map is very important and is keenly desired by all the men.

Finally, but with every evidence of creaking and groaning, the various elements of the attack began to draw together under the umbrella of a joint service command.

The 1st Regiment found itself assigned a landing at "Quisling Cove" where it was to mark the beaches for the main landing and then fight its way east toward the main Jap naval base at Kiska Harbor.

The next day, Walker's 3rd Regiment, in company with some of the other units assigned to the attack, would land on the western side of the island and attempt to serve as the other jaw of a pincers designed to crush Kiska's defenses.

The 2nd Regiment was to be held in reserve, ready to parachute in to any point that tactically demanded its presence.

Colonel Frederick was to go in with the 3rd Regiment. D-day was set for August 15, 1943.

The following entry from the diary of Sergeant A. W. Ovenden, 1st Reg., describes his feelings at the beginning of the invasion.

When the night came to attack we had been on the ship for two days. We were a queer-looking crew standing around our rubber boats inside of a huge barge the size of a ship, which had a ramp in the front where we slid our rubber boats out. Our faces were all covered in yellow-and-green camouflage paint and our clothes were daubed with green paint and our helmets were covered with dry tundra. At a given signal all lights go out and we wait in the dark for about half an hour, each with his own thoughts. I kidded myself by thinking that this was not my first time in action and can really say I wasn't frightened; all I wanted to do was to get the whole thing over with and get off these damned foggy islands. I forgot to mention everyone figured our platoon's job was a suicide mission.

It was an unusually clear moonlight night, which was bad; every minute we expected to be fired on and I was all set to jump over the side and take my chances in the water where it's hard to hit anyone. I was quite thrilled and couldn't believe we were at last in the spot for which we had trained so long.

Percy Crichlow gives an account of the preparations in his regiment:

Second Regiment was chosen as the parachute reserve. When the time came to put on all the equipment given to me I felt like a trussed chicken, hardly able to move. The Alaska Scout who had been with us and who used to keep most of his possessions in the back of his blouse was to be envied.

Then eventually I went to the planes and got ready for the wait. I was not too impressed by the transport even if they did have combat tanks in them. I was really annoyed when I found that I just had to have a crap. It was a major operation to get-off all the top layers, starting with the Mae West and the parachutes until some time later I was able to get down to my trousers and underwear. God knows what would have happened if we had got the order just then to go into the planes.

I also had elaborate instructions to see that everyone jumped and was told that I would be provided with a pistol other than my own for use on anyone that froze in the door. As soon as the rest jumped I was to drop that pistol and jump as quickly as possible. The lieutenant was supposed to throw out the equipment and jump first. But after a long wait nothing happened, we went back to the tents and had a long sleep.

In a day or two I just hated the name of Amchitka and Kiska.

August 15 came, and the troops went in. And, in a stunning anticlimax to months of preparation, they found that the last contingent of Japs had cleared out a few hours before they got there.

The intelligence preparation for the invasion could have led to a catastrophe. Where the Navy had supplied the information that one of the landing beaches was flat and covered only with pebbles, the beach was, in fact, covered with large boulders, some of them sixteen feet high. This meant that the task force, painfully threading its way to the shore through entangling kelp and landing in small rubber boats crammed with guns and supplies, was almost immobilized during the laborious unloading process.

Worse still, the unexpected bright moonlight silhouetted the men as splendid targets, while they struggled to pull the gear over the boulders in readiness for the long slogging trip to their objectives. A defending force, even of minimum size and ability, could hardly have helped making mincemeat of them. If the airdrop had gone through, many of the parachut-

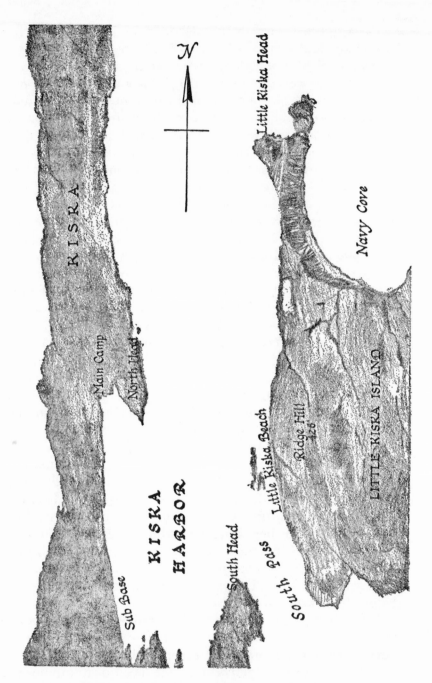

Kiska Harbor, showing where the Force landed.

ists would have been hurled to their death against the bare rocks and crags.

The Navy compounded the intelligence failure by inordinately sloppy landing tactics. When the LSTs dropped their front loading ramps, the slipping chains emitted a screaming series of creaks which completely nullified the tactical advantage of surprise. This was, in retrospect, the attack's one chance for success.

One naval officer was so oblivious to this need, that when the chain was momentarily stuck, he began to pound at it with a hammer in order to secure its release. Colonel Frederick looked at the Forceman nearest him, and, with a shrug, sent the man to where the hammering was taking place. Shortly afterwards, there was silence followed by a splash as the hammer went overboard. But when one of the destroyers blew two sharp whistles as the Forcemen were leaving it, all hands thereafter discounted surprise as one of their weapons.

Irrepressible Finn Roll (who, on the trip from the States to Amchitka, had earned everybody's envy by striking up such a strong bond of kinship with the Norwegian skipper that he had spent the voyage drinking like a king) managed during the landing to add Colonel Frederick to his list of ill-wishers. Roll, Frederick, Pat O'Neill and Colonel Eschenberg and a few others had been slated to make the landing in a twelve-man rubber boat. Instead, "I talked Eschenberg out of using the twelve-man rubber raft," Roll said, "and use two small ones, instead. I said we'd get in faster. The Colonel changed his plan. What I did not know was that the current around Kiska was outgoing, a small detail. And as a result, I got Frederick and us into shore after five hours paddling and Eschenberg and O'Neill did not make it at all. They were picked up by the Navy next morning drifting to sea. The cold water had paralyzed them and they were hoisted on board with nets like cargo. Meanwhile, back on Kiska, Frederick was madder than hell. We only had one half of the radio equipment, so he could not report to ship of mission accomplished. On the way back, everyone got promoted except me."

Roll, of course, thought the incident was funny; but, then, Roll thought everything was funny. Most of the other

Forcemen lost their sense of humor that night. It is a credit to both their training and courage that they went through with a mission containing abundant advance evidence that they would all be dead before morning.

A regimental clerk: "I still think with special horror how little history there would have been for the Force had the Japs still been on Kiska in the strength they were supposed to have been. I think few realize how close to a suicidal assignment our part of the operation was."

John McKay: "The only casualties that I recall was a Forceman whose grenade went off in his back pocket. Six of us carried him back down the ridge to the stretcher on the beach. Also on the beachhead we came across a grave. The Japs had put a marker on it. Can't recall the name of the soldier or airman but the inscription read 'To a Brave American Flier.'

"The mountain division who followed us in got into a fire fight amongst themselves in the fog. I knew at least seven or eight of them got killed. That landing taught us a lesson which was later to pay off when we hit the beaches in Italy."

The rest of that night saw the Forcemen carrying their loads of ammunition up the mountains to their assigned objectives. It was during this exercise that the men began referring to themselves as "Freddy's Freighters," a name which achieved permanent status during the early days of the Italian campaign.

The next morning, following a cold, wet and uncomfortable night, Arthur Vautour won immortality of a sort. On a sudden impulse he jumped out of the foxhole he had dug in the slimy muskeg and which had served as his bed and declaimed:

> *"It is not raining rain to me*
> *It's raining daffodils*
> *And with every dimpled drop I see*
> *Wild flowers on the hill."*

In spite of their aching misery, the men began to laugh until the tears came. They laughed, not at Vautour, or themselves, but at the relief they felt in being alive. They faced the rest of the day in high good humor, zooming around the beaches in the Japanese motorcycles and trucks which were among the hoard of souvenirs they quickly amassed.

There was one bright side to the mission. The Force had proven its awareness of the need for combat discipline, by debarking and reaching its objectives with maximum speed. Further, when other units were trigger happy in the darkness, they alone held their fire. There is one case of a guard detail posted by another infantry unit which fired on every squad sent out to relieve them.

A description of one of the tragedies, caused by the impulse of undertrained troops to fire on anything that moved, is recalled by Sergeant Simms: "After Kiska, one of the Forcemen went back on leave to San Francisco, where he lived several doors away from a friend who had been killed by the trigger-happy 47th. The father of the dead boy continually kept after the Forceman to tell him of the fighting in Kiska. He just couldn't tell the old man that his son had died as the result of Americans firing on their own troops through stupidity. He cut his leave short and came back to the Brigade."

On August 18, Frederick and the Force returned to Amchitka where they found a radiogram from Fleet Headquarters at Pearl Harbor awaiting them. It read:

HIGHEST AUTHORITY DIRECTS THAT YOU RETURN
SPECIAL SERVICE FORCE TO SAN FRANCISCO WITHOUT
DELAY. NIMITZ

This message was the result of a meeting at Quebec where Lord Mountbatten, learning of the Kiska debacle and evidently unwilling to let so fine a blade become imperiled by further misuse or disuse, suggested that they be sent to Eisenhower for employment in the Mediterranean. The sudden freedom of the Force also answered another leader's purpose. Lieutenant General Mark Clark had returned to Washington in order to plead for more help in the coming Italian campaign. He was meeting with little success because, by this time, almost all of the planners had agreed that the main thrust against Germany would be delivered across the English Channel from England into France. Therefore, Allied armies and navies everywhere were being drained to build up the primary invasion force designed for Western Europe.

Having few remaining resources from which to supply him, the high brass offered Frederick and his Force to Clark. The offer was accepted with alacrity, not just because of the Brigade's growing reputation but also because, at this point, Clark was desperate and would have probably jumped at the prospect of acquiring a detachment of cooks.

Frederick, on receiving the telegram, secured the release of the Brigade from Major General Corlett and his superior, Lieutenant General John L. DeWitt.

General Corlett summarized the impression that Frederick and the Force had made on the other Allied units and their commanders in this campaign by sending the following letter, through channels, to the Adjutant General:

1. In the occupation of the Island of Kiska, the First Special Service Force was under my command. They performed all missions according to plan and even though no actual enemy was encountered, their missions were difficult and dangerous. They landed in rubber boats at unknown beaches during the hours of darkness against what was presumed to be hostile shore. They moved across difficult terrain and positions where cleverly-concealed traps had been left by the enemy. They reached their objectives on schedule according to plan.

2. To accomplish their missions it was impractical for them to carry packs to provide the ordinary comforts of soldiers in the field. As a consequence, they were exposed to extreme discomfort for long periods of time.

3. It is desired to commend all officers and men of the First Special Service Force for their fine spirit and unselfishness.

4. It is especially desired to commend Col. Robert T. Frederick for his splendid leadership and devotion to duty. Colonel Frederick has a force that should be of great value in any difficult battle situation.

VI

The Six Bloody Days

In mountain passes the Germans constructed defenses almost impregnable to attack. Yankee ingenuity and resourcefulness were tested to the limit. Shortly after the capture of Mt. Camino, I was taken to a spot where, in order to outflank on these mountain strongpoints, a small detachment had put on a remarkable exhibition of mountain climbing. With the aid of ropes, a few of them climbed steep cliffs of great height. I have never understood how, encumbered by their equipment, they were able to do it. In fact, I think that any Alpine climber would have examined the place doubtfully before attempting to scale it. Nevertheless, the detachment reached the top and ferreted out the German Company Headquarters. They entered and seized the Captain, who ejaculated, "You can't be here. It is impossible to come up those rocks."

—General of the Army DWIGHT D. EISENHOWER describing
part of the Force's battle for Monte la Difensa.*

Upon returning to America, half the Force was furloughed and the other half sent directly back to Fort Ethan

* From *Crusade in Europe*, by Dwight D. Eisenhower. Copyright 1948 by Doubleday & Company, Inc. Reprinted by permission of the publisher.

Allen. Then came a month of general tightening up. Frederick had been given the rare opportunity of evaluating his command under perfectly simulated combat conditions and although he was generally satisfied, it had been obvious that certain of the men would not do under the strains that lay ahead.

One officer had incurred Frederick's dislike by getting drunk and disappearing for a few days after the ships docked in San Francisco. He had Adams file charges and then named himself as the President of the Court. This irregularity was challenged by the officer's defense counsel, but, even so, the man's trial ended with his disappearance from the Force. Which was all that Frederick wanted. He was just as ruthless in his treatment of several of the individuals who had no military duties. One of the chaplains had been discovered selling communion wine to the men on the way to Kiska and was replaced immediately upon landing in the States.

Getty Page became one of the two new Red Cross representatives assigned to the unit. He recalls coming to the Force: "We went to Fort Ethan Allen and told the two Red Cross men who were there that we were to relieve them. We were sent there because when General Frederick returned from the Aleutians, one of the first things he said to our headquarters was, 'The two Red Cross men we have are yellow. Give us two new ones.' "

After the weak officers and men had been dropped, new uniforms and gear were issued, and the corrections in procedure indicated as necessary by the Kiska exercise were made. The Force then sat back to await its expected overseas orders.

General Eisenhower, again contemplating the use of the Force for raids, sabotage or guerrilla operations in Italy, Southern France or the Balkans, sent for it in October. He was too late. As a result of Mark Clark's frantic scrounging for additional men in the impending Italian campaign, the Brigade had been assigned to his Fifth Army. In mid-October, Colonel Frederick and two junior officers left by plane as the advance detail for the Brigade's trip to Europe. Shortly afterwards, orders arrived at Force Headquarters sending the unit to the Hampton Roads Port of Embarkation.

By October 27, 1943, the entire First Special Service

Force was aboard *The Empress of Scotland,* a captured liner which had been formerly known as *The Empress of Japan.* Also making the trip were 3,000 casual replacements destined for other units and two companies of Wacs.

From the diary of Wilson K. Wheatley, Jr., another recorder from the ranks:

October 28, 1943

There were some Wacs in camp, but they were in a special section. Some of the boys managed to see some. A few were leaving the same day we were.

When we got to the ship, she certainly was a large one . . . a big three-stacker. This ship had eight decks, with the top decks for the officers and the company of Wacs.

Well, we sailed in the early part of the morning. The infantry and engineers aboard couldn't understand that the officers and men in our outfit were proud of each other. We didn't have the hard feelings about officers as in most infantry companies. Our officers were all very good guys and we all palled around together. They got us every break they could. We couldn't get near the Wacs on board but a lot of the guys sure tried to no avail.

October 30

One of the fellows that I palled around with was in the brig so I went up to see him once in a while. He had his trial on the high seas. They sure roasted him good . . . half of his pay for six months. But he knows that his slate will be clear as soon as we get into action so he didn't mind.

From the diary of Colonel Kenneth Wickham:

Also aboard the vessel were two W.A.C. companies totaling about 350 women. While the Wac's were quartered separately and placed off limits, our troops still made the most of their opportunities to visit with them, with the result that the voyage passed almost too quickly.

From the comments by Getty Page, Red Cross Man:

The fellows used to lie down on the decks below and watch the Wacs above—they in their playclothes of short dress and shorts underneath.

We also had a show and some of the skits the Wacs and the soldiers got up were rather suggestive. I remember one where the scene was a dentist's office and the person in the waiting room thought he was in a physician's office and overheard the dentist explaining to the girl to open wider and things like that. Very humorous.

When *The Empress of Scotland* put into Casablanca on November 5, Frederick, as usual, was on hand to meet it. He told the troop commanders that the whole Force would move directly to Oran in Algeria. Part of the men were to go by rail and the rest by truck.

The elements which went by train found the accommodations on a par with the "40 and 8's" in which some of their fathers had journeyed during the First World War. In fact, many of these cars were holdovers from that period. To the uninitiated, the description simply means that the car was built to hold 40 men or 8 horses and, as a result, offered few of the niceties of American railroad transportation. In spite of the primitive arrangements, the men were so absorbed in the colorful sights and sounds of North Africa that there was little griping. Colonel Wickham, in his restrained diary, describes it:

This trip is probably one of the most interesting railroad trips ever made by the Force. At every turn, each man could see something that was entirely new and different in his experiences. The members of the Force took a great deal of interest in the Arabs and the native French troops whom they passed along the way.

The "interest" that Colonel Wickham mentions had more colorful dimensions for most of the men. To them, the ride was chiefly notable for the interminable bargaining with the Arabs who swarmed over the train at each stop. Each time the train would come to a halt, the boys would sell their boots to the Arabs. After the sale, the MP's would retrieve the boots and return them to the seller.

A thriving business went on all along the way with mattress covers, an Army item much in demand among the Arabs, because of the ease with which they could be converted into clothing. The Force's favorite selling tactic in this particular transaction was to wait until the train slowed to a crawling speed, and then offer the cover to the Arabs who were running alongside. When the Arab gave his money, the boys would give over the mattress cover. After the exchange, the Forceman would sharply jerk the string he had prudently kept attached to his mattress cover, reel it back in, and thus preserve his wares for another "conditional sale" further down the tracks.

At one point along the journey, another train bearing huge wine casks had the misfortune to pull into a way station alongside the Force's vehicle. The men, at first, couldn't believe their luck. Then, with one mind, they pulled out their bayonets and knives and plunged them into the sides of the wooden casks. Some men, in their eagerness, shot out the plugs. Wine began spurting everywhere and the Forcemen caught it in their helmets, canteens or simply opened their mouths in the way of the spurting streams. One of the participants described the scene simply by saying, "We bathed in the goddam stuff."

Colonel Walker, out on the platform for a leg stretching, got caught in the general melee and in a few seconds his uniform was a purple dripping mess. Walter Grabiec reports, "Walker's only reaction, however, was a few curses as he walked away."

It was a raucous group that finally pulled into Oran. Colonel Frederick, after surveying them, immediately confined everyone to camp. That evening, some of the men promptly made it over the fence to a nearby native village where, by using Army supplies as specie (a mattress cover now brought $10), they were able to enter into the local scene. A bottle of brandy cost a quarter. The friendship of a native woman cost fifty cents. Some of the more prodigal Forcemen went as high as two dollars for the favors of the few French girls available.

One of the Forcemen had his throat cut. But since his

assailant missed the jugular vein and simply slit the man's vocal chords, the incident was shrugged off as a rather high price
for a night's fun and thereafter the men went over the fence
in pairs.

From the diary of Wilson K. Wheatley, Jr.:

Nov. 12, 1943

All the way from the Aleutians to the States to Africa our
regiment had very few AWOLs, but the other regiments had
quite a few. In this place, our regiment waited for the other two
regts. to catch up with us so we rested and took a few hikes to
limber up and a few drills.

We were warned not to go off. We were a secret outfit in
these parts and we were to tell no one about our training at all.
But of course we never mentioned anything because we were
very proud of our outfit. We just told everyone that it was none
of their business. Everywhere we went everyone wanted to know
who we were, why the big packs? why the U. S. and Canadian
insignia? They knew we were troopers, but why the big packs?

Everyone wanted our combat knives. Man, they were certainly dangerous weapons with the long needle-point shaft and
the pointed handle.

Well, the other regiments had arrived by now and the boys
in our [1st] Regiment had begun to get restless. We had been
there three days doing nothing. We had a hike down to one of
the towns and had seen a few girls and we all began to get ideas.
So that night practically everybody started to town, some to
Oran and some to little towns we had passed through while on
our hikes. Swifty and me decided to go to Oran and see the
sights, so off we went, starting about two in the afternoon. We
hitchhiked and got there and walked around taking in all the
different uniforms, etc.

We met a couple of nice-looking French girls, but we
couldn't speak French and they couldn't speak our language, so
we stood there for a few minutes until their mother came out
and they started walking away, saying something we couldn't understand. We just up and followed them. They went to a show so
we started to go in. The picture was all in French. The girls went

in the balcony and everyone was looking at us. There was no soldiers there so we figured we were in the wrong place so we got out. The acting was by American actors but they were speaking French so we got out.

We had a few beers in another place. Most everything in Oran was brass but Swifty and I never saluted and finally about one o'clock we decided to go home. We had to walk most of the night till we finally got a ride. We got to our row of tents when the guard said, "You men report to your company commander right away!"

Instead we went to our tent and saw our platoon commander and he told us that most of the regiment had been AWOL and we all had to see our regimental commander in the morning.

From the diary of A. W. Ovenden:

November 13

We found the journey through Oran more interesting this time as it was morning and people were busy going from here to there. As we were passing through in trucks the older French people looked at us with the expression on their faces which seemed to say "So young to die." I read it easily.

November 17

Here we are in Naples Harbour and it's quite a sight. More ships half under water than on top, most buildings smashed and hardly seem to be a good window left in the place. The Germans bombed it yesterday so maybe we'll see some excitement; while I won't ask for it, I imagine it would be interesting to see just how bombing is done. Our bivouac area is a huge college. It's a lovely building and camouflaged smartly with trees painted right up the building. All windows have been blown out, which means terrific bombs must have landed a mile or two away. The buildings around the docks were terribly mutilated and I noticed some very, very sad-faced older women. The younger bunch all seem to smile easily and the girls are healthy looking and extremely presentable; in fact, it's hard to find one with bad looks or bad figure. The boys are quite restless to get into town, but if our outfit acts normally I can see no passes.

Right now a few of us are sitting around a fire in the cellar of the college heating up our rations. An outfit left the college just as we arrived and left a lot of their rations, which we immediately scrounged and I'm full of candies and junk. This outfit is moving up to the front where I expect we will go shortly.

They're having quite a time this afternoon keeping the boys from drinking wine, we're having many roll calls to keep track of the men and it's quite funny how they all dash down and get vino. They're all mildly plastered. The big shots better get us out of here soon or they'll have a tough bunch to control.

At Santa Maria, the Force was given some replacements in preparation for the battles that lay ahead. Among them was Bill Slawson. He describes his reaction to the Force: "In replacement depot in Italy saw a poster that said join 1st S.S.F. Asked what that was, and was told 'suicide squad.' I said I'd take it, anything to get out of the Repple Depple [Replacement Depot].

"I thought they were a little odd and edgy, and neurotic. The first day I joined the outfit we were staying in some old school sleeping on marble floors and some Forceman was chasing another with a machine gun."

Finally, a sidelight on Robert Frederick during this period is supplied by Lester Forrest: "Now we can go to the village proper during the daytime, but nighttime is out. The General is curious why we want to go, is it the wine? the women? The General never blew his top except when we were sloppy, unshined shoes, bearded faces, no neckties, etc. His attitude was almost motherly at times. He would send his personal recon car to gather us up. We could see the distant firing, and hear the booms which set us to wondering as to when it was our turn. Then the word."

A chain of heavily fortified hills, linked together by some of the toughest German Army units in the European Theater, constituted Field Marshal Kesselring's "Winter Line." It was the Germans' main stand in front of Rome, and had stalled the advance of the Fifth Army through Italy.

The key to cracking this line was represented by two

formidable mountain masses named Monte la Difensa and Monte la Remetanea. No matter how ferocious a fighting force General Mark Clark hurled against these twin peaks, the attack had not only been repulsed, it had also resulted in heavy Allied casualties. The area was held by a crack Panzer (armored) Grenadier Division, with the Hermann Goering Division in reserve.* These were among the best German troops anywhere.

This was the situation when the First Special Service Force arrived in the sector. The latest attack, twelve driving days of sustained onslaughts, had just failed. The Fifth Army had fallen back to bandage its wounds and to eye, hungrily, the broad flat expanse which lay beyond the mountains. This was the valley of the Liri River. Once reached, it presented few geographical obstacles to an army thrusting toward Rome.

But first the mountain chain had to be breached. And 3,000 feet high, apparently impregnable, the well-named Monte la Difensa looming over the surrounding terrain was the stumbling block. A menacing bastion, its summit was generally cloaked in clouds or swirling snowstorms. Above its 1,000-foot tree line, there was nothing but bare crags.

Sustained Allied air and artillery pounding had produced little or no effect. The German defense was too well dug in among the sheer cliffs and crevices in the granite to be affected by bombs and shells. The closely-knit gun emplacements studded the upper heights and were connected by a series of concealed trails which gave infinite mobility to the defenders.

This was the situation when the Force was assigned on November 22 to the 36th Division, a component of Major General Geoffrey Keyes' II Corps. The assignment had been made by Fifth Army headquarters as part of "Operation Raincoat," the code name for the plan to breach the mountain passes.

Under the plan, Frederick's Force had been given Monte

* This unit was originally a *Fallschirmjager* (paratroop) division, but had been reorganized as an armored division.

la Difensa and its adjoining sister, Monte la Remetanea as targets. As in Kiska, they were to be the spearheads for the entire operation. If they could take these two objectives, the American and British forces would then pour through and engage the other German defenses. The most experienced headquarters officers felt, in light of the First Special Force's reputation, that there was a good possibility that it might take these targets in three days. Privately, they were convinced that if it did, the price would be almost complete extinction.

Frederick's first reaction on being given the target was characteristically unemotional. Instead of commenting on the difficulty of being given a job which had proven too much for units many times the size of his own, he simply gathered a few men about him and went up the mountain to see for himself. During the next week, under the cover of darkness, accompanied by a couple of his staff people or, occasionally, a handful of enlisted men, he crept up the mountain trails to choose the most advantageous assault route.

Apparently, the only militarily feasible approach to the summit was a trail leading up the south side. On the north side of the mountain stood a 200-foot cliff. Above the cliff was a series of six ledges averaging thirty feet in height. The Germans had comparatively little firepower on this flank because it was obvious that even a handful of men would have difficulty in scaling their way up. It would be next to impossible for a full-sized attacking force to come this way. Frederick accurately evaluated the German concept of the situation and chose the side with the series of ledges as the route for his Force. He reasoned that the Germans would have reserved this side as an escape hatch, and said, "If they can come down this way, then we can go up."

Frederick made only one miscalculation. He thought that mule trains would be able to pick their way up the south side in order to supply his attacking force. But the trails proved later to be too much for all but the hardiest of the four-footed animals. It was then that his 3rd Regiment slung the loads on their own backs and made the trip where the mules could not or would not go.

By November 25, the Force was in combat readiness for the job. The driving rain, which was turning the roads and fields of the area into a gummy mass, was no longer considered as a hateful source of discomfort. Now, it was reasoned, the downpour cloaking their movements could possibly add a certain depth to the element of surprise they needed for success.

The reconnaissance completed, Frederick called his staff officers and key commanders together and, pointing to a map of the mountain-turned-fortress, made the assignments for the coming battle. The 2nd Regiment, under Colonel Williamson, was given the D-day job of attacking and taking the hill. The 1st Regiment was assigned as a reserve to the commanding general of the 36th Division. The 3rd Regiment had a double mission . . . its First Battalion would become litter bearers and supply carriers for the 2nd Regiment, and its Second Battalion would form the Force's reserve, to be used wherever battle strategy might dictate.

D-day was December 2. All troops were to move out of the bivouac area under cover of darkness on the night of December 1.

The general disposition of the forces on the battlefield on both sides is simple enough to follow. The Germans occupied positions in the Monte Camino and Monte Maggiore area. They had a defense in depth, good artillery and the following troops: Third Battalion, 104th Panzer Grenadier Regt., Third Battalion 129th Panzer Grenadier Regt., Third Battalion, 382d Panzer Grenadier Regt., and the 115th Reconnaissance Battalion, all picked, veteran soldiers. They used these positions both as a bulwark against the Allied forces and as spotting posts from which they could radio targets to their heavy artillery located just to the rear. The spotters and the artillery worked with automatic precision. Any daylight movement by the Fifth Army units in front of them was immediately punished by a fearsome pounding.

Behind this German line stretched the pass which led to the pathway to Rome. On one side of the pass were la Difensa and la Remetanea. On the other were a cluster of peaks that had been given to the British as targets. These two salients were connected by a heavily mined ridge. Along the ridge were two smaller hills which the men called "warts" and the planners referred to as "knobs." Once both targets were taken, the other mountains in the range became vulnerable.

Monte la Difensa was the closest and toughest. When Frederick pointed out the importance of this target on the map, his officers saw that they had been given a job equal in every way to the training they had cursed so heartily in the States.

At 2:00 P.M. on December 1, all the officers of the Force were brought together for a final meeting. They were told that a high-ranking officer wanted to say a few words to them.

While waiting for the general, they talked quietly among themselves. One junior lieutenant asked Tom MacWilliams, who was to lead the assault battalion, a question about Canadian decorations. MacWilliams answered, "The hell with them all, the only one I want is a medal for long service."

Finally the general, followed by Frederick, walked into the compound. The men snapped to attention. The general waited for a few ominous seconds before beginning to speak:

"You men," he said, "have been preceded by a great reputation, but you haven't been blooded yet. War isn't Hollywood glamor, and men do not die dramatically."

A few of the men shifted their feet and glanced at each other out of the corners of their eyes. There were a few whispered remarks. These were professionals and they hadn't ever considered that their reputation would win battles for them.

The general looked about him. "Good luck!" And he strode off.

His farewell words had a good effect on the men. Perhaps it wasn't quite the effect he visualized, but it was enough to chase away some of the tenseness they were beginning to feel.

"Bullshit," said one young officer. "What's he trying to do, scare us?"

When reports of the speech filtered over to where the enlisted men were shooting craps, and otherwise occupying themselves before the movement, there was a general reaction of disbelief. Few of them had thought that the brass still stole their speeches from old World War I movies. Unemotional, casually profane, Frederick had spoiled them for the grandstanders.

From the diary of A. W. Ovenden:

Here it is—today is Dec. 1st.—we tore up all letters and left all identification behind except pay-book and dog-tags. We're all packed and tonight move up to the front, thank goodness, to do our job which is any job, as we are reserve battalion and fill in any gap which breaks down, the Force will take some mountain peaks which are holding up the Fifth Army.

We have been told part of what our mission is to be, it seems pretty rough and nasty. The Captain called all the staff sergeants together and told us in case of casualties we were potential officers, made in the field. You can imagine I was well pleased, at least it let me know I had been noticed.

We have just had instructions and a demonstration of how effective the land mines of the Germans are. In fact most of our casualties are caused by these mines. They're terribly effective from what we hear and our job is to travel through them at night —I just don't think of it. One type of mine goes up in the air, then explodes. We are told if we step on it to hold our foot down and stop it from coming up in the air, this way no one around would be hurt except the one holding it down, he, in nearly every case, will lose his foot. It will likely take nerve, but I hope I will be able to do it if necessary, but Christ knows how I hate to think of it.

Few of the men exhibited any signs of nervousness. This was an outgrowth of Frederick's open respect for them. His conduct as a commanding officer was marked by the belief that once he had selected and trained his type of man . . . that man became his partner in the enterprise . . . and was worthy of knowing the exact dimensions of the job to be done. This kind of honesty flowed in both directions. The commander and his men had great trust in each other. Neither side felt that there was any possibility that the other would let him down.

But, of course, the Forcemen were human beings, not automatons. Underneath the casual, professional air, the men made highly personal evaluations of the odds and each man decided for himself his conduct in relationship to the situation ahead.

At four o'clock that afternoon, the Force moved out. At hourly intervals, the 2nd Regiment, the 1st and then the 3rd loaded into trucks and rode part of the way to the base of the mountain. The men hiked the last ten miles in the heavy rain, as the falling night hid their movements from the German observers on the mountain.

The 1st Regiment deployed to the base of a hill and waited in their reserve position. The 2nd Regiment began the stealthy climb up Difensa, their objective being a point about halfway to the crest where they would wait, under the cover of darkness, to begin the attack. The 3rd Regiment, split in half, sent one battalion to the base of the hill to remain in readiness to back up the second. The remainder slipped into position to begin their packing duties. It was the eve of the first of the bloody days of Difensa.

The Allied guns, booming away to cover the attack, were answered by the enemy, who seemed to have assembled all the German guns in Italy to help them hold that miserable piece of muddy ground.

The 1st Regiment had a grandstand view of the spectacle. Bill Pharis stated, "Of all the pictures of World War II, I have often wondered how come someone didn't take a picture of Monte la Difensa. When we went in, it looked like the whole mountain was on fire. I think that all the fire power that was there, was turned on the mountain."

This is one description that has been repeated over and over again by the survivors—"It looked like the whole mountain was on fire."

By dawn of December 3, all the forward units had reached their assigned position and burrowed into concealment. Their stealthy arrival went undetected by the Germans. The Force stayed in hiding that day, waiting for other Allied troops to arrive at their positions in adjoining sectors. This

readiness of the entire line was essential. If the Force succeeded in taking its objective, the British and American infantry on their flanks would have to move in order to preserve
the victory. Otherwise, German reinforcements might arrive
in time to cut off and isolate the Force as a prelude to re-
capturing the mountain.

The importance of the target had been underlined by
General Clark, who left his command post at the Fifth Army
Headquarters in order to visit Frederick at 10:00 A.M., December 2. Clark told Frederick that all available air and
artillery fire power would be brought to bear on the sector.
The top of Difensa would be hit, as well as German entrench-
ments on surrounding peaks. This would provide a diversion,
and hopefully, a softening up of the enemy.

At 4:00 that afternoon, the men began to prepare for
their night's work. Grenades were checked, knives received
a final honing, and rations were distributed.

A half an hour later, Frederick stepped out of his command post, nodded to Pat O'Neill, Finn Roll, and the Force's
Chief Scout, a tall, slender man named Wright, and said,
"Let's go." Turning to Colonel Adams, he said casually,
"Look after things, Paul," and he and his small group began
taking the trail the rest of the way up the mountain. He was
followed shortly afterwards by the Force's combat units moving to assigned positions.

At dusk, the final barrage began.

The 2nd Regiment, which would carry the brunt of this
phase of the fighting, reached the base of the Difensa crown
by 10:30 that evening. Their path was accompanied by an
increasing volume of German shells. It seemed as if every
German artillery commander in the area had been supplied
with a map listing Difensa's trails, and had zeroed in accordingly.

Percy Crichlow supplies a graphic description of the
climb and the fight: "My section was to be the head section in
the attack. Two of my section, Van Ausdale and Tommy
Fenton (who had originally belonged to the same regiment
as I in Canada), were to be the scouts. We went up first by

truck and then on foot to concealment on the side of Difensa. It was a nervous day of waiting. Toward evening some of the men were sent to string ropes on the more difficult parts of the ascent. 'Van' told me when he came back that he could hear a German giving orders or directions not far above him as he worked.

"That night we just climbed. I could never have made it without the help of the ropes."

Harry Hoffman contributed a terse, but equally vivid description of the night. He said, ". . . no fear of death, just sheer exhaustion and survival. I can still see us climbing the hill and watching German mortars bracket us."

The 600 men of the 2nd Regiment moved upward silently, as silently as they had infiltrated the Coast Artillery post while training in the States. There were no signs that the Germans entrenched above were aware of their approach. At midnight, most of the men had reached concealment among the rocky ledges. The lead company of the assault force, scarcely daring to breath, lay well within range of the German positions.

Sgt. Bobby Gold was told by Lieutenant Adna Underhill to bring his men further up the climb in order to establish a position just behind the advance unit. Gold's men, their fingers almost numbed by the chilling cold, knotted the ropes about them and moved up.

The difficulty involved in this move comes into sharp focus when it is remembered the cliff face of Difensa begins at the 2,000 foot level and extends upwards at a pitch of 60 or 70 degrees for approximately another 1,000 feet. The peasants of the nearby villages never used anything but the well-cut trails on the opposite side when they took their flocks to the summit to graze. Since the winter of 1943, only two persons have tried to get to the top by means of the northeast face. These were two young men from Northern Italy, and the peasants who extricated them from the cleft in the rock wall where they had become stranded, cursed them for fools.

This was the cleft that 600 riflemen, carrying packs which would have forced lesser men to the ground, negotiated without a sound. They groped for crevices with frozen hands while stretching their muscles to the aching point to keep from sliding backwards. Like so many snakes, the sections crawled over the cliff face and, singly, broke over the rim.

Sergeant Gold's section reached their position and untied themselves. They sprawled out exhausted, the perspiration freezing to their bodies in the icy air. One man reached for his rifle and found that he was too tired to lift it. He whispered across to Gold who helped him slip the sling over his head. They rested for a few minutes, and then wriggled forward into the darkness to take their place on the flanks of their advance company. There was still no sound from the enemy. The only noise that broke the air was a burp gun (machine pistol) firing at regular fifteen-minute intervals. The Forcemen thought it to be some kind of signal to the unsleeping German artillery batteries on nearby slopes, who kept their guns trained on the trails going up Difensa.

Finally, the group was joined by another handful of men. It was Frederick and his staff, inching their way to a ledge close enough to the enemy to smell the cooking odors from the mess area. The shelf that Frederick and his group picked out was so narrow that it spanned just a bit more than one man's width. So they bunched down on top of one another and remained motionless in that position in the freezing rain. Their uniforms congealed in an icy mass to the rocks and to each other.

When all elements were in position, Frederick gave the signal for another stealthy advance. The forward elements crept to the crest which was a saucer-shaped area the size of a football field. There were hundreds of the best German troops here, some grouped in underground emplacements and supported by others in foxholes. The men of the Force slipped forward in the darkness, their blackened faces and dirt-stained uniforms making them almost completely invisible. Although in the distance, the rumble and cough of artillery could be heard, the only sound being made on the crest was the soft gurgle vented by German sentries who had their throats cut by the Forcemen gliding past them in the darkness.

At 4:30 A.M., Colonel MacWilliams, a mild-mannered Canadian history professor in peacetime, now commanding

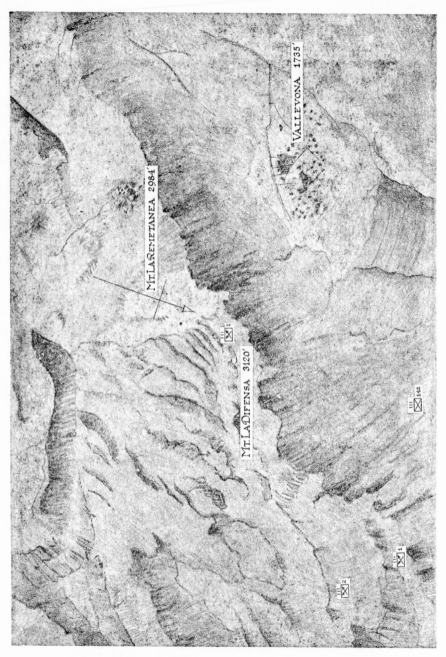

The terrain of Mts. la Difensa and la Remetanea, Southern Italy, where the Force became a legend.

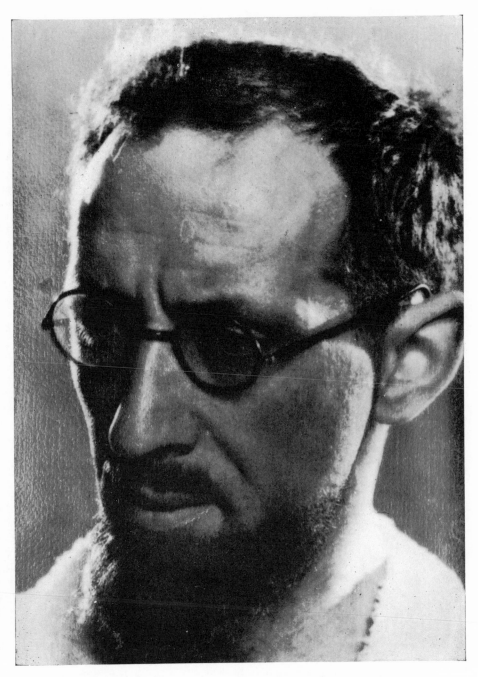

Geoffrey Pyke.   *Through the courtesy of David Lampe*

Robert T. Frederick as a colonel, in 1942.   *Official U.S. Army photo*

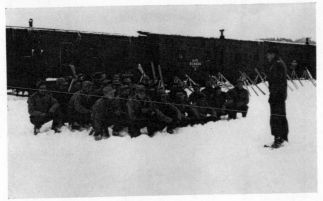

(*Above*)   Frederick at Helena, with Shinberger: 1942.   *Frederick*
(*Center*) Boxcar living at Helena; notice skis in background.
Frederick   (*Below*) The Force blows a bridge for practice in
Montana.   *Frederick*

(*Above*) O'Neil gives lessons to two trainees at Helena.   *Frederick*
(*Below*) Landing on Kiska.   *Frederick*

(*Above*) Firing the Johnson automatic rifle, Mt. Difensa. *Official U.S. Army photo*   (*Below, left*) Two Forcemen load a usual weight for the trip up Difensa. *Official U.S. Army photo*   (*Below, right*) Colonel Edwin Walker issues tactical orders: Difensa. *Frederick*

(*Above*) Wounded, coming down Mt. Difensa.   *Frederick*
(*Below*) Finn Roll awaits some Germans for interrogation: Difensa.
Frederick

(*Top, left*) Frederick used an undamaged eye on Mt. Radicosa. *Official U.S. Army photo* (*Top, right*) Finn Roll, but not as seen by Germans. *Frederick* (*Bottom, left*) Tagging the dead after Radicosa. *Frederick* (*Bottom, right*) Colonel Walker, up front on Radicosa; with him Majors Robert Walker and Jack Sector, and Captain Frank Erickson. *Official U.S. Army photo.*

(*Above*) Frederick checks on incoming patrol, with "guests."
Frederick (*Below*) Dug in on the Mussolini Canal, Anzio.
Official U.S. Army photo

the lead battalion, whispered word to his men to hold their fire until 6:00 A.M. He directed that knives and bayonets be used on any German that stumbled into their positions.

But a rockfall gave them away. The Germans had surrounded their emplacements with loose stones for this very purpose, and, as some of the riflemen began sliding into the ravines, the blackness of the sky was split and shattered by the flashes and noise of gunfire.

A green flare went up, followed by a red one of equal brilliance. Then came a blinding flash as two magnesium flares sharply illuminated the entire scene. The men of the Force, caught in the glare, stood silhouetted like so many menacing statues. The battle was on.

Crichlow describes the part of it that he saw: "All hell broke loose. I dived for cover and my section, who were laboriously climbing over the ledge behind me, started to crawl into position to my left as soon as they were on the ledge in front of the topmost lump.

"Lieutenant Piette gave me the order to lay down a base of fire while he got McGinty's section to circle to the right. My section started to return the Jerries' fire. In the dark it seemed that there was a kind of fort ahead of me from which came the flashes of German machine guns and submachine guns. There was a quick intake of breath near by and I knew somebody was hit. I kept firing my Tommy gun at the gun-flashes ahead of me and then the forms spread to my right. Apparently McGinty's section was getting into action.

"There was a strong point ahead of me and to the right and another to the left just below the very crest between boulders. Then it became clear that an attack was developing from my left; it turned out to be Number One platoon, but I didn't know that then. As the attack started from the left it was beginning to get light. I saw and spoke to Captain Rothlin for a short time and then started to move forward with the Johnson gun pair. We managed to get into the depression between the strong points as Number One was obviously getting control of the main area of resistance to the left. I recognized Bernstein throwing a grenade and turning away.

"I still had Deyette near me, but had lost touch with Daigle as we got into the saucerlike area. Deyette and I started to move up the side of the hill when he called, 'They're below here,' and then he went down. I found he had a bullet in his forehead and was sucking in his breath with a loud snoring sound. I never knew where the bullet came from and I never saw Daigle again.

"I went back to Buck Palmer and asked for somebody to cover me and he sent Belts. We went to Deyette again and brought away the Johnson gun and the ammunition.

"As there were men below and it was not clear who they were, we moved over to the rest of the company on the left and speeded up a couple of fleeing Jerries with a burst or two. I joined up with some of my section who had now moved into position on the crest. Hotenko of H Company stopped me and I took the unused Tommy gun magazines out of his pouches and left my empty magazines.

"Just then mortar [fire] started to come and we heard a plane. I helped put down some panels in case they could be seen. As more mortar came in, I moved back into better cover and awaited orders. I waited a long dismal night with my left knee stiffening up where pieces of flying stones had cut and bruised it and with my wrist and hand slightly hurt by mortar splinters.

"I found that my section had taken a real beating. Sergeant Fisher, my Browning gun squad leader, was completely blind—struck by stone fragments; Lewis had been sliced across his back by a bullet and then had been shot in the hand; Joe Dauphinais had a bullet through his arm; Clarke had a long gouge running back from the area just behind his eye; Deyette and Daigle were dead. In a neighboring platoon, poor Casey, who could have stayed behind as a cook but insisted on going to a combat platoon, was killed by a direct hit of a dud mortar bomb that cracked his skull."

Robert Neal contributes a poignant vignette which occurred during that hectic two hours: "When we first got up at the top and pinned down I ran a little way and lay down beside a soldier and talked to him for a long time before I found out that he was dead. I wondered why he did not talk back to me. It was too dark to tell at first who he was."

Most shock troops are rarely prepared to take prisoners. But this was the Force's first time in action. They found it hard to gun down a man who had raised his hands in surrender. This reluctance stopped abruptly after the death of Captain Rothlin.

Rothlin and his squad had flushed out a nest of Germans who had been hiding in an emplacement. The first German stepped up, a white flag raised in his hands. Rothlin went forward to collar the man and then one of the remaining Germans blasted a shot right into his face. Rothlin fell back, dying without another sound. His men opened up at the remaining Germans with all the firepower they had, killing every one.

Thereafter, the Force never took prisoners, unless specifically ordered to by Burhans, Roll or one of the other Intelligence officers, who needed the enemy for interrogation purposes.

The furious fighting continued on every side . . . and it wasn't being waged only by enlisted men and junior officers. Frederick seemed to be everywhere on that battlefield. The mild Tommy MacWilliams, the battalion commander, was killed in the early moments. Other senior officers fought as savagely and unremittingly as the Pfc's alongside them.

The next wave of Forcemen, the Second Battalion of the 1st Regiment which had been waiting in reserve, now came up and over the crest. John Dawson describes their arrival:

"The crest was cleared, roughly, when we got to it. Jesse Thorpe, a sharpshooting hillbilly, picked a sniper out of the rocks and claimed first blood for Sixth Company. Then it was 'Reinforcement on the Double!', and, for awhile, we were shuttled here and there as the fortunes of battle shifted."

James ("Stoney") Wines, now the police chief at Helena, but then a platoon leader on Difensa, posted his heavy machine gun man in as strategic a spot as he could find through the fog which occasionally sifted down the summit. The gunner's name was Jack Wray. When Wines motioned to the declivity where the gun should go, Wray protested. Wines insisted that it was the right position, and went on to rejoin the close-quarters fighting. When the fog lifted a few minutes later, Wines noticed that Wray's gun was not firing. He raced back only to find Wray lying beside the gun, a bullet in his head. Since he was too seriously wounded to be moved, Wray's companions raised a rough shelter made of their coats over him. Wray, in his delirium, turned and pushed it over. He died shortly afterwards. Wines never forgave himself for choosing the position which led to the death of his closest friend.

A former cowboy named Stone recalls Frederick in that fight, ". . . on Million Dollar Mountain, the Colonel was in the front line on the assault and got just as dirty and wet and miserable as anyone. He was always in the lead on the times I saw him up there."

It didn't take the three days that the experts had predicted. In just two hours of actual fighting, the German stronghold on Monte la Difensa ceased to exist. It had held back the progress of an army, repelled many determined and extended attacks, but the Force took it in two hours. Battle-wise historians still regard this feat as a mission they would have labeled impossible had it not actually happened.

At dawn, the fog parted momentarily. It revealed the Germans swarming away from the crest, down the slope and across the connecting ridge to the Force's second target, Monte la Remetanea. But this sudden-found visibility proved to be a curse rather than a respite. The German artillery observers found the 2nd Regiment still clumped together in the basin they had just taken, and on signal, artillery began showering death on the victors.

Major Edward H. Thomas, who had command of the battalion after MacWilliams died, looked over to Frederick for orders. Frederick waved the men to take shelter in the concrete pillboxes deserted by the Germans and then ducked into his forward command post on the shelf below the rope scramble. From here he signaled to the 2nd Regiment to hold up any further advance until the ammunition packers could arrive. He then radioed to the supply caves down the road to get the packers started with ammunition, water, rations, blankets and litters for the wounded.

Because it was a minimum six-hour trip, the Force dug in as best they could in the pillboxes and between the rocks for the rest of the day while awaiting supplies.

Captain "Pat" O'Neill comments on the battle:

"Perhaps we lost more officers than we should, as they needlessly exposed themselves. I recall borrowing Captain Border's rifle when I came across him in a kneeling position observing the enemy through binoculars on the opposite ridge. When I returned with his rifle, some thirty minutes later, he was dead with a sniper's bullet in the head.

"Problems piled up fast for Colonel Frederick when we found that the difficulty of supplying us would keep us on Difensa much longer than anticipated. His casual indifference to enemy fire was hard to explain, as there were times when a heavy barrage of mortar fire would send us scurrying for cover only to come back and find him smoking a cigarette—in the same sitting position and place we had vacated in a hurry.

"No one in my position then would presume to advise Colonel Frederick. However, when the question of resupply became critical I hinted the Service Battalion might be pressed into service to help out in supplying our front-line troops and carrying down the wounded. Luckily, at that particular time the field telephone to Colonel Adams was not cut.

"To this day I am not clear how Colonel Adams managed to get these troops from Santa Maria, our rear base, to our fighting forces loaded down with everything that was needed in record time—thus contributing to the success of our first and most vital mission."

Other members of the 3rd Regiment describe that nightmarish packing trip up and down the mountain:

Bill Rachui: "A soldier would carry either a five-gallon can of water, case of rations or a box of ammunition, and we made two trips a day for seven days using the same trail on which we had to pass dead bodies of men from units that tried to take the high ground before and our own dead every trip we made."

Leo Mitchell: "We were stretcher company—a Red

Cross on one's helmet is not nearly as comforting as a Tommy gun. Getting out of the foxhole at 2 A.M. and making time with stretchers on back was not pleasant; then the climb up for three hours and carrying the wounded down was hard work. Lieutenant Leske in our company surprised a German sniper by jumping on his back and taking him prisoner. He was a big one, complete with Schmeisser gun and Iron Cross—Les had nothing.

"Colonel Frederick stayed on the top all the time. Colonel Adams stayed at bottom keeping supplies going up. I remember when the trench feet cases were hobbling down, feeling sorry for themselves, Colonel Adams would say 'Where is your rifle and water bottle?' They thought he was crazy— but afterwards we all knew he had a better hold on the situation than anyone—an unarmed soldier is useless."

John Bourne indicated that the rest of the men shared a moment of sober realization when he said, "At first, the men felt that this was not what they had been trained to do and, in fact, were a little insulted. Their attitude changed, however, when they found that ordinary supply troops or medical orderlies would never have been able to withstand the rigors and hardships involved when battling that mountain. As an example, it took eight men about ten hours using mountain climbing ropes, etc., to bring a wounded man from the top of the mountain to a point where he could be placed on an ambulance jeep.

"Most men who were detailed to carry supplies made two trips up the mountain each day. Each pack-board load was about fifty pounds, such as a five-gallon can of water. Some of the stronger men were able to make three trips a day, but this was unusual."

The celebrated war correspondent, Ernie Pyle, was at the foot of the mountain during this period. In his book, *Brave Men,* he gives this description:

> The pack outfit I was with supplied a battalion that was fighting on a bald, rocky ridge nearly four thousand feet high. That battalion fought constantly for ten days and nights, and when the men finally came down, less than a third of them were left.

All through those terrible days every ounce of their supplies had to go up to them on the backs of mules and men. Mules took it the first third of the way. Men took it the last bitter two-thirds, because the trail was too steep even for mules.*

Roy Cuff, another Canadian, adds to this: "On the top of the mountain, the first 2nd Regiment position I stumbled upon in the mist or fog appeared to be quiet and peaceful as I saw quite a number of our boys who appeared to be resting after a hard night's battle. They were all dead, and looked so peaceful in the eerie setting."

Next morning Frederick received the welcome news that the British had taken their objective and were now in position to help consolidate the advantage the Allies had realized by taking one side of the gap.

The attack could now be extended to the west and the south. But first, because of the certainty of a German counterattack, intelligence was needed concerning the strength and disposition of the enemy forces. From the information that Finn Roll was able to piece together from his prisoner of war interrogations, it became clear that the escaping Germans had fled to the ridge and to adjoining Monte la Remetanea or had gone south to reinforce a German-held monastery at the top of the hill which was the next objective.

The morning merged into the afternoon, and the expected German counterattack had not materialized. Every time a mortar barrage began, Frederick felt it signaled the beginning of an enemy rush to retake Difensa. But none came.

Because the phone wires to the rear command post had been cut during the battle, the packers brought another important commodity with them . . . news of the combat situation in other sectors. One item was disquieting. Colonel Adams sent word that the British had been dislodged from the monastery which occupied one of the adjoining heights. The Germans whom the Force had chased off the mountain had joined their comrades in a counterattack, and now had sufficient strength to present an assault problem that, if left unsolved, would result in the Force's being isolated and finally cut to pieces atop Difensa.

* Ernie Pyle, *Brave Men* (New York, Henry Holt & Co., 1944).

This information reinforced Frederick's determination to take Remetanea as soon as possible. Instead of bracing himself for the enemy's charge, he decided to do some attacking on his own. He sent some 2nd Regiment men out on patrol down the ridge to Remetanea to clean out snipers and bring back some prisoners from whom they could extract information as to the strength of the enemy. Placing some of his men in outposts in the general area where a counterattack might come, he told the rest to dig in for the night. They would storm Remetanea at dawn.

Darkness fell early. The wind came up whistling through the pitch-blackness of the night bringing more icy rain with it. By 9:00 P.M. the downpour had increased the discomfort of the Forcemen to where it actually approached physical pain. There was no shelter, few blankets, insufficient food and, above all, a continuous barrage of mortar fire on their positions which never seemed to let up. Difensa had become a cold and lonely island cut off from the rest of the world.

And then, unimaginably, a new dimension was added to their misery. The Germans introduced them to the dread "screaming meemies." Ernie Pyle describes it this way:

> The Germans called the gun the *"Nebelwerfer."* It was a six-barreled rocket rack which fired one rocket after another, electrically. The gun didn't go off with a roar, but the shells swished forward with a sound of unparalleled viciousness and power, as though gigantic gears were grinding. Actually it sounded as though some mammoth man were grinding them out of a huge machine. . . .
>
> The screaming meanies made a frightful noise when they were coming head on, and even when they were going off at an angle some distance away they made a long-drawn-out moaning sound that was bloodcurdling.*

This was a sound to which the Forcemen were to become increasingly accustomed in the next few days.

Lieutenant Colonel Marshall's 1st Regiment, which had been spending an uneventful day in reserve, now began to

* *Ibid.*

get the attention of the German artillery. As the cannonading stepped up, it became imperative that the unit be moved elsewhere to escape the impact of the barrage.

At 11:00 P.M. that night, Brigadier General William H. Wilbur of the 36th Division, sent word to get moving. Lieutenant Colonel Beckett got his battalion in order and sent A Company up the trail to lead the way to their new position. A German machine gunner, concealed on the mountain, spotted them, and squeezed off a burst of tracers to signal his artillery. Shells literally cascaded down on the whole 1st Regiment. The barrage was a lethal mixture of every shell in the German armory; high explosive, air burst, dead head armor-piercing, and searing white phosphorus gushed from the skies . . . making movement of any kind an impossibility.

Robert Shafer stated: "All hell broke loose. They really had us zeroed in. I still think a German patrol was guiding their artillery because the old burp gun would burp a little and we'd get Boom Boom! We started to dig in a little. I was digging and a mortar shell came in and blew me and my shovel onto a lieutenant just below me on the hill. I don't know . . . at that time I didn't feel afraid at all. I says, 'Pardon me,' and crawled back because I didn't think another would land that close at that spot. I wasn't even nicked. Zann and Bundel were hurt. Bundel's arm was half shot off. He looked at his arm and his high-priced watch and said, 'I don't suppose I'll wear the watch on that hand again.' He was taken down the hill and died a little later. Zann had a hunk tore out of his shoulder blade. He was worried about it affecting his pitching arm. I just dozed a little the rest of the night and next morning went with Dr. Neeseman up the hill to help get wounded out. Oh, what a mess. The Third Company tried to dig in and really got clobbered."

As soon as Frederick learned of the pounding his 1st Regiment was getting, he streaked out of his command post in order to be with his men. Actually, he could contribute nothing to them at this point, but his presence among them helped them execute a professional withdrawal instead of surrendering to panic. Two of the men still remember their first sight of him:

137 *

"I saw General Frederick in the next hole, dirty, grimy, with his water bottle holder split, taking it like the rest of us," says an enlisted survivor of that barrage named Fred Pike.

Sergeant Allan H. Jamison said, "I'll never forget Colonel Frederick walking by our position and telling me to keep my head down, and here he was up in full view of the enemy himself!"

The Force responded to this kind of leadership. Major S. V. Ojala and fourteen other officers and men moved out into the darkness to find the snipers who were directing the barrage. Ojala's strategy was quite simple. He and his detachment would move up the slope of the mountain in the direction of the snipers who would certainly fire at them in self-protection. This fire would disclose their position to the rest of the Forcemen.

As Ojala and his men, weighed down with rifles, machine guns, and a supply of hand grenades, spidered their way up and over the icy crags, the German snipers reacted as expected. Their first hit was Major Ojala. His body began slipping down slowly over the cliffs and then, gaining momentum, it turned and bounced, finally plummeting into the wooded area below.

But the diversion worked. Other patrols trailing Ojala's party saw the German fire, and wormed their way to the emplacements. With hand grenades, they blew every German sniper to death. Shortly afterwards, the shelling stopped. The initial barrage had lasted less than an hour. But in those fire-filled minutes, the 1st Regiment had been rendered 40 per cent ineffective.

Midnight came, bringing to a close the first phase of the Force's initial entry into combat. Frederick was satisfied . . . not so much because his men had taken Difensa in a few hours when others had failed to take it in weeks, but because of the manner in which the victory had been won. The First Special Service Force had arrived in this theater of operations preceded by their reputation as potentially tough and vicious fighters. They had proved a right to that estimate.

This was an opinion Frederick had kept to himself.

Throughout his career, he seemed to shrink from portraying himself or his men as colorful characters in the General "Blood and Guts" Patton mold. When a war correspondent later asked him how the Force was able to take Difensa so quickly, Frederick offered no vainglorious description of the action. Instead, he made it sound uncomplicated by explaining in his casually subdued manner, "We simply tried a route that their division commanders didn't think of."

This attitude was characteristic of almost every member of the command. They were never glory hunters or braggarts. They eschewed fancy names and, later, when the Germans gave them the description "Devil's Brigade," they repeated it only with deprecatory grins. The Force, instead of glowing after an improbable victory, soberly counted their dead and wounded. They missed these casualties as friends, but, more important, saw the loss as a possible lessening of the whole unit's combat efficiency.

Heavy casualties forced Frederick to wait another day before beginning the attack on Monte la Remetanea. In the meantime, he placed his men in defensive positions and began moving the reserve units up into attack formations. Patrols were sent out into the rain to comb every sector, to bring back prisoners and to knock out sniper emplacements wherever they could be found.

Robert Neal said: "It was dark as pitch and we had stopped for a short rest, laying beside the narrow trail with our feet close by the trail when some guy came walking up the patch and tripped over my feet. We were all tired and griping; so when this guy hit my feet I said, 'Watch where you are going, you damn nut!' There was a guy just behind him; he stopped and leaned over and said to me, 'Don't you know who that was?' And I said, 'No.' He informed me that was Colonel Frederick. The Colonel stopped and said, 'Pardon me, soldier,' and continued up the trail."

Some of the patrols ran into heavy sniper concentrations. The dense fog added a note of unreality to the dangerous work. Sergeant Stan Slatumas, leading a detachment through the mist, was apparently suddenly blinded when a strong wind momentarily blew away the veil of fog. His patrol found them-selves face to face with a group of Germans in a sniper pocket. The Germans, crouching behind their embankment, opened up with machine pistols. The fire was immediately returned. Slatumas had been a fine fighting man. His body was never found.

The fog played no favorites. Once it parted to reveal a German sniper silhouetted against the skyline, and a Force-man promptly squeezed off a shot that hit the German in the shoulder, toppling him to the rocks below. He was later found lodged head down in a crevice, but with no bones broken. Oddly enough, he had been choked to death by his high collar.

That afternoon, the shifting fog added to the tension and the infighting that took place whenever visibility brought two groups together, was the dirtiest and bloodiest variety. But it was the kind of frontier fighting for which the Force had been trained. Armed with knives, guns and grenades, they moved silently through the mists, killing some of the toughest men the Germans had.

Once a rumor spread that Frederick had been taken pris-oner. A French Canadian recalls the feeling this aroused: "We thought a lot of him. Everyone loved him. When we heard the Colonel was taken prisoner or cut off from the Force, our platoon ran and ran until we cut the enemy off. We made the run about five or eight miles before we stopped. I think if we were not told that the Colonel was O.K. and was recaptured by our Force, that we would have run and fought until there was no more enemy left in the area; in fact, none in Italy."

Platoon leader Lieutenant Zabski, remembers in this kind of fighting, the Force temporarily departed from its pol-icy of silence in combat: "There was a strong German ma-chine-gun defense set up on the ridge. In my platoon were Sergeant Ray Gaither and Sergeant Harvey, a Canadian. These two machine gunners, with half the platoon gone, were able to knock out three or four machine guns, but when the effort cost Harvey his life, the remaining Forcemen bellowed, hollered and raised hell, throwing grenades and attacked with abandon. The enemy was finally outflanked. The success of this type of attack was tremendous, and the Forcemen gave vent to screaming and bellowing in a series of small attacks which were most effective in killing and confusing the enemy."

Lieutenant "Moose" McNair, a strapping six-footer was hit across the back in one of these engagements. His flesh was so badly torn that he could not stand up. Sergeant Juan Mendoza, five feet three inches high, picked McNair up (after Mendoza had silenced the enemy) and carried him ten miles back to an aid station.

The rains had set in again that afternoon, but the men found that this night would be far easier to get through than the preceding one. This was not because the screaming meemies and the sniper attacks had abated, but simply because, that morning, Frederick had contacted Colonel Adams at the foot of the mountain and told him that he didn't give a damn where Adams got it, he wanted some whiskey for his fighters by nightfall. The news of the Force's stand on top of the mountain made the job comparatively easy for Adams. Fifth Army personnel okayed with straight faces his requisition for "15 cases of Bourbon for medicinal purposes."

"I was Frederick's tommy-gun man," says Sergeant Mantino in recalling this incident, "during all these raids. We was right on top of this mountain when the Colonel ordered whiskey for everybody and then made sure everybody got his share."

Colonel Wickham has a different recollection of the requisition, although the results were substantially the same: "Frederick thought it would be good for the men's morale if they could be given some whiskey. He also thought it would be a good idea to get some prophylactics, or 'rubbers,' to put over the gun barrels to protect them from the rain. Fifth Army Quartermaster supplied the whiskey and a dozen gross of strippers but viewed the whole proceedings with a jaundiced eye."

The pack train that brought the whiskey brought another item that was a tremendous help to the men's morale. With them came the first batch of mail received by the Forcemen on Difensa. Practically everyone got a letter, including

Frederick. But his solitary missive did not appreciably raise his morale. It read, "Dear Sir: Corporal B—— of your command on a recent furlough left my maid with child. I would like to know what steps you are taking to correct this offensive action. . . . "

The dawn finally came, bringing with it the realization that the Force's patrols had cleared the southern slope of the mountain to a point where there were no Germans left on the topmost part of the ridge. Frederick decided that the fight could be carried forward without waiting for darkness. A quick push to the south down the saddle would tie together II Corps and X Corps, while an assault down the ridge westward to Monte la Remetanea would cover the British flank in their move forward.

This saddle area had been particularly troublesome to the Force because from it had come most of the harassing mortar fire. The Allied artillery had been kept from pounding it by the very real British apprehension that the shells might fall on their own troops. Two companies of German infantry occupied a monastery in the middle of that area and, until they were liquidated, further advance would be impossible.

Toward midafternoon, the 1st Regiment was ready for the mean job of clearing the enemy from the saddle. Their objective was a pair of small heavily fortified hills. There was to be nothing scientific about this assault nor would it contain any of the colorful elements of the original raid on Difensa. It was to be a straight, head-on battering of the enemy, killing in twos and threes, and being killed at the same rate.

Don McKinnon, a Canadian, described the Force's onslaught: "Our battle cries never ceased from the time of take-off until final attack uphill to enemy positions. I'm sure the howling and baying we did on that attack scared hell out of the Kraut; the howling was as much a release of pent-up emotions held up for several days as it was a battle cry. It seemed to me that we had no thought of anything but to take that hill, and at no time let anything stop us. If there was any way of measuring savageness of an attack I dare say that this attack would measure up with anything during the war. There was nothing skillful or intelligent, it was straight frontal and brutal, asking no quarter, giving none. The enemy was completely demoralized and withdrew under the overpowering wave coming at them. Enemy grenades were picked up and thrown right back at them, without, I believe, anyone even thinking about what could happen if it went off before being thrown back. Riflemen had fixed bayonets, and many used them. No prisoners were taken, as actually there was no chance for an enemy to give up and possibly if he had he would have been cut down by someone. His only chance was to run and that is finally what they did.

"I and many others were completely exhausted when the position was taken. This was the most complete exhaustion I've ever known in my life. After taking up positions on the hill we could see many of the enemy still going in complete confusion down the other side. From their numbers it was easy to see that they had outnumbered us possibly three or four to one."

Lieutenant W. E. Boyce, the leader of this murderous attack, was hit by three bullets as he and his men raced to the final attack. He remained alive only long enough to direct his men into the successful assault.

The regiment spent that night on the two costly knobs. The mortar fire became only sporadic, telling the tired men that the German grip on the area was slipping away. But fatigue was turning them into wooden-faced automatons who could be roused only by victory and removal to rear rest areas.

The next morning came clear and warm. The Germans were obviously backing away. The attack was now launched down the other ridge and Monte la Remetanea was taken and consolidated by noon. Although the end of the battle was in sight, there still existed a very real danger that lack of support could snatch victory from the hands of the Forcemen.

The best summary of the situation at that moment is contained in the message Frederick sent to Adams to be relayed to the 36th Division:

Situation at present (Dec 6—1200 hours). We have troops down to our left boundary at [the saddle] and have consolidated for defense of the area south of la Difensa. Our attack to the west against Hill 907 [la Remetanea] has progressed beyond the crest of 907. We are receiving much machine gun and mortar fire from several directions, principally from the draw running southwest from la Difensa, from west foothills of Maggiore and from north slopes of Camino. We are endeavoring to place artillery support fire on the troublesome areas, but it is difficult due to very low visibility and the British restrictions on our artillery fire.

I shall push the attack on to the west past 907 as far as condition of men will permit. Men are getting in bad shape from fatigue, exposure and cold.

German snipers are giving us hell and it is extremely difficult to catch them. They are hidden all through the area and shoot bursts at any target.

Please press relief of troops from this position as every additional day here will mean two days necessary for recuperation before next mission. They are willing and eager, but are becoming exhausted.

Communications are heartbreaking. Mortar fire (and travel on trail) knock out lines faster than we can repair them. Every time we transmit by radio, enemy drops mortar on locations.

In my opinion, unless British take Camino before dark today it should be promptly attacked by us from the north. The locations we hold are going to be uncomfortable as long as enemy holds north slope of Camino.

That night the British succeeded in taking Monte Camino. By noon the next day, British officers were coming through the saddle to compare notes with the Force. One Guards captain told Colonel Williamson that he was sursurprised by the number of American majors and colonels in so forward a combat zone. Williamson replied that the Force had the theory that leaders should lead.

Throughout the next day, the Force sent patrols down the slopes to consolidate and integrate their victories. The German artillery barrages had subsided to a trickle, but the area still remained infested with pockets of snipers. As before, flushing them out proved dirty and costly work. The job was finished that night. Nothing remained for the weary, filthy, mud- and blood-caked Force but the arrival of their relief and the trudge back down the mountain to where their trucks were waiting.

The story of the operation is obviously a story of individual and collective heroism. The work of the 3rd Regiment and the Service Battalion was a study in man straining past the limits of physical endurance in order to build the stock of supplies the fighters needed.

Colonel Burhans describing an erstwhile foul-up, said, "All the men in this first fight came to hold vast respect for the Medical Corps aid men. Theirs were the same hardships and, if anything, longer hours, for there were wounded men every hour, day and night. Sergeant Jake Walkmeister with the flowing handlebar mustaches was typical of all the medics; he worked without sleep four days running before coming down as an exhaustion case, himself."

Sergeant Randle of the 3rd Regiment said, "The Colonel was a wonderful man . . . he carried a wounded man off of Difensa by his own self."

In this action 532 Forcemen were killed, wounded or injured. If the percentage of casualties seems small in light of the fierce fighting, it must be remembered that it represented approximately one-third of the *total fighting echelon* of the First Special Service Force.

The price was worth paying. The southern jaw that the Germans had used to hold Highway 6, comprising the Camino-Difensa-Maggiore mountain pass, was now firmly in Allied hands. The next job was the snapping of the northern jaw as represented by San Pietro, Mte. Lungo and Mte. Sammucro. By seizing la Difensa and la Remetanea, the Force had gained an Allied triumph on the whole mass. A major advance was rendered virtually certain by the Force's victory. Difensa was the key to the later success of all the Allied armies in that part of Italy.

War correspondent Clark Lee reported, "This feat captured the imagination of the entire Fifth Army and overnight Frederick and his soldiers became almost legendary figures in a battle area where heroism was commonplace. Despite two wounds, Frederick had gone on fighting with pistol and grenade at the side of his men. The Difensa attack [is] destined to live in military annals because of the endurance, daring and fighting skill it involved."

But as the sun rose on December 9, no Forceman, not even Frederick, felt particularly triumphant. After spending the night staggering back down Difensa's slopes, the men just climbed or were boosted into the waiting trucks. No one looked back as they drove away.

VII

The Meat Grinder

*Here comes one of the stupidest, brutish stories of the war—
the misuse of an unparalleled weapon. . . .*

*In everything the Force did, it earned extraordinary laurels.
But, looking back, it is no less than tragic that this North American "corps d'elite" could not have been employed in the lightning, staggering blow for which it had been trained.*
—SHOLTO WATT, correspondent for the Montreal *Standard.*

General George Marshall had been opposed to any large-
scale Allied commitment in Italy. He saw it as "a vacuum
into which America's great military might could be drawn
off until there is nothing left with which to deal the decisive
blow against the Continent."

The history of the Italian campaign is continuing testimony to the accuracy of Marshall's judgment. The early
months of 1944 saw the Allied forces being methodically
chewed to bits in an effort to take a few miles of unneeded
real estate. During this period, the Fifth Army advanced only
seven miles in a month and a half . . . at a cost of 16,000
casualties.

The Allies had already secured every bit of tactical advantage this area could give them after they had invaded and taken Sicily. The over-all strategy of the war was satisfied after Naples. The airfields around Foggia were in our hands and from these huge bases our heavy bombers could reach Germany's industrial heart with comparative ease. Italy had nothing left to offer except the propaganda value of taking Rome, and the possibility of tying down large numbers of troops the Germans needed even worse on other fronts.

The subsequent fighting in France underlined the bitter worthlessness of the Italian campaign . . . even as a diversionary side show. A glimpse at the futility of the gesture is provided by watching the First Special Service Force for the few weeks surrounding Christmas in 1943. The Force was only a speck when measured against the vast armies that the military planners and statesmen shuffled around strategy maps, but by living with them and by watching them being fed like twigs into a roaring bonfire, it is easier to grasp the cruel magnitude of the waste that was involved in the entire operation.

The Force had 1,800 fighting men on Christmas Day. By January 17, 1,400 of them had become casualties.

On December 21, the Force moved from Santa Maria to just outside Venafro in a teeming rainstorm. In the higher grounds where they soon would be fighting, the rain had turned into sleet and snow. Medical reports no longer stressed "trench foot," but instead recited casualty lists dominated by men incapacitated with frozen feet and frozen hands. The weather had become a greater hazard than the mortar fire . . . and the mortar fire had not abated in any way.

The Germans were already skillfully utilizing every natural geographical advantage . . . giant boulders, ledges, caves, slopes and craggy peaks. Now, the weather gave them even more of an edge. They simply dug in and waited. Allied infantrymen who managed to get through the intense artillery fire blanketing the ground before the German positions, were making painfully slow headway in the small-arms fights which followed.

Both sides had dug in more deeply than at any other time previously in the war. The war had become an artillery duel and the British Broadcasting System was describing Venafro as "the hottest spot on earth."

The mission of the Force was to break the stalemate in this sector by seizing some of the peaks where the Germans had embedded their big guns. The Force had taken the first bastions . . . la Difensa and la Remetanea. Now came Sammucro and, further north, the Monte Majo Range.

The Force had gained a reputation for being ferociously efficient, but a tight security veil kept them from public attention. Mark Clark and his Fifth Army Headquarters staff were keenly aware that home-front criticism of Fifth Army's losses and slow progress was mounting to a crescendo. But the mission of the Force was considered too important to be blunted by the additional enemy forces that the needed publicity would bring.

Chief Warrant Officer Bush commented briefly: "We were at this location when Don Whitehead, Robert Capa and Ernie Pyle were up and wanted to put out some news releases on the Force, but they were not permitted to release anything."

From the notes of Percy Crichlow: "My company was in reserve. We moved up through Venafro and the rain poured down upon us as we sat on the trucks drawn up by a wall in Venafro. I kept thinking 'Where does Venafro appear in the classics?' Then we went on to camp in a olive grove, but eventually moved into the comfort of buildings in Ceppagna. Lieutenant Savage took over our platoon and set us up in a house in a corner. One turned off the main road on to a little square in front of a small church then went down a cobbled road with the gutter down the middle. The women emptied their dirty water into the street to run down the middle of the road and I used to think that somewhere in the background there must be the old medieval cry, 'Garde loo' (*Gardez l'eau* —watch out for the water).

"The woman who lived in the house before we came was obviously objecting to our taking over her house, but her protestations stopped cold when she saw Kroll start to chop up her cradle to start a fire. Her husband led her out of harm's way."

As usual before the Force went into battle, Frederick took it upon himself to personally reconnoiter the terrain. Sergeant Grey, a scout, told a correspondent: "I'm a reconnaissance sergeant with Force Headquarters . . . and Force Headquarters goes up forward. The Colonel's always with the forward echelon in the fighting lines. We stay with him and go out to find what's cooking. The Colonel gets closer to being shot than anybody. Sometimes he and I go with scouts, maybe for several days. . . . We infiltrate behind enemy lines and lie hidden in daytime and move around at night."

While on the mountain, making his estimate of the situation, Frederick discovered that other Army units in the area had not yet reached their position. This tactical weakness plus the severity of the weather led him to signal to his men who were camped halfway down Monte Sammucro to postpone the attack for another day. Through the night of December 23 and all next day the troops on Sammucro shivered in the penetrating fog and rain while waiting for rations to be sent up. It was the same difficulty that had plagued them on Difensa . . . to be certain of delivery, the supplies had to be carried on someone's back.

This day before Christmas, the Force's assault echelon was subjected to heavy and regular shelling. They dug in as best they could, to await the nightfall. At dusk the 1st Regiment began to move.

Sergeant Locke: "It was Christmas Eve. We were supposed to attack at midnight. It was put off until about six o'clock Christmas morning. Before the attack, well from the night of Christmas Eve until about four or five in the morning of Christmas, we were hit by shells darn near continuously. When we made our attack, we took the first hill in about thirty minutes."

The casualties began early. Another 1st Regiment man describes the charge: "The Germans were here in good positions waiting for us to come. They let us get within 100 yards of the top and cut everything they had loose at us. My company—Fourth Company 1st Regiment—was in the lead and we lost a lot of men, killed and wounded. I was wounded there Christmas eve of '43."

Carl Ward, of Fort Worth, Texas, was a platoon sergeant on Sammucro: "We were holding our own until the Germans cut us off. The Germans were all around us, so we bunched up in fives or fours in each foxhole and made 'em come to us. They came, but we made 'em fight for each hole. At night we would sneak from hole to hole and try to straighten out our line. We kept our dead in the holes with us and just threw blankets over them. It had been tough getting supplies to us before, but when the Germans cut us off, it really got bad.

"The four guys in my hole hadn't eaten for two days. This night the Germans hit the hill with everything they had and we dug in. After that the Jerries stopped shelling. We kept quiet and suddenly one of the kids yelled 'Hell, it's Christmas Eve!' And it was. We decided it would be a lousy Christmas without something to eat so we drew lots to see who would go over to the next hole and bum a can of C rations. I won the draw.

"I started to crawl across the snow to the next hole. When I got there everything was quiet. I climbed in and started to wake the kids up. I knew they had two dead boys, so when I shook a blanket and nothing happened I moved around and felt for the next one. The krauts began to pepper the hill with screaming meemies and I got a little panicky. I kept shaking the blankets and started to yell because I was damned mad that they could sleep through all of it. I stumbled around and shook every blanket before I realized all of the kids were dead. I got out and started back when I saw a guy light a match. I called him every name in the book. When I got through he said, 'Come over here, son.'

"I went over. It was Colonel Frederick and he was bending over a kid who had been hit pretty bad. 'I'm sorry about lighting that match, but this boy wants a smoke. I don't think it matters much tonight, do you?' the Colonel said. He asked me to help carry the kid down the mountain. I told him I thought we were cut off, but he said reinforcements had pushed the krauts back. We carried the kid down the mountain. Once when a mortar hit near by, we dropped him. When we picked him up the Colonel apologized. 'Hell, Colonel,' the kid said, 'when they come that close you gotta duck.' "

The Forcemen advanced toward the ridge at the peak of Sammucro. Mortar and machine-gun fire tore at them from up ahead and from their right side. On their left were nests of snipers who kept up a steady fusillade. In the faint dawning light, they had to run or crawl from one rock to another. They would stop long enough only to fire in return whenever the Germans gave away their positions.

The casualties continued to mount. Here are some random recollections of the men who were in that fight:

"That was some of the most ferocious fighting in Italy, I know there was not many headlines back home about it, but that is the way I saw it. I had twenty-five men in my platoon, and there was six of us that made the top. I don't know how many of the other platoons made it, but not a very big percentage."

"We got to the edge of the hill, when one of our boys from the company said let's go down and take the other hill. I was in charge of the company because all our officers and S. Sgts. were hit and myself I had been nicked on my shinbone. Just then Major Stewart came along and said he would go with his men. All we had left then in our company was no more than seven and eight men."

"Lt. Krasevac walked down the mountain with seven .30-cal. slugs thru him, helping a wounded enlisted man."

In one hour of savage fighting, the ridge was taken. All outposts were secured by eight that morning. The Germans launched several vicious counterattacks but were beaten back. The regiment remained under heavy shell and mortar fire for the rest of that Christmas Day.

The next day, at dawn, they were relieved by an infantry company, and the Forcemen returned to their bivouac to rest. They had won the fight for Sammucro without air support . . . by overwhelming the Germans with the speed of their attack.

Sholto Watt, a previously-quoted Canadian correspondent, who came to know the Force more intimately than any other reporter, said of them in a later dispatch:

> The evidence goes to show that the Germans were aston-ished by the speed of their attacks in each battle. They were not prepared, above all, for a speed which would have been reckless in soldiers of lesser stamina and abilities . . . less practiced in co-ordinated effort. The better men won.

The question of air support for the Force has been often raised. Colonel George Walton, one of the authors of this book, who was in a liaison position with the Force during this period, remembers: "At the time I was a captain and G-3 Air (Air Support Officer) of II Corps. Colonel Robert Porter, (now General Porter) the Deputy Chief of Staff of II Corps, told me that General Mark Clark, on his last trip to the States, had secured the assignment of the Force to Fifth Army and the unit was to be a part of the troops of II Corps. Porter said that the Force was an interesting outfit. It had been orig-inally designed for a hazardous duty, later abandoned. Many of its personnel were criminals recruited from American stock-ades and it had every conceivable type of training . . . that the men of this unit were so rough and tough that it was felt necessary to keep them as remote from civilization as possible while training them. Porter said they would be used as shock troops in attacks on the mountain redoubts of la Difensa, Sammucro and Majo in the Liri Valley. As Corps G-3 Air I was to contact Colonel Adams, the Force Chief of Staff, as to what air support could be used in the attacks on these ob-jectives.

"I saw both Colonel Adams as well as Colonel Frederick and explained how valueless was the use of air weapons in attacks on mountain objectives. Both men agreed with me and said if Corps air support was needed they would advise me."

After three days of rest at Ceppagno, the Force received its orders for the next phase of the campaign. The 2nd Regi-ment was given Monte Radicosa to take, the 3rd Regiment was assigned Monte Majo and the 1st Regiment, which had gotten badly chewed up on Sammucro, had two smaller hills as targets.

The Forcemen had become battle-wise veterans in the past few months. Although too numbed by fatigue to still feel the zest with which they had attacked Difensa, they methodically kept winning every engagement.

Clarence Sample spoke for most of the men when he said, "By this time it was just routine . . . a couple more hills to clear out. Only, every time out, we were four or five men less than the last one."

The Force had always been fighters, but now they added the dimension of experience. At every opportunity, the battle-field was thoroughly reconnoitered in advance by Frederick, his regimental commanders, or their scouts. Bits of ring craftiness like this kept their record intact.

One of the most enthusiastic scouts was "Chief" Wright who, on every occasion, labeled himself as "the old man's bodyguard." Wright followed Frederick like a shadow and on those occasions when he was sent out as the head of a scouting expedition, he invariably conducted himself as he thought that Frederick might under the same circumstances.

Sometimes his natural exuberance tempted him into an attempt to out-Frederick "the Old Man." While leading the handful of men scouting Radicosa's minefields for the coming battle, Wright and his men ran into a company of Germans who promptly turned all their firepower on the Americans. Gathering his men about him, the "Chief" scuttled back down the trail, pausing long enough at an intersecting path, where the Germans had erected troop bivouac signs, to turn all the signs around to where they pointed the way to American lines.

The weather, a bitter enemy during the assaults, was a friend in these scouting interludes. Winter now held central Italy firmly in its grasp, and the small detachments of infiltrators crept unnoticed up the trails, as strong gales whipped through the sector. Halfway up each of the mountains that the Force was to attack, lay at least three inches of snow. There was also zero temperature. The rest of the way up was covered with at least five inches, and occasionally much more where the stuff had piled in towering drifts. The icy wind-swept snow was blowing at almost gale force and the faces of the men were cut with particles of ice, driven by the wind. The attack on Monte Radicosa began a few days after New Year's Eve. The shepherds, peasants and farmers and their families who lived in those hills, and whose homes lay between the Force and its mountain objectives, began streaming past them back to safety.

From the notes of Percy Crichlow: "When we began to move up, I found myself in a group convoying wire-laying mules and pack mules. The wire played out and the drums squeaked. We gathered outside a farmhouse, and I and some others found a sheltered barn to have a smoke. It was really comfortable, but suddenly there were a couple of shots, then the door was thrown open and an excited senior officer cursed us for cowards, for hiding while the enemy ski troops (so he said) in white uniforms were surrounding us. Of course, it was pure bunkum, but anyhow I went out to a little copse and set a group of men to watch.

"When I was returning, I was just in time to see some rear-echelon Johnny with more stripes than brains about to fire at the copse. I told him that I had men out there. He had seen the enemy he was sure and intended to fire. I suggested to him that I had a Tommy gun and it made an awful mess if it went off by accident. He lost all interest in the copse.

"Later I had the opportunity of seeing Colonel Walker brilliantly directing the artillery fire. He had the misfortune to have one battery that kept firing short on our lines, but he calmly stopped each battery in turn until he caught the offenders without letting up his fire on the forward slopes. I still see in memory the artillery Fire Officer relaying his fast decisions, issued in an unflustered drawl."

The 2nd Regiment was now commanded by Lieutenant Colonel Bob Moore, succeeding Lieutenant Colonel Williamson who had returned to Canada. The men of the 2nd felt that Williamson was another victim of Adams' concepts concerning military decorum, but it remains the opinion of many junior officers that the Williamson brand of leadership did not conform to Frederick's insistence that anyone who commanded any unit under his wing should be the best soldier in the group. To Frederick's way of thinking, "command" was not an assignment, it was a post to be held only by all-around excellence.

He insisted on this quality and went to great lengths to assure himself that his leaders were, in fact, leading. During the assaults made in this campaign, one of the battalions knifed far into enemy lines to attain an objective. Once there, they found Colonel Frederick waiting for them. He had gone out in the hours preceding the attack, infiltrated to their target position, and then calmly watched and evaluated the performance of the unit.

The *Reader's Digest,* a publication not normally given to profanity, concluded a description of the incident with, ". . . any junior officer who wasn't out front that morning caught hell from Frederick later in the day!" *

On this attack, Colonel Moore's men had been assigned the job of first driving the enemy from an isolated town. Clark Lee, the correspondent whose later-released dispatches on the Force's exploits finally brought them a measure of the public attention from which they had been shut off by their "secret" status, reports a briefing. The discussion took place while the raiders lay hidden in front of their target:

> The commanding Colonel came up and stretched beside us in the snow.
>
> "This is part of the battle for Cassino," he said. "It won't do us any good to capture any of these little towns unless we get the high ground. We are attacking at nine o'clock. Part of our force is going over the high ridge on the right. The group there is going to make a surprise infiltration attack and get the hill just behind that village. That will leave the Germans on the hill just past the village, but I think if we creep beside them, they will crawl out."

The Colonel left the rest unspoken, but Clark Lee fully understood that once the Germans began to "crawl out," they

* November 1944. This story was written after the Force had left the sector.

all would be killed or captured. That was the purpose of this kind of warfare . . . chew the enemy up in a meat grinder. The ground that they were taking was valueless. Their only real reason for being here was to destroy as many of the enemy as possible.

The high-level planners spoke of "the psychological effect of having Rome in our hands," and "soft underbellies," but the miserably worn-out foot soldiers who squirmed through the freezing mud and fought in blinding snowstorms were not impressed with mystic phrases. They understood that they could either operate the meat grinder, or be put through it themselves.

Lieutenant Adna Underhill expressed it quite simply to Clark Lee. "We like to attack," he said, "because we don't get too many casualties then. We go straight into the Jerries until we get close enough to use grenades. We never let machine guns stop us or pin us down because we know that once we are stopped, we'll be murdered by their mortars. As long as we can keep going forward, there is less chance of getting hurt.

"That's the whole story of the Italian campaign. We (the Allied Army) stopped with one leg over these mountains, and we've been getting hell ever since. That's what happens when a platoon stops and if you multiply it by an army, you get the whole picture."

Roy Cuff, one of the Force's most skillful combat leaders, remembered a vignette that occurred during this phase of the campaign: "I recall being on patrol on a cold bitter night and moving over the moonlit snow, when we picked up a prisoner, a most cold and miserable-looking member of Hitler's elite. I turned him over to one of our large, tough, hard-boiled sergeants hoping that, when my back was turned, he wouldn't shoot the miserable creature. Instead the sergeant took off a woolen scarf he was wearing and offered it to the prisoner, who, mistaking the gesture, bent down and started tying the scarf around the sergeant's ankles. I wish I had a picture of the hard-boiled sergeant taking the scarf out of the prisoner's hands, and carefully tucking it around his neck for him."

This, of course, was an infrequent gesture. On another

occasion a surrendering enemy received quite different treatment from another group of Forcemen: "While dug in at Radicosa, we were bedded down and a kraut comes up to one of the boys' holes and says in broken English. 'Take me in, I want to give up, I'm lost.' The answer, 'Oh buzz the hell off, this hole is full.' "

Recitals of warfare are invariably studded with accounts of individual heroism. Therefore, it must again be stressed that the level of individual performance in the First Special Service Force was generally so high that a scrupulous setting-down of such incidents would result in a net effect of over-praise. The emphasis here should be on a team which, considered by its accomplishments, proved much greater than its not inconsiderable parts. Nevertheless, incidents occurred. They occurred with such regularity that it is only elementary fairness to mention some of them here.

Seeking to clear an outpost, Colonel Marshall sent Roy Woolhiser and eight men to silence a nest of enemy machine guns. The patrol returned that evening with four prisoners, having killed and scattered the rest of the Germans in the emplacement. The prisoners evidenced amazement at their experience. One of them said, "We were standing alertly at our machine guns when a voice said, 'Hands up!' The attack was very excellently accomplished."

Another account describes the activities of a private named Piatt who, while on a Radicosa patrol, had gotten lost in a snowstorm.

"A mouth of a cave opened up in front of him and he went inside. . . . He blinked. There in front of him was a fire and, on the other side of it, five Germans. Hastily they reached for their guns, but Piatt was faster. He yanked the pin out of a grenade, but held down the lever. 'Okay, you bastards,' he said. 'Shoot. We'll all go to hell together.' The Germans did not shoot. Fifteen more were in the rear of the cave, and Piatt marched his twenty prisoners back to the command post."

There were other contributions to the folklore of the Force. Some are funny in retrospect, although at the time the humor of the situation eluded the participants. For example, once when Frederick was at his command post on top of the mountain he received word that two high-ranking officers from the United States were waiting to see him at Fifth Army Headquarters. The laborious trip down took almost seven hours because of the gale winds and snow.

When he arrived at Headquarters, the two officers began questioning him about recreational facilities. Frederick looked at them incredulously until the light dawned on him. The name of his outfit had led the officers to believe that his job consisted of being in charge of recreation for the Fifth Army. "Special Service" to these men meant only the entertainment branch. He excused himself as politely as he could under the circumstances and went back up to the war, cursing every step of the way.

The final victory of this campaign was executed by the 3rd Regiment under Colonel Walker. The target was Monte Majo which for five weeks had been delaying the advance of the Fifth Army. Majo is the key to the country north and south of it and was needed as the maneuver pivot for the attack on Cassino. It was the third of the mountains guarding the road to Rome which the Allies had recently labeled "Highway 6," although twenty-five centuries ago it had been known as the *Via Casilina* to its builders. Down this road flowed the German sinews of war from Rome to Cassino.

The Force had stormed and taken la Difensa and Sammucro, using up the 1st and 2nd Regiments in the process. Monte Majo became the property of the 3rd Regiment.

Colonel Walker developed his attack in two stages . . . the first was to take the high ground between his assembly area and the peak, and the second was to take the mountain itself. This intervening high ground consisted of a series of lower peaks, capable of testing the skills and endurance of experienced mountain climbers. The chilling wind blew continuously, and the snow blanket made any objects moving over it so conspicuous that all infiltration had to be done by night. Once again, the Force's ability to move stealthily and purposefully in the dark served them in good stead.

On one hill, about a hundred Germans dug in among mortars and machine guns were taken completely by surprise.

The American detachment, under Captain D. P. Gallegher, had been reduced by previous casualties to only fifty-nine men. Gallegher's outfit crept through the early hours before dawn, reaching their objective by 3:00 A.M. There, waiting in the zero temperature for two hours, they could hear the Germans talking above them. At 5:00 A.M., the Forcemen attacked. Bursting grenades provided the first news of their presence to the Germans. Gallegher's men, split into small groups, fought silently and methodically until they had killed every one of the enemy.

Another group, under Lieutenant Radcliffe, a man shortly to gain Force-wide fame by virtue of the number of times he was captured and escaped in one night, were denied the advantage of surprise for their frontal assault. They fought from one rock to another until they gained the top of the hill assigned to them.

The next day the cold took its toll. Out of seventy-five officers and men under the command of Captain Fletcher, forty-four had to be brought down the hill with feet frozen so badly they could not walk.

By that night, the 3rd Regiment had secured all the intervening heights before Mte. Majo. Walker split his men into an assault unit and a support unit, and then, in order to execute a pincers attack, divided his assault unit into two subsections. Lieutenant Radcliffe commanded one section and Captain Berry took the other.

Once again the Force successfully used surprise as an element of their attack. Employing lessons learned at Difensa, Berry and his men went up a cliff face so steep that they were able to get within thirty yards of the summit of Mte. Majo before the Germans became aware of their danger. Using grenades, the advancing Forcemen cleaned up four machine-gun nests and had consolidated their position well before dawn, less than five hours since the beginning of their ascent.

Radcliffe once more had been given the route where unnoticed advance was an impossibility. He and his detachment ran the gamut of shelling, sniping, and machine-gunning from the moment they put foot on the base of the mountain. As they battered their way up, Radcliffe detached one, two or three men at a time to deal with machine gunners or snipers. At two in the morning they reached their objective, a spot high on the mountain's left shoulder. For the rest of the night they held off blistering counterattacks. By the dawn of January 7, the Majo peak was firmly in the hands of the Force. Despite an almost unbroken wave of German attacks, they continued to hold their ground for the next few days.

Again, air support had been impracticable. Even so, the Force's advance was so precipitate that the German commanding officers had been thrown into confusion by the hurtling nature of the assault. They ordered their men to retake the lost ground at any cost. Three-quarters of the German troops committed died in losing attempts. Frederick's men also suffered grave losses. Robert Capa, the celebrated combat photographer, in describing a visit to that battlefield wrote, ". . . every five yards a foxhole, in each at least one dead soldier. Around them empty cans of C rations and faded bits of letters from home. The bodies . . . were blocking my path."

The victory at Monte Majo was a military masterpiece. Because of their strongly entrenched positions among the rocks, the Germans had twice as much strength as the attacking Force. Yet the attack swept forward, swiftly overcame all defensive delays and reached the top of a towering mountain in a matter of hours. Then, the 3rd Regiment held it for almost three days of sustained counterattacks. Incidentally, it should be noted that one of the key elements in successfully holding the mountain peak for so long a period was that the Force had plenty of ammunition. By taking the peak so quickly, they were also able to get their hands on the German supplies. They made liberal use of German guns and bullets during most of the time of their stay. As each successive counterattack came over the lip of Majo the enemy fell in front of his own captured guns. Much of this accomplishment reflects the abilities of Colonel Walker. Anyone wishing to challenge his wartime achievements ought first to listen to the men who were with him in the fight for Majo.

"Red" Hindle: "I was seriously wounded and left to die in the snow. Colonel Walker found me and persuaded me to crawl down the hillside. We were between crossfire and I collapsed. Then Lt. Bill Story came along with some Germans and they carried me down to the hospital."

Arthur Vautour: "I was attached to the small staff of [Colonel] Edwin Walker. Regardless of his eccentric behavior at this present time, I found the man to be a wonderful military commander, the kind of man all Americans my be proud of as a preserver of their freedom. He knew what was going on at all times, and, looking at a map, he'd request the artillery to lay down a barrage at such and such a place, somewhere over the hills at a spot he had never seen. It usually proved effective. He was there, sick or well, and one dark night I was sure the man would die of exposure up in the hills. But he slugged it out with the best of them."

Pvt. Bursey, a Canadian, remembers: "A fellow and I were sleeping in our foxhole when we heard some guys hollering for help. We pulled on our boots and ran over. The Colonel was there already. The man had been hit by a phosphorous bomb and he was burning. I held my mitt over his face until it caught fire. The Colonel was burned, too."

Eugene Pelletier tells of being with Walker at the time Walker received his promotion to full Colonel. A shell fragment hit Walker's helmet a glancing blow, slicing away his new insignia of rank. Walker's reaction was not one of fright, but of anger. "The dirty krauts," he bellowed, "they've knocked off my new eagle!"

A 2nd Regiment man named Bennet was stationed at a supply dump located just behind Majo. "Our phone was connected," he recalls, "both to headquarters and up to Colonel Walker. One time we started to get shelled, but good, by our own artillery. One of my guys grabbed the phone and yelled, 'Give me Corps Headquarters.' When he was put through he ordered them to stop the shelling. Of course he didn't give his own name and I guess Corps thought it was Walker on the phone. Anyway, the shelling stopped.

"The phone immediately rang again. This time it was Walker. He was an ex-artillery man himself and he knew its value and he loved it so much that he thought it could do no wrong. When my guy told Walker what had happened, Walker said it was impossible . . . that it couldn't be *our* artillery. My guy answered, 'Then tell the Germans to get the hell out of *our* positions.' "

Another colorful personality was lost to the Force during this period. After the 3rd Regiment was relieved by an infantry outfit on January 10 and permitted to return for a few days rest in bivouac, "Chief Scout" Wright was killed while trying to help some reporters get an unusual story.

The episode had its beginning when Robert Capa, Ernie Pyle, and Clark Lee obtained permission to visit Force Headquarters. These three combat correspondents deserved as much respect for their bravery as almost any infantryman in the line. Perhaps more, because there were no regulations that forced them into the thick of the battle. Two-thirds of the trio, Pyle and Capa, died in later battles. These were men . . . fully as good as the men they had come to write about.

Clark Lee described how he accompanied Colonel Frederick on a patrol to occupy a village which was located right under the guns of the Germans a few hundred yards away. Lee listed the men of the patrol, among them "Lieutenant Finn Roll, and some others including myself and Robert Capa formerly of Hungary, the Spanish War, the London blitz, Club 21 and points between."

Starting down the path in single file, the group snaked through their own outposts and into no man's land. The party went on. At one point they had to take cover as an enemy emplacement barraged them for fifteen minutes with mortar shells. Frederick's hand was cut by flying rocks, but after sponging off the blood with his handkerchief he paid no further attention to it.

The patrol continued onward until Frederick was satisfied that he had the terrain fixed firmly in his mind. They then returned to his command post where he immediately got on the field phone to relay orders to his units. One of the men gave him some food, but "the Colonel got only a few bites between phone calls. The phone was essential in keeping things moving. The Colonel had to know where every mule would be at a given time, how long each trip took, how much ammo, rations or water it would carry."

Lee was surprised when the Colonel decided to go back. But, after a conversation with a captured prisoner, he had become convinced that the Germans were about to reoccupy a hill which they had previously abandoned.

The correspondent describes the ensuing action:

The colonel finished talking to the prisoner and turned to Lt. Finn Roll.

"Come on, Finn, get your gun. We're going."

"Yes, sir, where are we going?"

"Up Hill 650."

Then Frederick saw Bob Capa and myself.

"What are you doing here?"

"Going with you."

"No, there is an order against correspondents getting ahead of our lines."

"Hell, we're ahead of them right now, aren't we?"

"The point is that you might trip over a mine or give the rest of us away. Climb up near our forward machine-gun position and watch."

And with that, the Colonel went up the hill. The correspondents watched until he disappeared in the darkness. The willingness of Lee and Capa to take the risks of a hazardous patrol evidently impressed "Chief" Wright. Later, when Capa and a Signal Corps photographer named Gallegher were bemoaning the fact that below them in Cervaro some exciting street fighting was taking place and that they were missing a wonderful opportunity for pictures, Wright decided to bypass the brass and take them down himself.

The party, accompanied by two other scouts that Wright talked into accompanying them as bodyguards, went down to the valley below.

The photographers got their pictures, but Wright and a scout named Hill were killed in a gun duel with the enemy in the tiny village.

This phase of the campaign was over. Frederick, who had been wounded three times during the fight, received several decorations and a promotion to brigadier general as a result of the showing of the Force. In addition, for a brief time during the fight, General Keyes had placed him in command of "Task Force B," a group consisting of the Force, some infantry units, and a French outfit known as the "Bonjour Groupment." He had maneuvered this unit so efficiently that higher headquarters now recognized him as something more than an inspiring but foolhardy fighter. They began to see him as a tactician who could shuffle diverse units around a battlefield with imagination and skill. Nothing was said at the time, but Frederick was marked for later and larger commands—if he survived.

Very few trucks were needed to bring the Force back to its bivouac area at Santa Maria on the afternoon of January 17. Of its 1,800 combat personnel, 1,400 were either dead or in the hospital as casualties. The Service Battalion packers and litter men were reduced 50 per cent by fatigue and wounds.

VIII

The Black Devils
of Anzio

*During [this] period, I was the Commanding General of the
Fifth Army, of which the 1st Special Service Force was a part.
When it became apparent, shortly after the Anzio landings, that
a maximum economy in troops would have to be effected to hold
the extensive beachhead perimeter, the 1st Special Service Force
was selected to hold 13 kilometers on the southern flank of the
52 Kilometer Anzio-Nettuno front. This aggressive, fearless and
well-trained organization, then over 35 per cent under strength
in personnel, immediately undertook a series of raids and bold
probings of the enemy front. Repeated unsuccessful operations
by the Germans, to neutralize these devastating and terrifying
raids by small units of the 1st Special Service Force, gave birth
to the legend of the invincible "Black Devils."*

—MARK W. CLARK
General, U.S.A. (ret.)

Anzio was many things to many people in World War II.
To Adolf Hitler, it was "this abscess" to be excised from
Italy's body in order that Rome might be preserved as a sym-
bol of his unbroken domination of Europe.

To Field- Marshal Albert Kesselring, commander in Italy, one of the ablest of the German generals, it was a pie-shaped piece of land, perhaps thirty miles square, which the Allies had incomprehensibly selected for the beginning of an expensive assembly of Italian ground.

Kesselring and his almost equally capable associate, General Eberhard von Mackensen, welcomed the choice of the Anzio-Nettuno seaport area as the invasion point. Within a matter of days, they were able to surround the narrow beachhead with over 70,000 excellent troops. Among these were the 735th Grenadier Regiment, the Hermann Goering Division, the Reichsfuhrer (SS) Division, the 16th (SS) Division, the 35th Panzer Grenadier (SS) Regiment, and the 26th and 29th Panzer Grenadier Divisions. Kesselring also had numerous Italian units as well as more Germans in reserve.

Anzio represented the best compromise available to Winston Churchill. Intellectually and emotionally committed to the invasion of Europe through the Balkans, he had settled for a thrust through Italy to the south of France. To Churchill, Anzio signified that, at last, this concept was receiving the serious attention of the Allied high command.

Generals Marshall and Eisenhower questioned the continuance of the Italian campaign, however, because they were convinced that the only way Hitler could be beaten was by a frontal assault launched across the English Channel into France. They gloomily evaluated their Italian assignment and concluded that the most it had to offer was the prospect of partially eroding away the men and material that Hitler had at his command.

The subsequent unfolding of the pattern of World War II reinforces the view of the American generals. Although Allied forces prevailed in Italy and succeeded in lancing up through Southern France, there is little evidence that the campaign materially advanced the date of the final German surrender. And the psychological advantage gained by the taking of Rome must be balanced against the 72,000 Allied casualties shipped out of Anzio between February and June, 1944.

But the fact remains that an Ottawa Conference between

Roosevelt and Churchill resulted in a cablegram from Marshall to Eisenhower. This was to the effect that the Mediterranean Theater of Operations would be the scene for a continued Italian fight. Eisenhower was directed to go to London to assume command of the forthcoming cross-Channel invasion and to turn his present command over to the British general, Sir Harold Alexander. General Alexander, in turn, was advised to entrust the bulk of the fighting to General Mark Clark and his Fifth Army. Thus, the chain back to the First Special Service Force.

The Force, renewed to a strength of approximately 2,300 men by replacements and the return of some of its casualties from the hospitals, was idealized by Clark. He felt that Frederick and his men could do any job that he asked of them. At the Anzio beachhead, he asked the combat echelon of 1,300 men to defend 13 out of the 52 kilometers of front. This group . . . a drop in the bucket when measured against the approximately 40,000 men Clark had to crowd into the tiny perimeter, was asked to hold fully a quarter of the entire line. Which they did.

The Germans at Anzio should have been able to push their opponents back into the sea. Every square foot of the Allied position was under the surveillance of German artillery. The German units in the opposite lines were among the very best they had. But veteran outfits like the Hermann Goering Panzer Division faced the Forcemen and came off second-best in a series of fights which spanned 100 days.

Of course, the Force was far from the sole determining factor of the Allied victory at Anzio. But they kept such continual pressures on the Germans that Kesselring was forced to tie down large numbers of his men in their sector. Their uncanny ability to range unseen through the night behind enemy lines resulted in intelligence reports that played a large part in the Allies' ability to maintain what was, essentially, an untenable position.

It is a matter of record that the First Special Service Force was given twice as much of the front to hold as the entire 3rd Division . . . and the 3rd Division was considered one of the best in the U. S. Army.

Shortly after the victory at Monte Majo, the Force received its shipping orders for Anzio. Allowed ten days to rest and re-equip, most of the men contented themselves with the luxurious feeling produced by hot food, showers and clean clothes. Others felt that the word "re-equip" allowed them considerable latitude.

Sergeant Jake Walkmeister, for example, recruited a crew of prostitutes in the first few days and then devoted his remaining rest-time to figuring how to bring them with him to the battlefield.

Lieutenant L. Stuart, a 1st Regiment officer who was in charge of loading the Force aboard the Anzio transport, has offered a graphic description of the assembly and transportation of what subsequently became famous throughout the Fifth Army as "Walkmeister's Portable Whorehouse":

"I was dispatched to Pozzuoli to supervise the loading of one LST with twenty-six vehicles, and such other miscellaneous equipment as could be conveniently loaded without incident; the thirteenth driver, evidently full of vino, drove one wheel off the gangway. Jacking, lifting it back on course took a few minutes, which I spent in checking the remaining vehicles.

"One of them was an ambulance, neatly stenciled with 'MED. DET., 1st Regt., 1SSF.' It was driven by Sergeant Walkmeister. The sergeant had a long, sweeping handlebar mustache, which he constantly twisted with two fingers. He surveyed the chaotic scene with something of the same air which I imagined Gen. Mark Clark would have used, had he been present. I checked to be sure, and there was no ambulance on my list, neither was there a vehicle with the serial number boldly painted on the hood, which the ambulance had.

"I approached the driver and inquired if possibly he had been misdirected and was in the wrong line. This suggestion evoked a torrent of words which lasted for some five minutes.

"Summarized, it appeared that General Marshall had expressed a wish that the First Regiment of the 1st SSF should be equipped with an ambulance; that this wish had come down through a chain of command quite awesome in the

169   *

resounding titles which rolled off his tongue, and finally that these important people could hardly be expected to personally come down to these God-forsaken stinking docks to personally see that his ambulance was loaded. Of this latter argument I could find no fault, but I did point out that neither would they be present when we unloaded to explain the situation to a dockmaster, who would probably be a colonel, and, as a clincher, that there simply wasn't room on the boat for another vehicle.

"Sergeant Walkmeister did not deign to reply to this last argument, simply jumping from the seat and disappearing. 'Well,' I thought, 'that fixed him,' and went off to see about the truck on the gangway.

"A few minutes later the air-raid siren sounded, the trucks waiting to be loaded dispersed according to orders, and we all took a fifteen-minute break. When the all clear came, I noted with some little surprise that the ambulance, still driven by Sergeant Walkmeister, was at the head of the line, and that there were exactly enough vehicles behind it to make out my twenty-six.

"While I was considering another little chat with the sergeant, someone in a Navy jeep, equipped with a bull horn, came along, and bellowed something about getting them loaded—we sail in fifteen minutes. So loaded they were. I soon found that my own jeep, which I had placed next to the officers' country at the rear of the ship, had somehow been moved to a slot nearer the bow, and the ambulance reposed in its former place.

"Immediately after casting off, I busied myself with the details of securing the vehicles so that it was perhaps an hour before I went aft to the tiny wardroom where one of the two Navy junior lieutenants in charge of the ship had told me we would have a bite to eat.

"I recall, quite well, the scene that met my eyes when I opened the wardroom door and pushed aside the blackout curtain. Sergeant Walkmeister sat at one end of the table, about the size of a card table, before him were two quarts of alcohol plainly labeled 'for the use of the U. S. Army medical detachments only,' and two open cans of pineapple juice. A

Navy lieutenant was sitting on the edge of one of the two bunks holding the hand of a very pretty young lady. Behind her lay another pretty young lady, and on the other bunk lay one—or was it two?—more pretty young ladies. Old soldier that I was by that time, I wasted no time in inquiring how it happened that three or perhaps four such peaches were aboard one of the ugliest ships in the U. S. Navy, twenty miles off the shore of Italy, and reportedly heading for a very dangerous landing on an enemy coast the following morning.

"Instead, I reached for one of the free hands of the young things in the opposite bunk, scooped up a drink which Sergeant Walkmeister obligingly had ready with the other, and inquired after her health in my best Italian.

"Her health, it turned out was fine, and after a couple of shots of medical alcohol, which runs about 180 proof and in which, no doubt as a bow to the ladies, the sergeant sprinkled a few drops of pineapple juice, my own general outlook on life became much improved.

"The evening progressed and I lost whatever slight fear I may have had that some superior officer might inquire how it happened that an ambulance was on board, instead of the 4 x 4 the manifest called for. Steaks and French fries appeared, followed by ice cream. The Navy lived well in those days, I learned. I also learned, with my smattering of Italian—the girls spoke no English—that Signore Sargente (Walkmeister) had told them we would disembark the following morning in *belle Napoli* where they had friends. Far be it from me, a lowly lieutenant, to contradict as knowledgeable a man as the sergeant. Maybe we *were* going to Naples.

"The bunks had curtains which could be pulled together; the sergeant and the extra girl, or girls, disappeared to parts unknown and uncared for, and the young Navy lieutenant and the young Army lieutenant sank into the arms not of Morpheus but of Maria.

"The other Navy lieutenant fortunately was of the narrow-minded type. He looked in upon us early in the evening, spoke darkly of courts-martial and what Admiral Whatsis was going to say, and went back to running the ship. Which he did so efficiently that we were delivered in Anzio harbor at precisely the time the German Air Force chose for its daily demonstration.

"For this reason Sergeant Walkmeister did not have to again pull the air-raid siren, a privilege which had, he told me, cost a whole quart of 'alky' in Pozzouli. Disembarkation was quick and surprisingly efficient. No colonel appeared to ask awkward questions. The ambulance disappeared and I did not see it or Jake again for a matter of six weeks or so.

"I wonder sometimes what he told the girls when they first surveyed their new home. I don't imagine, though, that he was at a loss for words, even though his knowledge of the Italian language was about as sparse as my own."

The Force arrived at Anzio on February 1. Next day they moved to the front lines.

The area they were given to hold centered around the Mussolini Canal, a huge drainage ditch which stitched across the Littoria Plain. The canal was situated on one of the flattest pieces of land in all of Italy. Every move that the Forcemen made for the next four months was in the clear sight of the enemy watching from the mountains ringing the plain. Partial concealment could be secured only by burrowing into the sides of the canal, since any attempt to dig a foxhole in the plain was useless. If one dug as little as a foot one struck water. In short order their encampment became known to the Force as "the billiard table."

At its widest, the canal measured sixty yards. Its depth and swiftness rose considerably during the springtime months. The defense of the canal was of primary importance to the Allied operation, since it formed a natural barrier for the beachhead troops against the movement of the German tanks into their midst.

The only breaks in the landscape were the farmhouses and barns. When the Force arrived, most of these were occupied by Germans who used them as spotting and sniping points.

Frederick lost no time in putting his men to work. The 1st Regiment, approximately at half strength, was given one-

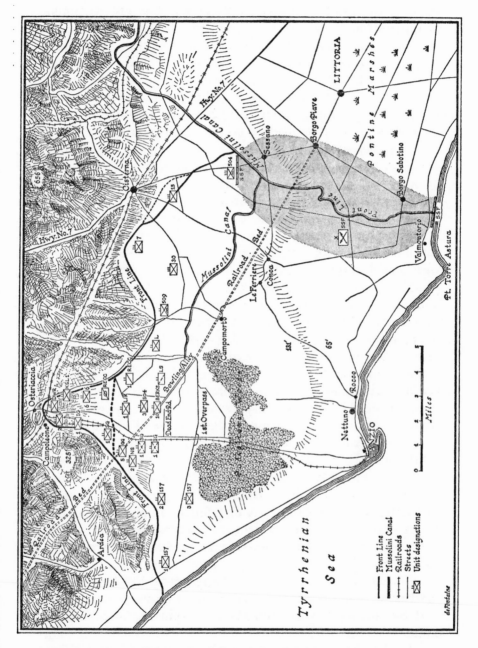

The flat, mountain-ringed plain of Anzio. The Force, at brigade strength, held the shaded area and raided beyond it daily. Three divisions held the rest. Here, the name "Black Devils" was born.

third of the Force's right front to cover. The 3rd Regiment was given the defense of the two-thirds remaining on the left side. The 2nd Regiment, now a skeleton of the outfit which had stormed up Mte. Radicosa, was put in reserve. Immediately behind them was the Service Battalion. But, on Anzio, "reserve" had an empty ring. There just wasn't enough ground to separate front and rear echelons into any meaningful division. The Service Battalion was alerted to the possibility of immediate combat duty.

During their first evening in position, the Forcemen became aware that the posture of defense was not to their liking. They lost men to mines and snipers and, evidently, were expected to simply burrow in more deeply until the Germans launched their inevitable counteroffensive. So, they decided the hell with it and by midnight had launched five patrols which penetrated as far as a thousand yards into the enemy position. Between the prisoners they brought back that night and the intelligence they accumulated concerning enemy concentrations, they were able to supply their own artillery with valuable target information. Next day, the American guns plastered the area and the Germans were on notice that the Mussolini Canal sector had become a particularly sore part of the Anzio abscess.

Within a week, the aggressiveness of Force patrols caused the Germans to pull back almost half a mile. The area in between the canal and the Germans' new position quickly became identified as no-man's-land, and its small villages and occasional farmhouses were the scenes of an almost manic turnover of tenants. The Germans occupied the houses by day, the Force drove them out at night. This deadly seesaw ended only after Frederick decided that the houses no longer had value as observation posts, and gave his men permission to blow them up. This was the kind of thing they had trained for in Helena and they jumped to the job with gusto. For the first time since their entry into combat, the Force came close to fulfilling its original design. At Anzio they operated as guerrillas on nightly patrols, disappeared when daylight came and, in between, blew up enemy installations whenever permitted.

The tenseness of combat was still present . . . the round-the-clock shelling by the German artillery insured that . . . but the freezing discomfort of mountain fighting which had turned them into numb automatons was gone. And their relish for this kind of fighting gave rise to escapades which quickly became legends on the beachhead.

For example: "Gus" Heilman's election as the mayor of Sabotino, a village whose name was promptly changed to honor a man whom he and the men of his company all thought singularly worthy of receiving this tribute—himself.

The town of Gusville was founded during one of the night patrols. Heilman and his men, skulking through the darkness in the no-man's-land between the lines, stumbled upon a deserted village which, on their maps, bore the name of Borgo Sabotino.

Surveying the solidly built row of farmhouses, one of the men commented, "I'd a hell of a lot rather be living here instead of that goddam mud back at camp." There was a general murmur of agreement from the other members of the patrol.

"Well, what the hell," Gus observed. "It's only a quarter of a mile or so inside the krauts' lines, let's move in."

A moment before the men had been dog tired. Now they were excited at the prospect of owning a town. One man yelled, "Hey . . . we got a city . . . who's gonna be mayor?"

"I nominate the lieutenant," yelled back another. The shouts of approval made the election unanimous.

One of the men, evidently a logical type, asked, "Mayor of what? Does this-here dump have a name?"

"I don't know what the hell the name of it was before," answered Sergeant Bernie Helming, "but I'll tell you what it is now. This-here town is hereby named Gusville."

From then on, Gusville was the home of the Second Company of the 1st Regiment. Correspondents on the beachhead heard about it, and it became a mark of status to inch down the road covered by German snipers and 88's in order to file stories bearing the dateline "Gusville."

The official army newspaper in Italy, *The Stars and Stripes,* even published an editorial about it. This read:

You won't find Gusville listed in your atlas, but for the moment this busy "township" is as deserving of a place on the map as Detroit, Rome or Proskurov.

Although it lacks some of the civic institutions customarily associated with a thriving community, Gusville can make a strong bid for recognition as a "model" town. Gusville has no strikes, no unemployment, no black market: and its residents are 100 per cent behind the war effort.

This location used to be a quiet spot in the Italian countryside: then one day Lt. Gus Heilman led the first Fifth Army unit into this advance sector of the Anzio beachhead and a new town was born that roars around the clock with the noise of battle.

On the surface, this fantastic community appears to be just a collection of huts and tents and a few buildings; the home of cows, chickens, horses and a few pigs. But it is also the home of sudden death—for Gusville is the base used by the reckless Anzio Commandos whose motto is "Killing is Our Business."

Every night the Black Devils of Gusville, American and Canadian troops steal quietly out of town, move over deep into enemy lines to kill or capture Germans. "Black Devils" is what the Nazis call them; the Fifth Army troops call them the wild men of the beachhead.

And these night raiders, proud of their front-line shantytown, are not lacking in civic enterprise. They issue their own newspaper, the *Gusville Herald-Tribune,* so that the troops in the town can follow the war outside the beachhead, and they have given picturesque names to their town's two streets—for example, "Tank Street," so named because a Nazi tank has a habit of moving forward at frequent intervals and pumping lead straight down the thoroughfare.

To us, these facts all add up to make Gusville an important place. It is another spot where it is being proved that the men of the Allied nations can be fused into a deadly fighting machine. And it is being demonstrated here that these fighting men do not lose their high courage, their lighthearted spirit and their sense of humor, even under the toughest battle conditions.

Gusville's existence as a community will be short-lived, but she needs no chamber of commerce. Her reputation is being assured by the deeds of her citizens.

The Tank Street mentioned in the above article was bisected by another thoroughfare which had been named "Prostitute Avenue." A dispatch by United Press correspondent Robert Vermillion explained, "The other gets its title because a man walking down it a little ways will find himself without visible means of support."

Vermillion's story ran in most of the papers in America under the heading "WITH THE 5TH'S BLACK DEVILS AT GUSVILLE." The correspondent concluded his report thus:

> This morning a patrol went out into no man's land. They returned with a wounded German, a wheelbarrow full of sweet potatoes, four bushels of peanuts, twenty-two eggs, and one rabbit shot while running. Gusville's livestock now boasts eight cows, fourteen chickens, six pigs and three horses, all stolen from the Germans. The boys are very kind to the cows and explain that they have to steal them because the Germans neglect to milk them.

True to his memory of past benefits, Mayor Heilman established a village bar immediately after he appointed a chief of police and other city officials from among the members of his company. The bar was stocked with the results of raids directed against German-held wine cellars and, as in Virginia, Gus became famous for selling good cheer at reasonable prices. Some of his other policies were not as popular. He attempted to levy taxes on Force battalions passing through his city limits on their way to patrols behind enemy lines and more than one transient Forcemen was heard to suggest an improbable filing place for his official decrees.

One of Gusville's most spirited citizens was Lieutenant George ("The Mustache") Krasevac, a tall character with a huge red soup strainer. He was not a member of Second Company, but was over there so often that the registered citizens appointed him city manager. Krasevac took his job seriously. He began to go out on solo patrols to pick up things. His first substantial pickup was the herd of cattle. Whenever the Force wanted to find out the whereabouts of German gun positions, the call would go out for Krasevac. "The Mustache" would then get his umbrella and bicycle and ride up and down Tank Street drawing German fire. "The Mustache" also led some of the toughest night patrols. He was wounded three times, the last one sending him out of combat.

There were, of course, some rumbles of resentment engendered by the success of Gusville. Rafael P. Montone, a rugged ex-resident of Laredo, Texas, had always been friendly with Heilman, and recalls, "We made a lot of patrols with Lieutenant Heilman. One time we got caught and ambushed. One of the boys got shot pretty bad, and old Gus Heilman crawled under fire to get him out and back to the company." But this friendship evidently faded under the grim realities of competition. Montone goes on to say, "I opened a wine bar and traded wine for eggs and chickens. It was known as Cisco's Bar. My bar went to hell when Lieutenant Heilman moved us across Mussolini's Canal and into no-man's-land."

However, the sheer pleasure of living in Gusville finally restored the bonds of friendship to Heilman and Montone. Again, Montone: "We had a lot of fun raiding the Germans at night. We used to come back loaded with eggs, chicken and fresh vegetables. I remember the day that some guy got drunk on patrol. I was his First Sergeant. We had a fight and he was sent to the hospital, and a week later he came back with a Purple Heart."

Gusville had a considerable effect on the morale of all the soldiers at the Anzio Beachhead. Subjected to continuous shelling, never certain whether or not they would be pushed back into the sea, the casual disinclination of Forcemen like Gus Heilman to consider their situation a serious predicament, made all Allied soldiers feel better. They saw that the Force was not only refusing to be content with self-preservation, they were enthusiastically launching and winning a series of offensive actions. More than one Allied commander observed that "the Force gave heart to everybody."

It was during this period that the Force got its name "The Black Devils' Brigade." A diary was found on the body of a German lieutenant, an officer in the Hermann Goering Division's Alarm [Scout] company who was killed during one of the patrols. In it was written, *"The Black Devils are all around us every time we come into the line, and we never hear them come."*

This comment was obviously a result of one of Frederick's rare dramatic gestures. He had ordered a printed supply of paper stickers upon which was reproduced the insignia of his Brigade and, underneath, was a statement in German to the effect that, "The Worst Is Yet to Come." The Forcemen, after killing a German, would paste one of these stickers on the German's forehead or helmet, and then go on. This tactic, executed by a band of blackfaced guerrillas moving soundlessly through the night, not only frightened the enemy, it also produced a mighty effect on the other beachhead soldiers and war correspondents.

One Canadian writer, evidently inspired by the feats of the Force into an outburst of high-keyed prose, sent home a dispatch which read, in part:

> You can't drag the exploits of any one outfit into a bull session over in Italy without someone mentioning the Black Devils of Anzio. But that's not hard to explain. These soldiers are probably the toughest, all-around fighting men ever created.
>
> When a tough job comes up, the "Black Devils" take to it like a duck to water. They revel in danger. With blackened faces and armed to the teeth with every conceivable death-dealing weapon from rifle to dagger, they stalk their prey, make their desperate silent killings, and come back as dawn streaks the Italian sky . . . bloody, weary, torn but grimly satisfied. These are the Black Devils . . . considered by many as the world's best fighters.

"Stoney" Wines observed, "The krauts were afraid of us. They had been told that we took no prisoners and that most of us were ex-convicts and would show them no mercy."

On one patrol, Lieutenant Krasevac and his men crept into the back of a house that the Germans were about to use as an assembly point. As groups of Germans showed up, the Forcemen took them prisoners and sent them back to Regiment headquarters. When daylight arrived, the Forcemen felt that their time was being used too productively to follow their usual practice of melting back to their own lines before daylight. So they stayed at the job of capturing the enemy.

By eight o'clock that morning they had captured 108 Germans and there didn't seem to be any more coming in. Satisfied, Krasevac's patrol started home. Just then, however, three more Germans walked into the area. Startled by the sight, they turned and ran toward their own lines. Krasevac, wanting a perfect record for this adventure, told two of his men to follow him and promptly sped after the retreating enemy. He chased them for almost a mile before nailing them. Although the run had been at top speed, he couldn't help noticing several desirable items of booty lying by the road as he raced by.

When Krasevac and his two men returned, their three prisoners, instead of uselessly holding their hands high, had been pressed into service. One bore a bed and mattress on his back, the second carried a large crate of chickens, and the third was pushing a baby carriage full of potatoes.

The 111 prisoners furnished a generous sampling of the enemy. Finn Roll found little difficulty in drawing from them a complete picture of past and proposed enemy operations in the sector. One of the German prisoners, a company commander named Lieutenant Holbein, confirmed Frederick's wisdom in naming his group a "Brigade" rather than a more accurate military description.

"We have had great trouble finding definite information," confessed the German lieutenant, "about the First Special Service Force. The best view in the Hermann Goering Division is that you are a division, by the frontage you hold."

Since an army division can normally number as many as 16,000 men, and the Hermann Goering Division was composed of seasoned professionals not given to unrealistic over-evaluations of enemy strength, the remarks by Lieutenant Holbein stand as a comment of the Force's impact in combat.

Yet another prisoner had on his person a directive from higher German headquarters which read:

You are fighting an elite Canadian-American Force. They are treacherous, unmerciful and clever. You cannot afford to re-

lax. The first soldier or group of soldiers capturing one of these men will be given a ten-day furlough.

Although the number of Forcemen actually captured by the enemy has never been officially established, all authorities agree that the number was less than thirty. Since approximately 4,000 men, at one time or another, wore the insignia of the Force, this number easily represents the lowest capture rate in the American army. The Forcemen never surrendered. No prisoners were taken in the mountain fighting, and it was only the last massive assault by the Germans against Anzio and the final breakout which resulted in a handful of Forcemen being isolated and captured.

One of these, a man named Minto of the 2nd Regiment, remembers the circumstances under which he fell into German hands:

"I was wounded and the Germans interrogated me for about seventeen hours without stop. I never met any other Forcemen until I got to Germany in Stalag Ulla. The German officers didn't like the Forcemen with baggy pants and dirty faces.

"It happened while I was on patrol. We had just finished blowing up a railroad bridge on Highway Six and were on our way back when I got hit. When I came to I was on a German stretcher. They carried me for at least two miles and then made me get off and walk. They were very rough and kept yelling and pushing me. They seemed to take a dislike to me for some reason. One NCO who was in charge wanted to know how many of us there were. But who was I to say?

"They also cut the soles out of my jump boots, and that is how I walked the thirty-five miles. There were about one hundred other prisoners [from other Allied units] with me on the march, but only about fifty-seven reached Rome. *The rest were shot or run over by vehicles or tanks* [authors' italics]."

Lieutenant Taylor Radcliffe was netted by the Germans one March night while on patrol, but his stay as a prisoner was so brief that he barely qualifies as a "captured" statistic. Overpowered by five Germans, he was bound, gagged and taken to the headquarters of the 7th Luftwaffe Battalion for inter-rogation by a member of the Hermann Goering Division named Ulrich.

Captain Ulrich began with the attempt to establish a friendly relationship. After untying Radcliffe he offered to shake hands and asked whether or not the Americans had received fair treatment. He told Radcliffe that he had lived for seven years in Philadelphia where, as a stockbroker, he had never made less than $30,000 a year. This, he obviously felt, indicated a community of interest between him and the American because he then again offered to shake hands. Radcliffe made no response to these overtures until a query was made concerning the disposition of the British troops in the area. Radcliffe's answer, which contained a graphic suggestion, so displeased the German that he smashed Radcliffe across the throat with a piece of rubber hose. Radcliffe was spared further punishment by the sudden beginning of an artillery barrage which bracketed the headquarters in a close enough pattern to send the Germans to their foxholes in an adjoining yard. They left one man behind as a guard.

When the guard went to the window to gauge the effects of the bombardment, Radcliffe picked up a board from the floor and knocked him cold. Stopping only long enough to free two other Allied prisoners in an adjoining room, Radcliffe ran out of the house and up the road. The three men hid themselves in a large tree, where they spent the rest of the night and all of the next day.

The following night they resumed their flight but, unfortunately, ran into a German patrol. The Germans cut loose at the escapees with their machine pistols. Radcliffe was hit in the foot. Rather than hamper the other two men he sent them on and dragged himself into an empty farmhouse where he was later found by the patrol of Forcemen sent to search for him.

Evidently the blow from the rubber hose had paralyzed a nerve in his throat. It was another week before Taylor Radcliffe could speak above a whisper. But this, of course, didn't keep him off other patrols.

From the diary of A. W. Ovenden:

Feb. 8.

Jerry is one-half mile away and we've been shelled quite a bit. Three nights ago were attacked by jerries at a point where the bridge was. Six of our men turned back 120 Heinies, and Bruce again was a standout, he pulled a machine gun from under our two men—one who was killed and one badly wounded—and turned it on the bastards and they turned tail and ran like hell—they'd come to blow up the bridge.

I was in a position fifty yards down the bank and resolved to sell my life dearly, only one man was with me—all I could hear was Heinies yelling, and Bruce had already yelled to me that our machine gun was wiped out and I couldn't leave in case they sneaked over my part of the bank. My feelings were that I'd stay in my spot till they finished me off—never thought I'd have such thoughts and figured maybe I might fail at such a moment, glad to know I won't—pride for our Force I guess—we don't retreat unless ordered.

From the notes of Percy Crichlow:

There was the scrounging of the men for food and one fellow even had a cage of chickens near by. We occupied ourselves with digging a posh dugout with stove (ration cans filled with earth and moistened with petrol from some unwary jeep) and improvising the comforts of home. By night we went out to do some job or other. One night we had to go to help Captain Underhill's lot bring back their dead and wounded from a raid on Sessuno across the Mussolini Canal.

Then the big raid when I got shot with a machine gun in the back of my leg as I attempted to walk up the road. We didn't achieve much, but I think Jerry had a busy time. They were all running around with tanks and trucks and flak wagons until they frightened the daylight out of me and I was quite glad to go home. I went to Anzio hospital and they cut a little piece out of the back of my leg and expected me to stick around, but Jerry kept bombing to try to hit the dump on one side or the airfield on the other (what a place for a hospital!). Finally a piece of something came through the tent when the ack-ack guns were popping off, so I decided it was much safer up on the line and told the doctor I was going to catch a ride back up on an ambulance. Actually I had to go back with a ration truck at night.

Before the breakout I was commissioned, but remained with my company.

House-blowing actions were a characteristic patrol function. Sergeant A. K. Morgan, reconnaissance sergeant, described a typical sortie:

"Reaching a point about seventy-five yards from some houses that were our targets, Sergeant Lee and his crew found German wire and, starting through it, were caught in a hot crossfire from about six machine guns. Then a Schmeisser [machine pistol] cut loose from the house itself. Something had to be done. The remedy, as per usual, was the old house-clearing bazooka. A few rockets through the windows and several more fired generally toward the machine guns to divert them quieted the situation enough for a fast break through the wire and into the house. There was a brief altercation with a German standing in the door.

"With an 88 still hammering away occasionally, and machine-gun rounds spitting off the walls, the crew went to work laying charges. It was too dark to see what was going on, so Morelli lit an old dago oil lamp, the boys had a cigarette apiece off the flame, and shortly the charges were in and fuses lit. Then they got out fast, started through the wire, and were met by a bright flash from House 10 next door. Shortly it was raining large lumps of masonry. That confused the Germans who stopped firing. Then House 11 exploded and the Germans were really confused. Major Jack Sector, Regimental Executive, armed with a swagger stick, was along for the fun.

"Captain Hubbard's company in the meantime had been shooting over on the left opposite Borgo Piave drawing fire off the operation at the houses. During that fight they had several casualties. So there we all were that night—taking on a fortified position with Force teamwork against the usual heavy odds."

(*Top*) Force patrol coming in, Anzio. *Official U.S. Army photo*
(*Center*) The Force needed a few things at Anzio. *Frederick*
(*Bottom*) One Forceman, and five fresh German prisoners, and the
night's booty. *Frederick*

(*Above*) Frederick, in Heilman's underground H.Q. at Gusville.
Frederick (*Below*) Four legends: L. to R., Heilman, Walk-
meister, Akehurst and McFadden, in the Gusville saloon, Anzio.
Frederick

(*Above*) One of the Force's bona fide farmers at Anzio. *Frederick*
(*Below*) Brigadier General Frederick and Captain G. N. McCall lead
the Force breakout toward Rome. *Official U.S. Army photo*

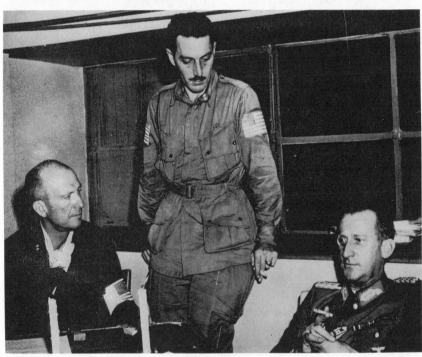

(*Above*) Mark Clark decorates Frederick, after Rome has fallen. *Official U.S. Army photo* (*Below*) General Patch, General Frederick and an unidentified German general captured in southern France. *Official U.S. Army photo*

The Force says goodby to General Frederick after Rome.   *Frederick*

Before starting on the subject of this period, I want to
to take advantage of this first opportunity/to give you a little
[above "opportunity/to": I have had]
insight into the "volunteer" matter which General O'Daniel
mentioned in his talk to you several weeks ago. You will
remember that General O'Daniel remarked somewhat caustically
that my unit was made up of volunteers that he needed in his
division for non-commissioned officers.

So that ~~Someone~~ you will better understand~~ing~~ the "volunteer"
system, I am going to read two messages I received when I
was ~~organi~~ forming the unit. From one post I received a telegram
that said: "All volunteers for your command have departed
this date. Direct the officer in charge and armed guards
to return to this station as soon as practicable."

From another post I received this message: "All personnel
transferred to your command are en route except 42 men AWOL,
26 men sick not in line of duty and requiring further
treatment, and 14 men in confinement awaiting final action
on remission of sentences. These ~~volunteers for your command~~ [above: volunteers for your command]
will be transferred ~~to your command~~ as soon as available."

I never quite got the whole story because almost all the
messages were received in code, and as we had no deciphering
equipment we could not read them. My adjutant had a large
desk drawer full of coded messages by the time we received
the codes and deciphering devices; but by that time I had
too many other problems to worry about old messages.

*And that is just about the way the
"volunteer" system worked.*

Facsimile of a memorandum by General Frederick, commenting on
Force recruitment.   *Frederick*

Don McKinnon: "After many of these patrols we would, on getting back to the canal, walk right in and wash the mud off our clothes and weapons.

"The most enjoyable patrols were the demolition patrols when we went out to blow up a house or some other structure used for outpost or observation. We always got a kick out of driving the jerries upstairs and then blowing the building out from beneath them."

Conrad Legault: "Due to the flatness of the country our number-one problem was concealment. As the land was too flat to permit daytime patrolling, we slept during the day and patrolled at night.

"We became masters at launching sharp raids and assaults from unlikely approaches at unlikely times and in unlikely weather conditions. Constant offensive attitude on our part proved successful. All our plans were prepared with two main purposes in mind: inflict casualties and capture prisoners.

"Our hold on this small piece of Italian soil was so weak that the Force was constantly kept in a state of alert. In the event of a German breakthrough, our plans of withdrawal were to sail down the Mussolini Canal into the Tyrrhenian Sea in whatever improvised rafts or floats we could find and with whatever equipment we could save.

"After four or five weeks of patrolling close to enemy positions our men became very proud of their skill at night attacks. We relied chiefly on the use of surprise and our successes were often due to the physical fitness and the rugged determination of the men. They became so accustomed to this type of warfare that much of the detail was left to the discretion of platoon commanders and section leaders."

"One staff sergeant, D. J. McLachlan from Vancouver, adopted an attitude typical of the force," recalled John Bourne. "His platoon commander, Lieut. D. W. Cuddy, was killed the night we moved into our lines when we arrived at Anzio. Later on he took over a rather dangerous defensive position on the enemy side of the Mussolini Canal. I visited him the first morning he was there and took the usual precautions to keep myself from coming under observation. To my surprise, Sergeant McLachlan was striding around on the road near the farmhouse that was his platoon headquarters as if there were no enemy for miles around. I questioned the wisdom of this and was told very politely that he considered the road to be his and wanted the Germans to know it. Unfortunately, a few weeks later he was killed on a patrol way out beyond our lines."

There were some lighter aspects to this constant round of patrols. Once an American B-24 crashed behind the German lines and it became a race between the Forcemen and the Germans as to who would get there first. Staff Sergeant Sol Biblowitz, along with Huffstutter, Farr, and Lloyd from his section, reached the scene of the crash and began searching for the survivors who had been seen parachuting to safety. Their search led them to a farmhouse where, in an adjoining haystack, they spotted the tail of a white parachute dangling over the sides.

"Hey," the sergeant called.

No answer.

"Hey, you!"

No answer.

Finally Biblowitz yelled, "Hey, Yank, get the hell out of there before we drag you out!"

A straw-festooned head poked its way out of the stack. Surveying these strange characters in baggy pants, parkas, and carrying a strange weapon (the Johnson light machine gun), the pilot finally said, "Kee-rist . . . are you guys Americans?"

On another occasion, Colonel Moore and his men were cut off and surrounded by the enemy. One German called on him to surrender. Moore was incredulous at this cheek. "Hell, no," he yelled proudly, "I got a battalion!" Moore's men then shot their way out of the trap.

General Frederick had an unpleasant chore to perform during this period. He had grown attached to the big, blond Norwegian Finn Roll, and "I received word to inform Roll that his father had just been murdered in Oslo by the Germans. From then on, any time we captured any Germans at Anzio, Roll would take them up to the second floor of the building across the street from our headquarters and throw them over the railing. After he had done that once or twice or three times, they'd talk. He'd ask them whether they were in Norway at any time. He'd keep throwing them over until they'd finally talk to him. He spoke German very well."

A 1st Regiment man recalls: "I remember about six of us making a raid on a farmhouse one day. We saw a white flag, so we stopped shooting. The krauts came out with their hands up. The first thing I knew, I was standing there by myself. The rest of my gang had gone in the house for souvenirs."

An Italian woman and her child, driven by the Germans from her home, had hidden along the banks of the canal. When she felt she was unobserved, the woman attempted to cross the stream into the American lines. But, on the bank, she stepped on a hidden mine. Both her legs were torn off. Forcemen Walsh and Ryan administered first-aid to her and then took turns carrying the mother and child to a field hospital. When they arrived, a medic told them, "We got enough to do trying to take care of the soldiers. We got no room for civilians. You had no business bringing them here."

Ryan replied, "Men can be left to die, but not a woman."

Bill Story, who was not an admirer of Colonel Edwin A. Walker, because he felt that his commanding officer was too prone to treat the members of his regiment as children, stated that Walker, under strain, spoke in the same high-pitched and garbled manner that years later he used before a Senate Investigating Committee.

Story remembers Walker as "a dirty unshaven man in a G.I. raincoat and a pulled-down knit cap who looked like a tramp and was an altogether miserable character."

Later at Anzio, Story contracted jaundice. He went to headquarters to report his malady. Walker began to tremble and ordered him out, screaming: "Don't you know it's contagious?" Of course, Walker's bad nerves may have been due to the constant shelling. Day or night, it never stopped. There is much other testimony to his personal courage.

Bernhard Alvestad later received the Silver Star for gallantry in action in France. He made 82 patrols at Anzio in 90 days, which certainly was a record even for the beachhead, and had this to say: "Our training in the States for night patrols helped us very much and there was always good control among the men. The German soldiers, as a group, were very poor at fighting in the dark and became confused very easily. They were also handicapped by their equipment, which was very noisy."

General Frederick predictably played a prominent part in these night patrols. Although it may seem incongruous that a general would go on routine patrols behind enemy lines alone or with a handful of men, this was his usual practice.

Colonel Wickham observed, "Frederick went on many actions at Anzio . . . often just to check the conduct of the night patrols. He had a sense of where and when he was needed. The men became aware that they would always find him in a critical area. He was quite dapper, and always wore an overseas cap instead of a helmet."

Sergeant Jim Kurtzhal remembers on one occasion he was slated for a patrol with Frederick. Before starting out, he said, "Wait a minute, General. I want to get a better weapon."

Frederick answered, "Ah, the hell with that. You've got a .38 and I've got a .45. Let's go!"

The Forcemen bragged to almost every man from almost every other outfit they met about the prowess of their leader. One frequently repeated story that is recalled by Ralph Randall deals with the time that a patrol of Forcemen was caught in a minefield. The Germans, waiting on the other side, opened up a terrific barrage as soon as the patrol was in midfield. The losses were high. One of the litter bearers carrying a stretcher was hit. The remaining bearer turned to the nearest soldier and said, "For Christ's sake, don't stand there. Grab the other end of this litter!" The other soldier promptly obeyed. After the litter team had taken the wounded man out of the minefield, the first bearer discovered the identity of the soldier he had pressed into service. It was, of course, General Frederick, who had seen nothing extraordinary in helping where he was needed.

The men would do anything for Frederick . . . follow him anywhere . . . and no job was too tough if it succeeded in earning his approval. Once, while in bivouac at Anzio,

Frederick wanted some heat in his hut. Several Forcemen scouted up a charcoal drum which served the purpose admirably. Unfortunately, no one thought to vent it to the outside and, when Frederick went to bed that night with his door shut, the fumes pushed him into unconsciousness. However, just before he passed out, he called the medic, Major Arthur C. Neeseman. By the time the latter arrived, Frederick was sprawled out on the bed, almost asphyxiated. Neeseman got Frederick to a hospital where the General stayed exactly one night before he picked up enough strength to tell the doctors that he couldn't spare any more time at the rear and went back to rejoin his unit.

Any organization which remains self-contained and under pressure for any length of time inevitably begins to assume certain easily recognizable traits which are a synthesis of the traits of a majority of its members. Obviously, the personality profile of the First Special Service Force would show it to be recklessly brave, quite often cruel, and, above all, eminently dependable in battle. There was also another trait which distinguished it from other Allied troops. As one correspondent put it, "That outfit is crazier than hell." The Forcemen might not have been crazy, but many of the things they did on or near the battlefield certainly constitute some of the oddest combat stories ever recorded.

Sergeant J. A. Izatt: "I'll never forget the night we made a company raid on one of the towns at Anzio. Dave Woon and myself took a prisoner and Dave searched this prisoner and came upon the picture of a pretty woman. When Dave threw the picture on the ground the German, who was a fair-sized boy, became quite violent and offered to take Dave on in a boxing match. So there and then Dave put down his Thompson and they proceeded to have one hell of a good scrap while I leaned against the building and looked on.

"At this time we were about two miles inside Jerry lines and the battle for the town was in full progress. Dave had just finished punching the Jerry out when a little guy by the name of Dutchysen came skidding around the corner and asked Dave and I if we had seen a couple of chickens that he was chasing, hoping for a chicken dinner I suppose.

"This was the same night that Buck Shearer came sneaking around the corner of a building and came upon one of his own men. They were both surprised and didn't recognize each other. Buck was a little slow and the other boy got off the first shot and creased Buck's skull knocking him on his back. Buck sat up slowly, looked at the other fellow and said, 'Now you've shot me, you b—— you can carry me back to the lines.'"

Sergeant Jamison: "When we were relieved by the British for the breakout we were reluctant to leave behind our horse and surrey so we decided to use this transportation for equipment. I can still recall the amazed look on the British officer's face when my section passed him with all our gear aboard and also a keg of wine and the usual black beard and outlandish clothes. He was still staring when we were some way down the road.

"One day we were inspected by a general and he came to my position—which was a dugout for five and right in the middle of an open field—and he said, 'Do you mean to say that you live in this?' I said, 'Sure the Heinies know we are crazy, but they don't think that we are this crazy and leave us alone,' and he just shook his head and walked away."

Sergeant Knox: "On one occasion, a company was caught in a minefield where the Germans had removed the safe-passage tapes. Most of the Forcemen were gotten out by some tanks that had been sent up, but, nevertheless, several of the men were severely injured by the antipersonnel mines which saturated the area. One of the tanks rumbled up to the surgeon, Evashwick. A boy was sitting on the tank with one leg up . . . the other having been blown off. The Forceman called to Evashwick, 'Hey, doc, got an extra foot around this place?'"

On other and less grim occasions, the Force would take all sorts of risks in order to secure fresh eggs and other farm supplies. Lieutenant Tom Zabski notes, "It was not unusual to see a soldier in a trench made large enough for himself and a cow."

Farming became a craze which swept the Force, even affecting those who originally came from the big cities. One officer complained, "I can't do a thing with those sons of bitches. They patrol all night and they farm all day."

One of the national magazines met widespread skepticism with a story about bearded doughfoots who were tending livestock and milking cows in no man's land. The story also featured the activities of one patrol that returned from behind German lines bringing back not only a brace of captured German soldiers, but also a sewing machine and a cow. The story might never have appeared in print but, by this time, well-known correspondents were making the Force's sector a standard visiting point every time they needed a colorful touch to liven up the day's dispatches. Among them, cartoonist Bill Mauldin, some of whose drawings of the Force appear in this book, found the doings of the Forcemen an unusually fertile source of ideas.

Sergeant Jim Kurtzhal, when asked to describe a patrol, skipped all the heroics and only stated, "Morgan, Lee and myself were out on a daylight patrol. We had already scrounged all the chickens and eggs we could find. The eggs we put in our shirts. We started to walk across a waddy when a machine gun began firing. As I got up, I told Lee and Morgan that that was it for me . . . I had gotten hit, and they should go on. They started to laugh. I put my hands in my shirt and pulled out eggs instead of blood."

Sergeant J. Gartner remembers coming off patrol one morning. "I'm sure if a German could have seen us he would have died laughing. Everyone was carrying something, a bag full of chickens, some eggs, one fellow even had a small pig in a bag. We had set up housekeeping on a farm, had a cow for our milk—plenty of fresh meat we had butchered. Sometimes you wouldn't think there was a war on."

The front line in the Force's sector at Anzio was dotted by farms, foxholes lined with rugs that the men had scrounged, cows, chickens . . . and portable stills. It even had a prophylactic station. Some of the men had found Italian families in farmhouses behind the German lines—families which contained either young mothers or older daughters.

When the Forcemen of the 3rd Regiment came back with stolen wine they found that their commanding officer was a paragon of fairness. Colonel Walker told them, "Certainly you can keep it . . . but let's divide it evenly. Half for you guys and half for me."

Sometimes the humor of the men became quite primitive. The Brigade barber, Thomas Garcia, used to make his rounds on bicycle, carrying his tools to the front. After one visit to Gusville, however, he gave up front-line operations. The men of Gusville, when Garcia asked the way to the next Force emplacement, gravely pointed toward Strada Litoranea which was still held by Germans. Garcia was halfway through no man's land before he realized his potential capture represented a Forceman's idea of a joke.

Lieutenant Stuart became aware of another chapter in the Walkmeister saga when: "Along in March our sector had a tank attack and Colonel Frederick sent for me to organize an anti-tank platoon. Seeking a place to give my gunners some target practice, I chanced upon the ambulance parked close to a small cottage in what appeared to be an enclosure of a large country estate. A large stone house loomed on top of the hill above the cottage and faced the sea, the whole enclosed by a high fence with Keep Out signs in English and Italian.

"As I watched, a figure, unmistakably that of Sergeant Walkmeister, came out of the house and approached the ambulance. I called him over and made inquiries. The big house was the country residence of 'The Staff,' whoever they might have been, and commandeered from a rich Italian. The small house was a gardener's cottage, and in it he had the girls quartered, ready, for a small fee, for parties, festivals, or anything needed to take the minds of the Big Brass off their duties for a few hours. It was connected to the villa by a tunnel, which, Jake told me, opened secretly into the wine cellar, although he was the only one who knew the combination, excluding the original owners. Jake also pointed out a short cut by which he could be back in his medical detachment within five minutes after receiving a call on his private telephone. 'That's quicker than The Brass can get to Anzio,' he said. The take was currently about five hundred a week, he concluded, but if the skipper of the liberty ship brought those four girls from Naples, as he had promised, he could double it."

When the warm spring days came to Anzio, some of the platoons and companies began devoting more time than ever to animal husbandry. Domesticated Brahma steers were hitched to plows and some units even had their own string of mules. Others had horses acquired from nearby farms, but these were used mostly for riding.

One night, Colonel Walker sent an urgent message to Lieutenant Zabski that he wanted to see him at once. Zabski saddled his own private horse and set off for headquarters at a gallop, skidding to a halt only when he got to Walker's tent. Walker muttered to an aide, "Isn't that a hell of a silly way for a full-grown man to act?"

The men being the products of a system of free enterprise, commercial, agricultural and dairy projects were soon in full swing. Gusville, in the middle of no man's land, had acres of cabbage and potatoes in its backyards. The Service Battalion had its own chicken-cleaning plant. Intense arguments took place in the 3rd Regiment over the legal issue of whether, when one company relieved another on the front line, did it not also relieve the old company of egg rights in certain henhouses.

The 2nd Regiment had a good herd of dairy cattle, but was forced to put out guards at night because of rustlers working in jeeps.

Jake Walkmeister took time from his medical and other duties to act as midwife for four baby mules.

These activities were by no means confined to the enlisted men. The Force Surgeon, Major George Evashwick, delivered five babies in farmhouses behind lines and was satisfied with his pay of two eggs each until he learned that Father Essig, the Catholic chaplain, was getting a chicken as a fee for a christening.

Father Essig set up his services right on the edge of the canal. He prefaced each service with the announcement that if enemy planes came over, Mass would cease and he could be reached for personal consultation at the foxhole located at the rear of the altar.

Services were also held each Sunday in Gusville. However, their popularity proved their undoing because so many

Forcemen squirmed out to attend that the German artillery found it an irresistible target. Since most of these activities were carried on in full view of the German observation posts, the question asked by Sergeant Kirk of the Service Battalion is quite cogent, "I wonder if the Germans thought they were dealing with madmen? After the breakout I was really impressed on seeing, from the vantage point recently held by the Germans, what a marvelously clear view they must have had of the whole nutty proceedings. The flat Anzio plain was completely and beautifully visible to the holders of those heights!"

Of course, such a thriving community found it only fitting to have its own newspapers. A few of the social notes from the newspapers some Forcemen published at Anzio have been preserved:

> *From Second:* After reading home-town clippings, Sgt. Arky Cameron was heard to exclaim, "My God, I'm another Sergeant York!"
>
> *From Communication Corners:* Sgt. Nick George, fugitive from malaria, jaundice, Neapolitan Nights and oversea-ism returned to the fold yesterday. He is quartered with the goat, "Bock Beer."
>
> *From First:* Sgt. Jack W. Stallings of Cerreto Alto outpost blasting fame is taking over the Victory Garden section of Gusville Farm Projects, Inc., and plans to start spring plowing in the near future.
>
> *From Service:* Since the Christian twins bought that cow, they are having trouble finding room for her in their foxhole.

Because many of the men had a country background, a great premium was put on horses. Horse races were regular events (remember, this was in plain sight of the German guns), and some of the men made so much money acting as bookies that their wives became quite worried about the funds mailed home, fearing that their husbands would be caught engaging in larcenous activity.

There were several occasions, however, when the extra-curricular activities of the Force seriously embarrassed higher commands. One of them involved two German finance officers who were riding out to their troops in order to conduct pay-day. They made a wrong turn and landed in the Force's lines. Possessing thousands of Italian lira, they represented too fine a haul to the Force to be sent further back for normal prisoner of war interrogation.

The story of the capturing unit's new-found riches swept the beachhead, because the Forcemen immediately fell prey to all the vices of the *nouveaux riches*. When the high brass began to hear stories about Frederick's men lighting their cigars with 1,000 lira notes, they demanded the persons of the paymasters and/or the money. Despite repeated and strin-gently worded orders, they never got either one.

On another occasion, certain Forcemen learned that a nearby cave was actually a mammoth wine cellar. The fact that it was also the headquarters of Major General Lucian K. Truscott didn't give them a moment's pause. They infiltrated the headquarters area, disarmed the general's sentries, pene-trated the top-secret map room and made off with as many casks as they could carry. Colonel Wickham noted, "Truscott, in his embarrassment, made only an informal complaint to Frederick and forgot about the whole thing."

Every so often the Germans sent over a barrage of propa-ganda leaflets. Although they never converted any Forcemen to their point of view, their leaflets became prize souvenirs. One of them, violently anti-Semitic, dealt with the mythical activities of a war profiteer named Abe Levy. The girls in this series were so lusciously drawn that Forcemen actually got into fights over ownership.

From the notes of the Red Cross man, Getty Page: "Spring came to us while we were in this part of the beach-head. I had two large tents which I put together and rolled up the center and went into the town of Nettuno and got some chairs from a bombed-out hotel. I had the only large area in the place. It was used for many things, including a court-martial. The court always seemed to favor my GI Hang-out, as it was called, to hold their trials until one day I called Colonel Walker and said I didn't think it was a very good

195 *

reputation for the Red Cross—a soldier might write home: 'Dear Ma, Got 30 years at the Red Cross GI Hangout yesterday.'

"I didn't hang around during the courts-martial. I know that some men had been previously court-martialed for murder, rape and other offenses.

"I had many of the difficult chores to do. I remember one time having to find one fellow to tell him that both his mother and his baby had died. I found him in a stockade. He said, 'Now, Mr. Page, let's see what you can do about getting me my PX rations. I haven't gotten any smokes since I have been in here.'

"I said, 'Aren't you concerned about your mother and baby?'

" 'No. My mother was an old woman and I have never seen the baby. I want you to see if you can get my PX rations.'

"My GI Hangout had a volleyball court, and we played a lot of volleyball. The area was one of the few large areas where we played volleyball by Anzio rules. Anzio rules were to jump into the net and try to come down on the feet of the fellow on the other team. This went very much against my training. I had been a Phys. Ed. major and I tried to teach the right rules for playing volleyball, and it was difficult for those who were exponents of the Anzio rules.

"One day there was a horse race, and I am sure there were many large wagers on it. Our horse raced against some Italian that was in our area. The fellow rode the horse quite like a jockey and it was the faster horse of the two. The Italian was waving his arms and kicking his heels as we came along. As it neared the finish line just to make sure of victory for the Force's horse, the soldiers ran into the horse of the Italian. It was quite courageous, but I thought quite unsportsmanlike."

During its stay on Anzio, the Force received a steady infusion of replacements in order to keep up a combat strength of somewhere between 1,300 and 1,700 men. The famed Ranger battalions supplied some of these recruits. In earlier engagements, they had been sent into battles which had resulted in their almost total decimation. Since the survivors were exceptionally tough, Frederick felt that they represented prime potential for the Force. The Rangers, however, were not easily assimilated by the Force. They felt that they had proven themselves by heroism in too many battles to be now regarded as recruits.

One Ranger, a Scot named MacKin, said: "I had heard of the Force quite some time before I joined them. I was filled with amazement and curiosity about these North Americans. We of the Rangers considered ourselves a pretty rough group. But here was an outfit trained not only as amphibious troops like we were but also as paratroops, ski and mountain troops. It was quite a surprise when I learned I was being sent to serve with them. Although I didn't relish thinking of what probably lay ahead for us I was proud to be a part of this bunch who wore the red, white and blue piping, the jump boots and wings, the cross arrows, the baggy pants, the rucksacks and pack boards, the long knife, drove Weasels, fired Johnny guns and fought under two flags.

"Relatively few had the privilege of serving with the North Americans and I am glad I was there with them. I found them to be a hard-fighting, versatile, quick-thinking unit who could operate well under all conditions whether as a unit or as individuals. They had above average intelligence and high esprit de corps."

Sergeant Sabine: "We [the Rangers] were amazed by the apparent lack of organization in the Force."

Perhaps a comment by W. G. Sheldon comes close to defining one of the basic reasons for the Force's unbroken string of successes: "For those under my command as a platoon leader or company commander, there were close bonds bordering on love and a sense of responsibility for their lives. The main problem with the men was keeping them from getting killed. Their courage and aggressiveness verged on the edge of foolhardiness at times. Utter disregard for their own lives was common."

Among the replacements was Raymond Hufft, who later gained notoriety when, as the Adjutant General of Louisiana, he flew Governor Earl Long out of the State and to a mental hospital. While on the plane, Long fired General Hufft and replaced him with a National Guard private. Colonel Wickham, who had taken Colonel Adams's place as the Force Executive Officer, describes Hufft as, "Absolutely fearless in combat as well as an experienced soldier. He was a killer who, on being shot at one time in Nuremberg, insisted on going ahead and killing the sniper himself."

The Canadian Government, having made no provisions for replacements, saw their participation in the First Special Service Force being dissipated to an incidental minority. The Canadians took such pride in the Force's accomplishments that it finally became a matter of national interest to restore the balance in the North American unit. Once again recruiting teams toured Canadian military establishments in order to secure qualified volunteers for Frederick.

The contribution of Canada to the Force's great record is underscored by the fact that during approximately one month, there were Canadian casualties of 18 officers and 194 enlisted men.

Sholto Watt, in one of his dispatches, reflected this feeling when he said:

Fifth Army Beachhead, May 25.

Canadian replacements have arrived for the U.S.-Canada formation which have been 90 days in the Italian campaign. The men of the formation take a tremendous pride in their international composition. They never tire of pointing out to visitors that Americans serve under Canadian officers and vice versa, that you couldn't tell whether you were talking to Americans or Canadians in the Force, and indeed the Force gives the impression of having formed something new, a synthesis of North America, but of North America at its best.

The Canadian reinforcements themselves, many of whom I have met both at the Force's base and in the line, are very happy men. Some of them have already seen action with the Canadian Corps in Italy, but the majority, these coming from what is the best trained army in the world, are in the line facing the enemy for the first time. Some of them went out on patrol in no man's land on the night of their arrival. On the call for volunteers—such is the reputation of the Force—six times as many men applied as were wanted. They arrived at the base, hitchhiking or on bicycles, from many miles across Italy; they were not always truthful about their ages.

Now that the balance of Canadians and Americans has been restored, men of the Force are strengthened in their desire to keep it an outstanding example of North American collaboration.

It is not, perhaps, out of place finally for a friend of this Force to suggest that for so long as the postwar world retains the need for armed forces, the tradition of the Force should not be lost. Picked men from all over North America, knit together by discipline and pride, are not likely to be inferior to any opponents, and their obliteration of harmful national distinctions must be a standing object lesson to a world rent by prejudice.

IX

The Breakout,
The Road to Rome
. . . and Beyond

During the breakout from Anzio, I remember watching one of the men firing a machine gun as he advanced. He had just killed a German when he became aware of my scrutiny. He yelled over to me, "Back in Kansas City I used to get $500 each for doing that!"

—Brigadier General Kenneth G. Wickham,
G-1 of the First Special Service Force throughout its existence.

It was time to break out. The Force, pulled back to the rear for a twelve-day period of regrouping and rest, was matter-of-factly aware that it would be employed as the cutting edge of the slash through the enemy front line. Its commanding officers felt that being paired for the advance with the exceptionally able 3rd Division was a merited recognition of its abilities.

Final organizational changes now took place, not because there were any remaining weak sisters left, but because the high casualty rate had made them inevitable. United States and Canadian replacements brought the complement of men to its highest point, almost 2,000 combat troops, and all the regiments were again composed of six companies at full strength. Colonel Marshall still commanded the 1st Regiment, but Lieutenant Colonel Jack Akehurst, senior Canadian, was given command of the 2nd. The 3rd Regiment remained unchanged, with Colonel Walker at its head and the Canadian, Major Jack Sector, as his executive. Additionally, four 75-mm. cannons mounted on half-tracks and a number of tanks were attached to Frederick's command in preparation for the battle.

At 6 A.M. on May 23, the Allied artillery began the concentrated barrage which signaled the opening note of the push. The Force, now attached to the VI Corps under Truscott's command, began streaking toward the German lines. Their speed cost them a high casualty rate because, in a relatively short time, they were far ahead of other units on their flanks. They became, in effect, the thin and terribly exposed spearhead of the whole attack.

An account by Lieutenant William G. Sheldon: "At last it came—H-hour! Our artillery reached a great crescendo and then lifted and Sixth Company jumped off. In about 15 minutes, Jack Jennings, my company commander, gave me the green light and I started out with my men in file behind me.

"The first day's objective was to cut Highway 7 to Rome, and when we had cleared the woods, it was about a mile across open fields. We advanced again—the tanks giving us great support and several Jerries surrendering to them. I felt confident—ever so confident then. We had cracked Jerry's main line and on occasion it appeared that my own little platoon was the tip of the spearpoint. I had suffered no battle casualties. With the tanks, it seemed easy. We crossed the field without resistance, and at about 2 P.M. came to Highway 7—our objective. I sent two scouts ahead and they reported all clear.

Just then a Jerry motorcyclist came boiling down the road and one of Dave's bazooka men made a direct hit, leaving the corpse lying grotesquely by the roadside charred and burnt.

"We crossed the highway still without opposition, and 200 yards beyond came to a high railroad bank where our company set up a defensive line—our final day's objective. It all seemed too terribly easy. I couldn't believe it. Then it began to rain—a thunderstorm and we got soaked. We were sniped at from a small ridge on the right, and I sent a patrol up to get the sniper.

"Suddenly things began to happen. My men spotted a big German Tiger [Mark VI] tank approaching beyond the tracks, then another and another—seventeen in all. Fifth company on our right was pinned down by fire, and began to withdraw. We were then forced to withdraw just to the other side of Highway 7, where we began to dig in.

"Then the big German tanks worked in closer and began machine-gunning us. It was at once apparent that our fate would be the same as that of the Rangers at Cisterna weeks ago when a whole battalion was cut off and captured or killed. The basic weakness of our position was that our left flank was wide open and the division which was supposed to be there was still in the rear. Finally, the order came to withdraw, and it was a wise move. We moved across to the woods we had left —machine gun bullets whistling by on all sides—miraculously none of us were hit."

Note by Jack Akehurst: "I believe we did a pretty fair job of creating the impression that we were a much larger force than we were, and when the breakout took place we were the only ones outside the perimeter in the first 24 hours (I don't think we could have got back if we wanted to)."

Note by Don McKennon: "After the holdup and we started again it was just go-go-go until we made our objective, the hills which overlooked the beachhead. We could realize then why we never dared to show ourselves on the beachhead too long or too often. It was just like looking down an alley. From there it was across the mountains to Cortina. It was a hard, hot march. A few days later I was wounded, on the first of June, or close to that date. A week later I jumped the hospital and caught up with my company."

As stated earlier, only a handful of the Forcemen were ever captured by the enemy, and this occurred when a man was wounded so badly that he could not move or when, as in the sole case of the breakout at Anzio, elements of the Force were trapped through their own fierce initiative. By driving so far ahead so fast (the Force advanced three miles in the first breakout and its neighboring division gained only a half mile in the same period), the men were cut off and isolated.

One of the men captured during that period was Sergeant J. G. Jacobson. Here is his description of the event:

"Since crossing the highway there was no contact with the companies on either flank and we had made a bad mistake in moving so far after losing contact. The German troops were sniping and firing at us and soon our tanks had expended their ammo. Immediately from a wooded area on our left front there came the roar of two Tiger tanks that pulled up on the railroad grade and fired pointblank at the light tanks that were attempting to withdraw.

"Surrender was inevitable with 88's pointed directly at us. German troops came over the top and that was it for twenty-eight of us. Several wounded were left, some dying. Among those was Sergeant Hulbert, who was burning alive from a white phosphorus grenade when a bullet mercifully took his life. Another was a boy named Sanders whose abdomen was torn open from a mortar shell. What helpless anguish it is to see the agony of a friend dying this way!

"As the Germans were marching us to the rear, a strange thing happened. A Canuck named Horricks from Manville, Alberta, Canada, who apparently had been wounded, jumped up at pointblank range and while shouting, 'Kill the s.o.b.'s, every damn one of them!' actually got off a few rounds before he was shot and left for dead. I still don't know why the Germans didn't gun us all down.

"The morning after our capture we were marched toward Rome under the watchful eyes of our German guards. The H. Goering Division troops treated us very well. We hadn't gone far before we were able to see the terrible havoc American artillery was wreaking on anything of value militarily around the beachhead. Any little settlement with a crossroads or *any* crossroads was under fire. Some of the shells were making craters ten or twelve feet across, so just getting past was a problem."

The 1st Regiment was forced to pull back and wait until it received badly needed replacement of its ammunition stores and for the other units to catch up. That night they counted their losses. Thirty-nine had been killed and many times that number were wounded. But the German dead lay in a long series of piles between the canal and the Force's stopping place at Highway 7. Again, the Force had punished the enemy severely, dealing infinitely more damage than it received.

Once outside the perimeter, the Allied forces spent little time in counting casualties or consolidating gains. Under the impatient goading of General Truscott, the men raced across the fields like a pack of suddenly released hounds. Jim Kurtzhal remembers charging along with one of the foremost elements. "I thought I was way out front," he said, "when I saw a jeep coming down the road toward me behind fourteen German prisoners. In the jeep shepherding them along was General Frederick and his driver."

James Ryan, now a minister of the Christian Church in Hyndman, Pa., saw his friend Walsh hit by sniper fire. Ryan crawled over to him, but "I could see he was hurt too bad. I went ahead and took eight or ten prisoners and held the BAR on them. Walsh died. I got rid of my prisoners and then went on. That night I hid in a cellar, where I tripped over something going in. Next morning when I woke up I found I had been sleeping among eight dead Germans."

Early next morning, as the 7th Infantry took the town of Cisterna, the First Special Service Force stormed across Highway 7 to the base of the Lepini Mountains. Its goal was the town of Cori. But, the same morning, other Allied units succeeded in closing the pincers and thus, at 7:30 A.M. after four months and three days, Anzio ceased to be an isolated beachhead.

This was not the moment for mutual congratulations. Plans now centered upon the capture of Rome. Clark had determined that the prize would be secured by American army units, so Frederick and his men were directed to march through the mule trails of Rocca Massima and advance on the town of Artena, situated in the Alban Hills at the very gateway to Rome.

Clark's use of the Force for this mission was evidently the result of a need for speed, determination and an unstoppable thrust, and the Force was superbly designed to provide all three requisites. Therefore, the decision was made to send the Force bowling down the road to Rome.

By May 25, the Force had taken Mt. Arrestina. Two days later it took Rocca Massina. In the meantime, the 1st Armored and 3rd Divisions had punched a wide hole in the German line, and other elements of the Fifth Army were pouring through.

At the little town of Artena, a stop on Highway 6 heading into Rome, the Force paused briefly to regroup and re-equip.

The next objective between Rome and Artena on Highway 6 was the town of Valmontone. But the Force was to pay a heavy toll in men before they could move these few miles. The Germans had momentarily stopped running, in order to lash back at the Force's position with a heavy artillery barrage and a series of counterattacks. This offensive was backed by a line of heavy and medium tanks which the Germans had placed along the railroad just north of the town. The fire from their lethal 88's, zeroed in at the crossroad of Artena, caught, wounded and killed many of the men from the 1st and 3rd Regiments.

The enemy resistance to the attack from Artena was one of the heaviest that the Force ever faced. It was a fantastically concentrated mass of weapons of all kinds, aimed directly at them. Used to mobility, the Force now found itself confined in comparatively narrow straits, looking squarely into the face of a massive array of weapons. A dozen tanks with self-propelled 88's, a horde of high-velocity 22-mm. flakwagons, and houses full of sharpshooting snipers from the Hermann Goering Division confronted the Force as they made their uncovered advance against the German positions.

One of the authors, Col. George Walton, was a member of General Keyes' II Corps headquarters staff during this period. A friend of his, now Lieutenant General Harvey Fischer, had just received an order to return temporarily to the States. Walton asked him to call his wife, Helen, and to tell her that he was fine. Fischer agreed to do so.

That night, Colonel Porter, of the command's operational section, assigned Walton to temporary duty with the First Special Service Force to act as the forward Air Observer. Porter told Walton that if he could succeed in setting up an observation post in the Force's position on the cliff overlooking Highway 6, he would not only have lucrative targets, but he would be able also to aid the Force's advance to Valmontone.

Walton recalls, "I'll never forget that ride to Artena. I had planned to arrive well before daylight, but because of the deep ruts and bomb craters in the road, it was almost dawn by the time I got there. During the last mile, an 88 spotted us and opened up.

"The ancient palace, where Frederick had established a command post, and the town of Artena were the hottest spots I've ever seen. The Germans were withdrawing, but seemed determined to use up all their remaining ammunition. There was rarely more than just a few seconds between the explosion of the shells being thrown in.

"The palace was on a cliff overlooking the broad valley, so my observation post gave me a splendid view of the whole area below. There were several holes in the walls made by the German shells, but I was told that it was dangerous to observe through these openings for more than a few seconds at a time. Also, the Forcemen were chary of my using the radio to relay target information for fear that the German detecting devices would use the signals as a guide for additional barrages.

"I was with the Force at Artena for several days, and I had good opportunity to observe the caliber of the men. They were about as rough and tough a group of men as I have ever known. As I said, this road that I came up was zeroed in by the German 88's. Sometimes it was necessary for Forcemen to go back over it to contact other units in the area. I actually heard these men watching their buddies making the trip and casually betting each other on the traveler's prospects '—Bill's got to go back, how much you put up that he won't make it?'

"The men had enormous respect for their officers and the respect was returned. The wide gulf between them that exists in most military units was completely absent. This was one outfit where rank existed primarily to define combat duties.

"When I later returned to II Corps Headquarters I found a note waiting for me from Colonel Fischer. It said, 'George, I'm not about to call your wife. I'll be damned if I'll tell Helen you are okay, then find out she's already gotten a telegram from the War Department "regretting to advise." As soon as I hear you're back, I'll tell her you're all right, but not before. I'm sorry, but anyone who's spending any amount of time with that outfit doesn't have many prospects. Let me know.'"

And, of course, there was Roy Cuff. "That big bastard," as his friend Pat Harrison describes him, was in continuing evidence in the fight. Harrison relates a story told him by Cuff's machine gunner:

"They were out on a night patrol . . . and they heard these Jerries clumping up the trail. Cuffy, in the dark, deployed his patrol into ambush formation on either side of the trail. He kept the machine gunner with him, telling the kid, 'I'll tap you on the shoulder when I want you to fire.' The kid told me he started to sweat when the Jerries kept coming closer and Cuffy gave him no sign at all. The kid thought the first German was going to step on the end of his gun barrel before Cuffy did anything. Finally, Cuff leaned over real calm, as if they were on a firing range back in camp, and said, 'Okay lad, let 'em have it.' There were about fifteen Germans coming up the trail in single file and they went down like ten pins."

Cuff himself thought of another patrol incident: "In the valley below Artena, I had the unnerving experience of having my opposite number in the German Army stumble into me and apologize. I had been assigned the task of occupying a farm on a prominent knoll in enemy territory. When I reached it about 2 A.M., I found it unoccupied, except for some unknown individual who disappeared in the darkness on a mule.

I had just got my men into position, with Tommy gun at the ready, when around the corner of a shed a German officer, leading his platoon in column, bumped into me. As we wore woollen caps and any old clothing when on patrol, he possibly took me for an Italian, as he muttered an apology, or something that sounded like it. In an instant I saw behind him a long line of glistening helmets and wasted no time in getting my weapons and patrol into action with very successful results. Almost the entire enemy platoon was killed or wounded."

The Force lost many good men at Artena and in the valley beyond. One of them was Major Jack Sector, the executive officer of the 3rd Regiment. Today, when Edwin A. Walker seems wedded to the point of bigotry to every far right cause, it should be remembered that his second-in-command, Sector, was a Jew and that the relationship between the two men was so close that Walker risked his own life to rush out in the midst of a fearsome shelling in an attempt to drag his dying executive back to safety.

Sector was a Canadian who had been one of the earliest members of the Force and had, in fact, led many recruiting parties through Canadian camps for Frederick. He is invariably recalled with deep affection.

Pat Harrison: "Artena . . . that's where we lost one of our finest officers, Major 'Black Jack' Sector. In the first days of the beachhead, when things were real hot up on Fizzle Road, Major Sector would come strolling along all by himself, just carrying his swagger stick and laugh and joke and buck up the boys, when all the time he really knew how tough it was and what a rough spot they were in."

Jim Kurtzhal: "Major Sector's last words when he was hit at Artena by an 88 were, 'Here, take my watch, I won't be needing it.' Sector had always carried a swagger stick but no weapon. He would tell the men with him where to shoot."

Captain Bennett: "I was with Jake Sector the instant he was killed. He was outside a hole in the bank in front of Artena. We, Walker [Col. Edwin Walker] and I, were inside this hole. The shrapnel was as thick as rain and Walker went out, pulled Sector in and dressed his wound. I was too shaken to be of much use."

The Force was not destined to remain bottled up in the Artena area for any length of time. Frederick sent out continuous patrols, some of them the strength of a battalion, to engage and destroy the enemy wherever they were encountered, and finally, with the support of a heavy artillery bombardment, seized the railway and broke through.

On the morning of June 3, with the various assault groups brought together as "Task Force Howze" attached to him, Frederick now commanded a front which spanned the width of the entire II Corps. It was a thin fighting line to be the front of the advance on Rome. As before stated, it had not been intended that the Force would spearhead the entry. That honor had been, for political and military reasons, reserved for several other infantry organizations. This plan was abruptly changed when the Germans, despite Field Marshal Kesselring's repeated assurances that Rome would be undefended in order to give it the status of an Open City, began to show signs of girding themselves for a fight.

Mark Clark lost no time in speculation. He informed General Keyes that the latter's II Corps would go in prepared for anything. In turn, General Keyes directed that Frederick's Force lead the way.

The men, though excited by the prospect of going after one of the biggest prizes in the war, plainly showed the strain to the experienced eye of Captain Sheldon Sommers, a medical officer who replaced Major Evashwick, after the latter had been wounded by shrapnel at Artena: "Compared to the Rangers I thought the FSSF in the last four days into Rome looked more tired, worn down, lean and ragged than any infantry I had worked with. They moved under fire very well, like experienced infantry, and operated beautifully with tanks. The last day into Rome I did not have a 2nd Regiment casualty in spite of vigorous fire fights. On the other hand, there was a Canadian Indian in that action who was the drunkest combatant I ever saw. He was operating without a helmet and I could not find him one because nobody got hurt and sent back."

Colonel Frederick, as could be expected, remained far out in front of the advancing Force. He had elected to stay with Task Force Howze and spent the time ranging far ahead of even the pathfinding group. The Canadian regimental commander, Colonel Akehurst, took it upon himself to suggest to the Colonel, who had received a slight wound, "Please don't get in front of my regiment again."

The next time Frederick was hit, he told Akehurst, "Jack, I kept my word, I didn't get in front of *your* regiment. This one happened while I was in front of another outfit."

A noncom, Sergeant Johnson of the Service Battalion, showed that he understood Frederick's propensity to be where it was the toughest when he said, "General Frederick wouldn't want us to go any place unless he was close by."

Another enlisted man attempting to describe the same phenomenon, said, "General Frederick was not the kind of man most folks picture as an Army general. You couldn't tell where he was going to be. You might ask a buddy for a match or a cigarette in the dark, and it might be the General that gave it to you."

Lieutenant Crichlow's description of the ride was graphic. "After Colle Ferro we made the sudden move by trucks up the highway where the Germans broke at Valmontone. A few German planes bombed and strafed about nightfall and leaving the trucks we traveled all night toward Tor Sapienza. When we came near, there was some enemy activity. Moving along the back of the houses we found a German tank knocked out and its crew dead near it. This had been done by Italians, I believe, for there were no troops ahead of us.

"By dawn the Italians were welcoming us with coffee but doing a little stealing, including my whole pack. A few prisoners were picked up. It was understood that our Regiment would stop here, but in the early afternoon, we were called on to go with a tank force into Rome."

Incidentally, Taylor Radcliffe later reported a comment by the Force barber, Thomas Garcia, who, on seeing the Coliseum for the first time, said, "My God, they bombed that, too!"

Captain Sheldon Sommers: "We were held at Tor Sapienza until 1 P.M. The tank-infantry attack under artillery and small-arms fire from Tor Sapienza into Rome was one of the most beautifully co-ordinated daylight attacks I ever saw. Colonel Akehurst ran it perfectly. By the time we got to one Rome city limits sign, there was no opposition, and my part of one column got about four blocks short of the railroad station, when Colonel Akehurst drove up and withdrew us to Tor Sapienza for the night, at about five P.M. All I had from dawn on were German casualties and one unidentified Forceman asking what was a good cure for drinking gasoline."

By midnight of June 3, the Force had assembled just outside Rome. Frederick, who had established his command post in a farmhouse in the suburb of Finocchio, was disinclined to take another offensive step until a message he had received from General Clark a few hours before was clarified. The message had read:

> Fifth Army forces are rapidly approaching the city of Rome. The intentions of the enemy are not known; he may decide to fight within the city or he may withdraw to the North. It is my most urgent desire the Fifth Army troops protect both public and private property in the city of Rome. However, the deciding factor is the enemy's disposition and actions. If the Germans oppose our advance—battalion and all higher commanders are authorized to take private action without delay to defeat the opposing enemy . . .

Frederick was not left without direction for long. At 1:06 A.M. on June 4, he received a radio message from General Keyes tersely ordering him to fire the opening gun. The message read, "Secure bridges over the Tiber River above 68 Northing within the City of Rome."

At 6:30 A.M. on June 4, the first elements of the Force entered the city. Because there were many claims as to the units involved in the initial entry, Frederick and several of his men were directed to make official affidavits concerning the time of the event. Among the affidavits in the War Department files is the following:

Sworn Statement

Personally appeared before me, the undersigned authority for administering oaths of this nature, one Brigadier General

Robert T. Frederick, ASN O-17196, Hq., 1st Airborne Task Force, APO 758, U. S. Army, who being duly sworn, deposes and says:

"Early on 4 June 1944, the First Special Service Force was directed to enter the city of Rome and to secure bridges over the Tiber River. Elements of the First Special Service Force with attached elements of the 1st Armored Division proceeded toward Rome from the East, the assault force attacking along Highway 6.

"At 0620 hours, 4 June 1944, the head of the assault force column passed the city limits of Rome and entered the city. This column was preceded by reconnaissance personnel who worked into the city as far as the main railroad station before returning to report their observations. The assault column consisted of 1st Armored Division vehicles on which personnel of the First Special Service Force were riding, with personnel of the First Special Force on foot ahead and on the flanks of the motor column.

"When a portion of the assault column had entered the city, the enemy opened fire with anti-tank artillery which prevented further forward movement of the Armored Division vehicles until after the enemy defenses had been neutralized. However, troops of the First Special Service Force continued on into the city in a maneuver to outflank the enemy defenses. I can state the time of entering the city with certainty as I was in a radio vehicle near the head of the column and checked the time frequently during the advance. I definitely remember that it was 0620 hours on 4 June 1944, when the leading vehicles crossed the city limits."

This entry into the city was marked by a loss which saddened every Forceman. Alfred Cook ("Cooky") Marshall, at the head, as usual, of his 1st Regiment, was killed by the enemy.

Colonel Bob Burhans was a close friend of Marshall's. He describes him as ". . . a decent and honest man. After graduation from West Point, 'Cooky' had been dragooned into the Quartermaster Corps which he hated. He jumped at the opportunity of coming with the Force. His troops really loved him and his officers swore by him.

"Cooky had quite a sense of humor. As an illustration

. . . one time Baldwin received a large shipment of beer from the Fifth Army . . . enough to give each enlisted man two cans. 'Fussy' Baldwin, however, when he delivered the beer to Marshall cautioned him that the men should not have more than one can at a time. Cooky promptly issued each man his two cans, but spent the next few hours calling Baldwin up at 15-minute intervals to ask if his men might have another sip.

"He was killed by a 20-mm. shell from a kraut flakwagon as the Regiment was entering Rome. They found him laid out with another dead American on a couple of desks in a schoolhouse where he had been taken by Italians. Around the desks had been placed many bunches of flowers."

Bob Shafer: "On entering the outskirts of Rome we were delayed a little by a few tanks, but got rid of them and continued on. We pulled up by a highway and had four or five tanks with us. The Jerry had a few tanks and troops coming down the road below us. We just slaughtered them, knocked out two tanks and there were dead Jerries all over the road and field. Before this happened, Sergeant Helming and I went with Colonel Marshall to locate the 2nd Battalion. Helming and I were running and dropping behind cover as we found it, and Colonel Marshall was just walking straight down the field as though he was on Main Street.

"I told him once, 'Cripes, Colonel, you better be careful. There's snipers out there.' He just smiled and kept on.

"Finally we saw a tank with the 2nd Battalion, and the Colonel said for us to report back to our battalion.

"Anyway, about 15 minutes later he was dead. He just had too much guts or pride to keep down."

Bill Rachui: "We finally broke through late in the day and started a long march through the city. When we reached the more populated portion of the city, people lined the street on both sides of us. As we marched in double file, they would hand us everything imaginable to drink, but it didn't matter, it was a hot day and we would sweat it out as we walked along. At times the young ladies would join us and march a ways with us, but two or three times snipers opened fire on the column from buildings, and every civilian would disappear in a matter of seconds, doors would lock and we were left on the open streets, but, sending a party to roust out the snipers, would soon continue the march again. At dark 6th Company reached St. Peter's Square and from there we moved by platoon to our platoon objective, which each platoon had a bridge on the Tiber River to take and hold until relieved by another unit.

"Our platoon moved down the street toward our objective with a column on each side trying to stay in the shadows. We picked up two local policemen that promised to lead us, but after a while they disappeared. About this time we reached a large intersection, on one corner we could see three men, but could not identify them, so myself and two other members, including the platoon sergeant, decided to walk over to them.

"When we got near we saw that they were German soldiers; since it was too late to turn back, we walked right up to them, and I informed them in German who we were, that there were many more American soldiers coming down the street behind us, and for them to surrender, but about this time one started to ease his submachine pistol into firing position which I noted and yelled, 'Let them have it.' As we fired, in the direction of our firing was a park covered with hedges, German soldiers raised up from behind all of them from a rest and sleep. Dazed by the firing, they ran to the high ground on the other side of the park, hollering at us, asking if we were German or American. We answered, 'German,' and kept shooting.

"While the battle was on, two German half-tracks, pulling self-propelled guns, came by; we engaged them in battle, they threw out their wounded and continued on down the street."

Anthony Skripac: "The people were so glad to see us that they all gave us fresh bread and wine. Our platoon captured 5 Czech prisoners and as this was as far as we were to fight, we were to keep the prisoners with us and guard them. The wine was plentiful, so we gave the prisoners some too. We moved into some building to sleep. We were to guard the prisoners one hour each. The first man to start the guard fell asleep, so the next thing we knew it was morning and the prisoners woke us up."

Roy Cuff: "I remember our trying to slip through the streets of Rome with a patrol assigned to seize a bridge over the Tiber . . . being descended upon by hordes of happy Italians, who impeded our progress until fire from enemy parachutists, left to fight a delaying action, broke up the welcome. I remember proceeding carefully up a street carrying a Tommy gun, when one of our tanks with a large gun sticking out the front rumbled up behind me. The tank commander unbuttoned his hatch, stuck his head out and asked how far we were behind the leading troops. When I informed him that we *were* the leading troops in this area, he slammed down the hatch, did a quick turn around, and that was the last I saw of him. His disappearance made my Tommy gun seem awfully small."

Percy Crichlow: "We came under fire and the truck ahead of me had a wheel blown through the air. A machine gunner had a good try at eliminating me, but without success. Unfortunately, in the rush the base plate of the platoon mortar was mislaid, but the ammunition went to help another mortar crew. After a little fighting we moved forward. My platoon now took the lead as Captain Gordon, our company commander, had been shot in the body and seriously wounded, and Kaasch, who had the lead platoon, took over, calling on me to take the lead. We went along the houses, up a deserted main street where a couple of German tanks were burning. Some girls rushed out as I moved the platoon continuously up the street, they kissed us and stuck flowers in our belts and equipment, but when a shot went off they disappeared completely. I was told some Germans had escaped down a tunnel, but had no intention of following. We moved forward as far as the railway station and watched American troops coming into the city."

Sgt. Rafael P. Montone: "Gus Heilman lost his pants in Artena so he made Rome in his G.I. long johns. We raided a German O.P. and hit them for fifteen cases of cognac and three hams. We had a feast before rolling into Rome.

"I was with Frederick when we took Rome. We were the

first ones in, all the way to the Tiber River. It was here that Frederick got hit on the leg and I got me a Bronze Star . . ."

John Bourne: "The 2nd Regiment moved through the First as far as the Victor Emmanuel Monument. My battalion was ordered to proceed through the center of Rome down the 'Corso' to take six bridges across the Tiber. Orders were given to two companies to take these bridges—three each. The Third Company was kept in reserve with Battalion H.Q. which stayed on the main axis of advance.

"There was little or no resistance at the outset and it was indeed thrilling to receive such a tumultuous welcome from the Romans. The cheering and happiness were quite moving. Every now and then, the crowds on the street would suddenly disappear and some die-hard Germans in an armored car would turn a corner and start shooting. It was rather uncomfortable, as there was no cover to be taken, but skillful use of bazookas, grenades and machine-gun fire quickly disposed of the enemy—then the crowd would appear again.

"General Frederick showed extreme courage in advancing well ahead of his troops in a half-track, for the purpose of making a personal reconnaissance. By so doing, he was lightly wounded, but if I remember well his driver was killed."

War correspondent Eric Severeid, writing in *Not So Wild a Dream:* *

> Late in the afternoon of the day of liberation [Rome] I checked in at the luxurious Grand Hotel. The suave clerks receiving us with perfect composure, as if this were all in the day's business, though German officers had that very morning checked out; their names were still fresh on the register. The swank bars of the city were already doing business with its new customers, and one had to fight his way through the street girls on the corners. At midnight I wandered toward my hotel and in the moonlight came upon two American paratroopers from Frederick's outfit, who were sitting disconsolately on the curbing. They were lost, had no place to sleep, and were under orders to report to their outfit, somewhere outside the city, by six in the morning.
>
> I took them to my room and they stretched out on the floor.

* Eric Severeid, *Not So Wild a Dream* (N.Y.: Alfred A. Knopf, 1960).

We talked a while, and one of them, a brawny St. Louis man, who had been a milk driver, said: "You know, I been reading how the F.B.I. is organizing special squads to take care of us boys when we get home. I got an idea it will be needed all right. See this pistol? I killed a man this morning just to get it. Ran into a German officer in a hotel near the edge of town. He surrendered, but he wouldn't give me his pistol. You know, it kind of scares me. It's so easy to kill. It solves all your problems, and there's no question asked. I think I'm getting the habit."

Toward dawn I thought I heard the sound of running water and came full awake to discover that the bathroom faucets useless after the water supply went down, had started functioning in the night. The two paratroopers were sleeping soundly in an inch of icy water, and the beautiful flooring of inlaid hardwood tiles was ruined. Uncertain of the new conquerors, the management said nothing.

Frederick's orders had been to secure the bridges across the Tiber. That afternoon, even though his leg was bound up after being hit by a shell fragment, he, his driver, his aide (who was a handy machine gunner) Captain Newt McCall, and two enlisted men ranged up and down the banks of the Tiber River checking the bridges for demolition charges left by the Germans.

Later in the day at the Margherita Bridge, Frederick and his handful of men ran into a German battalion bent on holding the bridge open while their comrades retreated to the west. The Germans advanced toward Frederick, and he and his men opened fire. Several adventure magazines later presented highly colored accounts of this event, but Frederick's own description is far less heroic: "First," he recalls, "I hollered to them to halt. Frankly I couldn't think of another damn thing to say. When they didn't stop, we began shooting. We killed three of them and captured twelve while the rest were running away . . . evidently figuring us for a much larger group than we actually were. My driver was killed and I got hit in the leg and arm."

Frederick then went back to his own lines and secured a much larger group which he then took to the Littorio Bridge, north of the Margherita, in order to continue his inspection.

His medical officer, Major Arthur Neeseman, finally got Frederick to stop disregarding his wounds and to turn himself in to the hospital.

Frederick had been hit three times that day. Added to his six previous wounds, he could now lay undisputed claim to being the most-shot-at-and-hit general in American history and he was finally willing to concede his mortality.

Major Neeseman sent him to a hospital in the rear at Anzio. One night was enough. He got Neeseman on the phone early next morning and told him, "These goddamn German prisoners kept me awake all night with their moaning. I'd advise you to get me the hell out of here fast!"

Neeseman never questioned the sincerity of Frederick's advice. He was back at the hospital within an hour and, without the formality of checking Frederick out, had him flown in a Cub back to a hotel in Rome where the General impatiently passed a few days waiting to get his strength back.

The story has an epilogue. Just a few years ago, Frederick visited a civilian hospital in order to make arrangements for his mother. A surgeon there looked at him critically for a few minutes and then broke into a wide grin, saying, "You know, you're still AWOL and you owe the Government all the salary you've been drawing since the end of World War II!" The surgeon had been the commandant of the hospital which Frederick had left so abruptly.

By 11:00 P.M. on June 4, the Force had taken and secured the bridges assigned to them. The 85th Division had secured the other eight bridges to the south and Rome was firmly in the hands of General Mark Clark's Fifth Army. But the Force was not permitted to remain in Rome to participate in the orgy of celebrations which swept through the city. They were told to withdraw back to the suburb of Tor Sapienza and await further orders. The men slept that night as if they were drugged.

Next day, June 5, there were a few incidents which showed that the march and the fight had not extinguished the spark which characterized most of their activities. One officer found himself an Italian girl and solemnly assured her that he couldn't wait until he married her. He prevailed on another Forceman to act as the clergyman, and he and his girl and the pseudo-priest and a handful of other men immediately began to celebrate the impending nuptials. Everyone got drunk. The supposed priest insisted that he could not marry this couple until he was certain that the girl was clean. Thereupon, and with her consent, the men immersed her in a wine barrel and gave her a bath. The ceremony which followed was pronounced a ringing success by all concerned. The bridal couple signed a hastily produced "register," and some Canadian Forcemen who had gotten hold of some bagpipes escorted them to the bridal chamber.

Another Forceman awoke in the bed of a prostitute. Not remembering that the city had changed hands, she wished him a good morning in German. That day, every prophylactic station had a long line in front of it. Bill Story recalls, "In them was every rank from private to major general." That night, the men slept at Sapienza. They awoke on the morning of June 6 to the news of the invasion of France.

The men were almost completely spent. They moved around the bivouac at Tor Sapienza like so many zombies and the dull fog didn't lift until the announcement came that the organization would be sent to the shores of Lake Albano, where the Pope kept a summer residence. Regimental surgeons had reported that the men were listless, perilously close to exhaustion and infested with lice. The prescription indicated was relief from combat and some swimming in Albano's blue waters. And generous dustings with DDT.

Frederick took great pains to see that his men were furnished every possible accommodation at Albano, and passed the word around to his officers to look the other way whenever any but the most flagrant breaches of military discipline were being committed. As for the food, the richness of it proved a hardship at first. Tony Skomski recalls, "Our stomachs were so shrunken from emergency rations that when we rested at Lake Albano, our stomachs hurt from the big meals. We laid on the ground and groaned after the first meals. We also had a parade in honor of the dead we lost in Italy."

There was another factor which added to the general air of ease in the camp. Almost every man had his own personal vehicle. It is true, of course, that these were not officially issued to the Forcemen, but the transportation problem was solved by the men (and quite a few of the officers), who stole every unattended vehicle they could find.

This outbreak of modern rustling slowed down to a trickle after the Episode of the Major General. Bill Story, who had been in Rome on pass, came back that night to sign in in the book kept for that purpose in the headquarters tent. Story was mildly amazed to find a jeep parked in the middle of the tent. "I saw the jeep," he said, "and in it was a helmet. On both were stenciled two stars. One of the men had been to Rome and had returned in a general's jeep. That night the stars were taken off and the jeep repainted. The helmet was thrown in the lake. As a result of this story getting around next day, an inventory was taken, and it was found that the Force had almost twice as many jeeps as it was authorized."

Story also recalls the Forcemen's habit of tensing for a fight every time they were asked by other soldiers the identity of their unit. Their answer, "The First Special Service Force," immediately conjured up in the minds of the other soldiers a unit devoted to passing out doughnuts, magazines and baseball gear.

Sergeant Jordan: "We were often, mistakenly, identified as members of the Special Service group of entertainers sent over to entertain the troops. Upon being asked about the red, white and blue stripes on the braid of our service caps, our answer was that we were members of a barber detachment."

Another of the interesting features of the stay at Albano was the proximity of the Pope's summer residence. Some of the men stole everything that wasn't nailed down in or about the papal premises. Quite a few pieces of the Pope's summer furniture were used to add a decorator's touch to the bivouac area, and so many of the men's sleeping bags were lined with sheets adorned by a papal crest that a general "shakedown" inspection was ordered. All the pilfered items were returned, including a gold statue which one Canadian had reverently placed at the entrance to his tent.

The men not only stole furniture from the Pope, they

also stole the Pope's furniture from the General. Frederick and Wickham had been assigned a villa which they occupied while waiting for their wounds to heal. Through a letter of introduction from the Roman Catholic Bishop in Helena, they were able to borrow quite a few items legitimately from Castel Gandolfo. When the villa was returned to the Italian authorities it was discovered, with great embarrassment, that almost half of the items loaned by the Pope were missing. After a series of showdown inspections and a succession of dire threats, the missing items were found and returned to the Vatican authorities.

Wickham, who has enormous respect for Frederick, recalls those days at the Villa: "His leg was in a cast and so was my arm, so I did the walking and he did the writing. Frederick liked to talk and was hungry for company. Good talk, to Frederick, was as necessary as food and I learned more about the man in those few weeks than I had in the previous year. A rare man."

Now came one of the most traumatic events in the Force's brief history. On June 23, at a ceremony which everyone thought would be confined to the presentation of awards won in battle, Brigadier General Frederick announced that he was leaving for another command.

The reaction to this news was one of shock. The majority of the Forcemen looked upon Frederick as a father figure and the unexpected news left them stunned. Sergeant Kirk describes the scene: "I'll never forget the collective gasp that arose when General Frederick assembled us and announced that he was leaving us. A part of the Force died at that time, for I know of no one who did not respect and admire him. We all felt a physical loss at this news. To me, at least, this had a greater impact than the actual disbanding of the Force. We were losing a man whom we all loved."

Rough and tough Sergeant Montone said, "It was here that all Forcemen cried like babies, when we said good-bye to General Frederick."

In a recent conversation, Frederick's own description of his severance from the Force seemed typically understated.

"After all," he said, "I felt quite a bit of regret. I had formed the Force and had been with them ever since. I had taken such a liking to them that I felt badly, even though it meant a promotion which I hadn't expected.

"At the time, I had my leg tied to a board so I was getting around only with difficulty. I stood throughout the ceremonies while the decorations were awarded, and then, at the end, I told them I was leaving. I heard some of them say, 'Oh, no!'

"Some of the men wanted to know where I was going, so they could transfer under me. But I didn't tell them that I had been directed to raise and command the 1st Airborne Task Force for the Southern France invasion. They weren't supposed to know. I simply told them that I was leaving and that Colonel Walker would assume command."

This statement is a reflection of Frederick's dislike for emotional descriptions. Actually, according to some other participants in the ceremony, the scene was a dramatic one. More than a few men cried openly. There are some reports that Frederick's own eyes were not dry.

Perhaps a measure of the men's affection for Frederick is a description of the general reaction after the departure. It became known that Frederick's new assignment would carry with it a promotion to major general, and the men were glad that Frederick had been given his much deserved advancement. At the time, Frederick was thirty-seven years old. Within a few weeks he was to become the youngest major general in the Army Ground Forces.

One of the best descriptions and summations of Frederick as a combat leader was written after the war by veteran INS correspondent Clark Lee:

> It is difficult to write about Frederick's exploits without suggesting a wild-eyed composite of Sergeant York and General George (Blood and Guts) Patton. But the comparison is misleading. Frederick certainly saw as much combat as the average infantryman, and more than most, and, in common with Patton, he demanded the best effort from those in his command and believed that the way to win battles was by incessantly attacking, getting the enemy on the run and keeping him there.
>
> His military fame is founded on his own fighting record,

rather than any striking of attitudes, display of showy uniforms and flashy bodyguards, or employment of a highly-colored vocabulary. Even in action he is quietly alert, usually soft-spoken.

As could be expected, there were, and are, many conflicting opinions about Edwin A. Walker who now assumed command. There is a general agreement that he was an outstanding combat leader, but quite a few of his fellow officers found traits which they considered unattractive.

Gus Heilman, by this time a captain, thought that Walker, although a fine professional soldier, was disparaged by others because of a poor and inadequate speaking voice.

Another officer said that Walker was too excitable and "not at all composed like Frederick. What's more, he consistently gave out poor efficiency reports on almost all of his officers."

The same officer produced several examples that Walker's anti-Negro bias was strong, even then. One day a high Red Cross official, who happened to be colored, was visiting the Force and was spotted by Walker as he entered the officers' mess. Walker sent over an orderly to tell him that he would not be allowed to eat there . . . that he must eat in the public rooms.

Colonel Wickham disagrees with these harsh previous estimates of Walker. He says that "Walker was an able soldier. Frederick, although two years older, saw eye to eye with Walker. Walker was a pleasant and dedicated man and an excellent commander of troops. He was highly respected by his men. Even in combat, he always wore a tie which was sometimes cocked halfway around his neck."

And perhaps one of the most authoritative sources for comments concerning Edwin A. Walker must be his superior, General Robert Frederick.

Speaking in 1965 to a friend, Frederick observed, "He was an outstanding soldier. He wore himself to a thin shell doing the best job he could. His campaigns while leading the Force were excellent. After the war, I went to hear him lecture on several occasions. When he was out here to talk at Stanford University, my wife and I went over to hear him. He was lecturing on an anti-United Nations theme. After his talk, when questions were asked, his answers sometimes did not relate to the points raised. Two years before, when he was in San Francisco, I went to the Commonwealth Club to hear him. It was the same sort of a talk. But I think he retains a certain regard for me, even though he turned to the right after the war."

His preoccupation with right-wing causes later led Walker into a series of ignoble situations. After winning additional fame as a combat general in the Korean War, he was assigned as a senior commander in the U.S. Seventh Army in Europe. While there, it was alleged that he instituted a series of required lectures for all military personnel which reflected his ultraconservative views. When this news reached the American public, the reaction was so strong that Walker was relieved from command and recalled home. Walker resigned from the Army in order to initiate his career as a spokesman for the far right.

Upon returning to the states, Walker promptly became identified with many anti-integration disturbances. His actions were so violent that he was later forcibly examined by a battery of psychiatrists to evaluate his sanity.

Pat Davis, a former Forceman who writes with the pen of a highly sensitive poet, forwards this comment: "I remember most the mild-mannered, almost timid Colonel Walker at Lake Albano. I talked with him for quite a while in the doorway of an old house one night as the units were moving in along the shore of the lake and the moonlight came and went with fitful irregularity.

"And now he has been charged with insurrection against the United States and found 'not guilty' by the white supremacists. This is the real tragedy . . . the tragedy of General Walker. He was the victim, somewhat like the Italians, of his own political extremism. I cannot believe that his postwar conduct was the result of rational behavior. It is in the classic Greek tradition of tragedy . . . a fall from high estate to low degree."

On July 1, 1944, the Force departed from Lake Albano for a return voyage to Naples. Just before leaving, a highly complimentary letter was received from General Clark in which he described them as an "elite" group and told them that their activities while under his command had resulted "in a bright new link in our military tradition."

Two days later, the Force was in another bivouac at Santa Maria Castelabate, a fishing village located forty miles south of Salerno, where training for the next action began in earnest.

At first, it was considered that the Force would be landed farther north in Italy in order to cut off and further demoralize the retreating Germans, but after a series of changes in plans, the assignment was made to have them spearhead an invasion of Southern France. This move was designed to ease the pressure on Eisenhower's invasion troops, now painfully inching their way through the hedgerows of Normandy.

As a footnote for the record, General Clark bitterly protested the use of American troops for this invasion, which had been labeled OPERATION ANVIL. He felt that the job could have been handled easily by French troops and that his Fifth Army should be left intact in order to pursue and utterly smash the fleeing enemy.

As a matter of fact, this conclusion was later endorsed by the German commander, Albert Kesselring. In his book on the war, *A Soldier's Decision,** he states, at considerable length, his opinion that the Allies lost a priceless opportunity to thoroughly decimate his troops before their later withdrawal into Germany for the last stand.

The training for OPERATION ANVIL went on. John Bourne furnishes a concise description of its nature: "Besides the amphibious training, we brushed up on our assault work and generally got into first-class shape for what lay ahead."

But Forcemen remained Forcemen no matter what training was given them for what grim or misadvised goals. Sergeant Pope remembers this about the assault course: "That real pretty gal that rode in each evening on a motorcycle and out again the next morning . . . having spent a profitable night."

* Albert Kesselring, *A Soldier's Decision* (New York: William Morrow & Co. Inc. 1954).

X

The Champagne Campaign
and the End of the Trail

*There were two cemeteries . . . the Canadians of the Force
had been moved from the U. S. to the British. Both were beautifully kept, and there were many flashbacks as I read the names.
The living were separated at Villeneuve-Loubet and the dead at
Anzio, but the ties still bind us all. It was, as is, the Force.*
      —Colonel JACK AKEHURST, the Canadian
      regimental commander, after a 1959
      return to Anzio to visit the graves of the
      Forcemen who fell in Italian battles

The invasion of Southern France was probably one of
the war's worst kept secrets. The Italian civilians behind them
and the German soldiers in front of them speculated only on
the place and the time . . . two matters which General Sir
Henry Maitland and his American commander, General Alexander Patch had resolved in favor of the Riviera area in the
middle of August.

The Force was assigned the job of seizing two of the Hyères Islands, three small land masses between the French naval base of Toulon and the Riviera, which had been established as the left flank of the Allied landings.

Neither of these islands had beachfronts of any size. As a result, the Germans had skipped fortifying them in order to dig more deeply into the forts which Napoleon had built on the high grounds. Here the defending gun emplacements were surrounded by walls which were, in some places, twelve feet thick with concrete.

The Force left from Corsica and headed toward their target in a fleet of destroyers. By now the Force was so solidly professional that one more invasion failed to excite them to any degree. Aboard ship most of the boys gave little thought to the landing. Some played poker and some slept or read. One section fell asleep in the landing craft and had to be awakened just before they touched shore.

Mickey Flynn, 1st Regiment: "That night before the landing, we were below decks and the music was coming over the PA system. We were all jitterbugs in them days and the Little Chief (he was an Indian) and myself were dancing.

"Then my buddy, Tommy Irving, got to talking to one of the seamen, a Scotchman, and I'll be damned if he didn't know his cousin in Glasgow. So we wind up, just before going over the side into the boat, Scotty comes up with a jug of African rum."

The fights for the forts of Iles d'Hyères resembled nothing so much as an early Errol Flynn movie. It was the besiegement of a well dug-in enemy whose relatively small numbers were more than compensated for by the excellence of his fortifications.

The Force lost many good men at the gates of these forts. It wasn't until they got substantial assistance from the big guns of the Navy and from the Air Force bombers that they were able to batter their way through the doors.

Mickey Flynn tells about the assault on Fort Del Eminence: "We left that morning and started to circle around the fort. They were all forts of the medieval days. We were creeping and crawling and went right under a machine-gun position. They never fired on us. We bypassed the fort and came up behind it.

"We went into a graveyard and got locked up there by either mortar or rifle grenades. We lay behind the wall and not one of them came inside—my section leader, Jerry Rasconne, said, 'Let's go,' and away we went. He threw a phosphorus bomb and we charged. Thank God, the trenches were empty. Jerry says to me, 'Take out their guns, Mick.' I started to take them out—just myself and a guy from the 48th Highlanders of Canada, Norm Brown.

"All of a sudden they started to counterattack. We started running. Brownie falls on his face and I stopped, ran back and says, 'You okay, Brownie?' He says, 'Yea, Mick, I'm okay.' By this time the mortars are coming in pretty steady. Brownie and I run along the trench and start counting the shells coming in. We can hear them. We hear pup, pup, pup. We can hear them.

"So we wait for a couple to fall and I says to Brownie, 'Let's go.' So we run over the drawbridge and into a small room, a food closet. It was full of weiners and sauerkraut. When we get in there I meet Jerry Rasconne, Lacasse, Meathead, and a few more guys. All of a sudden we were cut off.

"Meathead is hurting and we need some morphine—who is going to go for it. Lacasse says, 'Flynn and I will go for it.' Well, being a member of my outfit I could not say no. So I says, 'Give me an extra couple of mags (I had a Tommy gun at this time) and I'll go.' Lacasse says he knows an easy way down. I says 'O.K.' We left to bring help, but never made it. Actually, he did not know where he was going. We started out and the machine guns opened up. I said to Lacasse, 'Where do we go now?' He says, 'I don't know.' I says, 'To hell with you! Don't take me on patrol again!'

"I went back. I met Sgt. Frank Welch, an American, both legs broken, hit in the back. I went to take Welch out and I got hit. He looked after me until we were taken out."

Major W. Winston Mair, a Canadian who had joined the Force while it was training at Santa Maria Castelabate, was the 1st Regiment assistant executive officer during this attack. His reactions to the Forcemen are interesting.

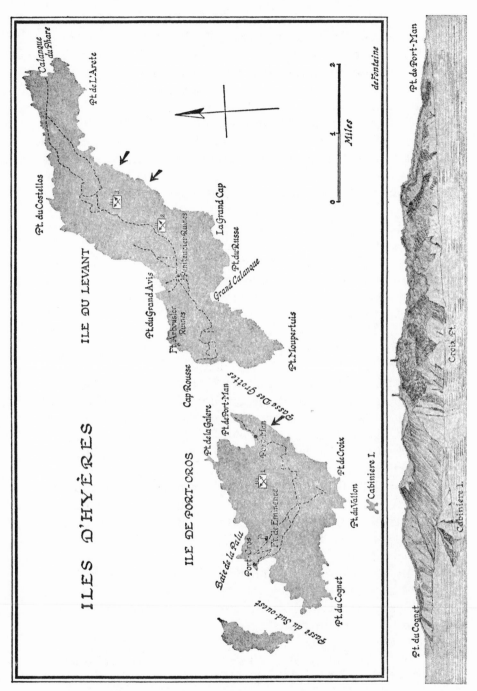

The Iles d'Hyères. The miles of German bunkers, gun emplacements and tunnels do not show, but the coast was studded with them.

"The men were too courageous," he says. "They had a mistaken concept that courage and physical fitness were all that was necessary. For example, a group of the Forcemen were surrounding a ravine in which there were a number of Germans. All they had to do was shoot down into the ravine and toss in a few hand grenades and sooner or later the krauts would have surrendered. Instead, after tossing in a few grenades, they rushed into the ravine, taking some prisoners, but suffering unnecessary casualties themselves. It was unnecessary and foolish courage. Another thing, if a boy got himself hurt in a minefield, the problem was not to get someone to rescue him, but to hold back a multitude."

Major Mair recites another example of the Force's casual attitude when he recalls, "during the fighting on Port Cros, there was a lull during the assault waves. I stretched out behind some rocks in order to get a quick nap. I was just about dozing when a soldier started to take a piss in my face. I told the chap to move over."

Gus Heilman, who was now a major, supplied another example of the Forceman's misguided courage. The Germans confronting his battalion were holed up in a fortified château with a well-armed group of men. Sergeant Bernie Helming happened to find a telephone wire leading to the château. He tapped it, asked to speak to the commander, and when that perplexed officer came to the phone Helming demanded that he surrender. The German wanted a prisoner brought to the phone to prove prisoners were not killed. Word was sent back to Colonel Walker, who oblingingly found a prisoner for the commander. But in the meantime, Major Heilman became impatient. "Oh, the hell with it," he said, "let's go on in." In thirty minutes the fighting was over and the big guns had been silenced.

By August 16 the island had fallen to the Force. Other Allied assignments had been carried out with equal success and General Alexander Patch's invasion army began its steady march through Southern France.

Note by Major W. Winston Mair: "We were shelled shortly after we landed on Port Cros. An American medical sergeant, J. L. Walkmeister, who had a handlebar mustache, was hit. I pulled him behind a building, but it was too late. The sergeant died."

Sergeant Jake Walkmeister was later described by Colonel Burhans as "1st Regiment's friendly, mustachioed medic who was one of the best liked men in the Force." In an organization noted for its colorful characters, Sergeant Jake stood out. He was a workhorse during battle, but at other times he showed an uncanny ability to twist almost every situation to his own benefit.

Sergeant Walkmeister had been killed by a burst of shrapnel from a shell which had detonated against a cement cistern cover. He had gone out of the aid station to lead a wounded soldier to safety. The recollections of Walkmeister were completed by Lewis Stuart, who wrote:

"Jake was no storybook hero. He lived solely, in his own words, to make a buck, and he was not particular in the means employed. On the opposite side, his quick wit and deft hands, plus a judicious mixture of alcohol and pineapple juice, eased the lot of many a mangled soldier who passed through his aid station.

"There are many wearing the Silver Star and higher honors who did less than Jake to merit them, and there are many behind bars who did less than Jake to merit their punishment. Had he lived, by now he would have a $250,000 house in Miami Beach, or Los Angeles, or be in jail, or possibly both."

After the fall of the islands, the Force was once again brought into contact with General Frederick. Frederick had formed a fine combat unit out of the odds and ends which had been assigned to his 1st Airborne Task Force and had handled it so successfully that only a handful of men had been lost in the invasion drop. He was now in the process of relieving the 36th Division to continue the drive east to the Italian border. The General, understandably, was overjoyed at the reunion. He made many trips to Force Headquarters and, on the first one, he greeted the men massed in parade ranks with, "I'm sure glad to see you."

Force discipline faltered at this point. One man yelled, "General, you can say that again . . . we're sure as hell glad to see you!" And the remaining ranks broke into wild cheering.

On another occasion, the General was touring the Force sector in a jeep. He stopped to talk to a few of his old Forcemen, and, as usual, asked if there was anything that anyone needed. John Bourne recalls, "A man from the 3rd Regiment, a Southerner, said he hadn't had any 'Snoose' since he got to France. That night, two cartons of Copenhagen snuff came up with the rations. This was typical of the man."

After the invasion of Southern France, Frederick was again moved to a higher post when, in December 1944, he became commander of the 45th Division. After a series of postwar appointments in the United States, he became the commanding general of the headquarters command of the U. S. Forces in Austria. This was May 1948. The following February he was given command of the 4th Division at Fort Ord, California, and remained with the unit after its redesignation as the 6th Infantry (Training) Division.

In May 1951, he was named chief of the joint U. S. Military Aid Group to Greece. General Frederick retired after this assignment.

In a report issued by the Canadian Government,* a description of the next few months receives scant attention. The entire campaign is dismissed with one terse paragraph which reads:

> The force's D-day task of capturing the two easternmost of the Iles d'Hyères was easily accomplished on 15 August 1944. After transferring a few days later to the mainland, the force advanced rapidly eastward along the Riviera coast and by 9 September had taken up a line of positions behind the Franco-Italian boundary. Positions were held here until 28 November.

Of course, it is a cliché to once again say that no action is a fringe action to the men who die in it. And, although the

* Colonel Stanley W. Dziuban, Chief of Military History, *United States Military Collaboration with Canada in World War II* (Washington, D.C., 1955).

* 232

enemy remained sparse and scattered, the fact remains that men were wounded and killed in the drive north to Le Veyans, the eastward turn toward Grasse, and on to the banks of the Var River.

This Force drive eastward throughout the Riviera country was only part of Patch's Seventh Army "show." The rest of his units fared about the same. Progress was good, much ground was taken, but some men died. The resistance to the advance was never along one solid line . . . it was a matter of stumbling over a strong point here and a rear-guard action there.

Most of the back-pedaling was being executed by German divisions, half of whose personnel were Poles, other Slavs and second-line troops in similar categories. But when a Forceman was hit by a bullet from an enemy gun, cliché or not, the damage was of course the same, even though a discouraged and beaten man's hand was on the trigger.

Account by John R. Dawson, 2nd Regiment: "We were hauled down the coast to a place called Bylvabelle to get ready for the march east. The French First Army was moving through the same area, mostly North Africans and coal-black Senegalese, who made our quartermaster truck drivers look practically Nordic by comparison. They also had the novel, by our standards, custom of trailing their women and goats behind them, and the lack of glamor of the former led some of our men to speculate that perhaps the officers got the goats and the enlisted men had to make-do with the women. There was at least one public-accommodations establishment of French girls, I'm told, that had two queues of prospective customers, one French and one Force. Race-conscious Yanks and Canadians wouldn't allow coloreds in our line, but the extra-black Senegalese were readily admitted to the French line, and both lines converged to the same waiting (and bed) rooms.

"The trip across the Riviera was more like an extended route march than a battle to Rangers and Forcemen who were used to a rougher grade of competition. Our biggest scrap was at Villeneuve-Loubet. We forded the river, and as we came into town in the early morning, it looked like another of those occasions when the Germans had pulled out on us. We started down a street which had houses on one side and an open park on the other. Frenchmen came out of their houses in considerable numbers to see the Americans or relieve their bladders, the second seeming to preoccupy them most, for there was a solid rank of peeing Frenchmen. About that time some fire started coming from some cleverly camouflaged foxholes. They were designed to cover the river, and the Jerries were as surprised as we were, and though we had two or three wounded, they had let too many of us get too close. They were grenaded out fast.

"The town's M.D., Dr. Lefebvre, was very active as the day wore on, in patching up our wounded. I don't recall where our medics were, but he was with our company, and I imagine the townspeople acted as stretcher-bearers to get casualties back. Anyhow, as dusk approached and we expected a counterattack, my platoon was holed up in and around the doc's house. He and his wife were giving us wine and brandy, the full V.I.P. treatment. A bit later, they turned sour and sullen, scarcely speaking. I had quite a time getting the story from them, but they finally told me their house had been looted by some of our men. I was embarrassed. It seemed too dirty after the events of the afternoon and besides, with a probable counterattack coming up, it is best to be on good terms with your sawbones.

"I called the guys together, told them what had happened, and said no charges would be made if the stuff reappeared in a certain room in ten minutes. It did, and the doc and his wife were pleased. I hope that it wasn't restolen as we left.

"Our battalion came out of the hills above Menton, and approached it via the coastal road. We became the extreme right flank, and first platoon, Sixth Company, were literally touching the water. We lived in a millionaire's mansion, which did depreciate a bit with artillery fire over the months. We settled down to patrolling, laying mines, and an occasional pass back to Nice."

Percy Crichlow: "For me the most interesting part of the chase was just before Grasse. We pushed forward by night with my platoon leading. With us was a Frenchman who was armed with a .22 pistol, who was going to guide us. Eventually I was told to halt and set up around a bend in the road and to send forward a party to reconnoiter. The patrol went out and after a long wait they started back through my outpost, but I could hear hobnail boots. So could my men around the road. But the patrol didn't seem to hear it. Then suddenly one of my lads, Martin, dashed forward and grasped the man in the hobnail boots on the tail of the patrol. He was a German.

"I learned later from the patrol that they went up to the higher road, and just as they were going to come back they had to duck for cover as a German company moved quickly down the road, obviously withdrawing hurriedly before our advance. The German apparently was one of the sad sacks that couldn't keep up, spotted our patrol which he mistook for the tail of his column, tried to catch up with it until Martin grabbed him.

"One night the same Frenchman turned up. He was guiding a patrol, but he wanted a safe line to patrol. He obviously was just going to be a nuisance. I tried to reason with him and show him that nobody goes out to find out what he already knows; the object of a patrol is to find out about an area which is not well-known. As he wouldn't listen, I sent him straight ahead. I never saw him or his pistol again."

There are a few other comments worth recording because they illustrate that although the personnel of the Force had drastically changed, the spirit remained substantially the same.

One ex-cowboy from Wyoming recalled that "Lt. Col. Moore, with the object of improving our morale, would walk along the top of the ridge of the French-Italian border in view of the enemy. After he'd gone, they'd throw all the artillery at where he'd been, that they could." Bill Mauldin subsequently used this incident as the basis for one of his most popular cartoons.

The story of Colonel Waters, who was the CO of the 2nd Battalion, 2nd Regiment, and had his command post in Averill Harriman's villa is also interesting. It was quite far forward and it was dangerous to go to headquarters during daylight hours, because of snipers. Enough wires still supplied sufficient electricity to the villa, but frequently they would be broken by artillery fire. Waters would phone back for French civilians to fix the electric wires . . . telling them it was an emergency as his beer was getting warm and his food was spoiling. The French electricians would present an itemized bill for repairs, showing so many feet of wire used, so many hours of labor, etc. Waters would sign the bill and say, "Send it to MacKenzie King (the Prime Minister of Canada)."

After the dissolution of the Force, an Inspector General arrived one day with a sheaf of these bills and an order from King that this officer should be court-martialed. The men told the IG that Waters had been killed. The IG was much relieved and so marked the file. The file had gone from the Prime Minister to the War Department, to the Canadian Army, to the British Army, to the American Army, and then to the Regiment.

Another anecdote illustrates that the Forcemen remained in character. Once, during a cold train trip, there was a stop-over at a way station. The trainmaster had a little stove in his shack. When the man's back was turned, the Forcemen removed the stove. When the loss was discovered, a detailed search of the train was made before it was permitted to depart . . . but no stove was found. A few miles out of the station, a stovepipe appeared out of the side of one of the boxcars. The stove, with a nice hot fire, had been successfully hidden. Walter Grabiec, who relayed the story, commented, "Only a Forceman could have figured out a way to steal a hot stove."

The greatest source of concern on this march was not the enemy, but fatigue. Skripac, of the 2nd Regiment, said, "As we pushed along the Riviera, we kept going day and night. One night, Butch Rohaly said, 'I wish those Jerries would open up on us pretty soon and stop us!' "

Sergeant Kubler almost solved the fatigue problem. "We grabbed us a bus someplace and went along almost like sightseers. Then we had to go uphill; the damn bus couldn't make it. We all got out and pushed it up. Captain Peters came up and reamed me out; said we were getting too far ahead of everything. He took our bus back with him. Pete was a real good Joe, but I still honestly think he pulled rank on that bus deal. On foot again we would go, up one hill and then down into the valley. We'd be dead tired approaching those quaint little villages. As we approached these small hamlets, the people would embrace us, give us fruit, bread and wine. By the time we got on the far side of those towns we were running, singing, dancing with the girls, revived and very unsoldierly. But we kept going."

A Canadian newspaperman was awed by the endurance of the Forcemen as he accompanied them part of the way on the march:

> I have seen them start marching with full packs under a broiling sun, trudge all afternoon along a dirty, dusty road, or throughout the forests of Southern France, in order to reach the starting line at nightfall, so they could fight.
>
> I have seen them fight for 60 hours straight to capture a town, then still have enough energy left to help the townspeople celebrate their liberation in an all-day party before they moved forward again at night.

More than one Forceman, when asked for his chief recollection of the French civilians, answers, emphatically, "The Hair-Lined Streets!" The reference is made to the shaved heads of the French girls who slept with the Germans during the Occupation.

A headquarters corporal: "The people here were really bitter toward the Germans, and we saw many of them hanged by the Resistance people before we could get to them. They also treated their own people who had collaborated with the Germans quite harshly. The women were shaved and paraded in mule carts naked through the streets. Many of the males were shot or hanged. In Nice we came upon several German officers hanging from the power poles on the streets."

Of course, the Forcemen could be depended upon to give their own type of recognition to the baldhead badge of shame. Major Frank Fryza remembers: "At the time it just seemed odd with all this hair lying on the streets and walks. We soon learned from some FFI guys, that any girl or woman who 'collaborated' was shorn of her locks. Girls wearing scarfs around their heads were then sought after by some of our men for a little 'collaborating.' "

Nice . . . Cannes . . . Menton . . . these were the exotic resorts where the Force now found themselves. The warm September sun saw the Forcemen maintaining a schedule of patrols and occasionally engaging the enemy, but it also saw the Forcemen luxuriating among surroundings that were light years away from the cold and lonely and bitter slopes of Monte la Difensa.

The First Special Service Force had always been noted for its high percentage of men who were Absent Without Official Leave. Of course, the men never stayed away from the Force when combat threatened . . . but whenever possible, they went AWOL from base hospitals and rest camps in order to be on hand with their friends when a battle was about to be joined.

Now the pendulum swung the other way. Many Forcemen, bored with the inactivity and aware that there was no further prospect for the Devils' Brigade other than disbandment, slipped away to follow personal trails which were neither blessed nor understood by the American and Canadian higher commands.

Colonel Burhans went back to Southern France just a few years ago on a sentimental visit to review the scenes and retrace the paths that the Force had known during the war. While there he met more than a dozen Forcemen who had gone AWOL during this period and were still living in France. Most of them were married and had families. This might have been expected. The ideal Forceman was not a creature who would meekly submit to the dictates of the rear-echelon administrators whose star was now in the ascendant.

But it should never be forgotten that no Forceman ever deserted a *battlefield*. The Canadian correspondent who had accompanied the Force on its march through France and who had marveled at its endurance, also commented on this strange facet of the Force's proud record. He said:

> They often go A.W.O.L. from hospitals. Occasionally a letter concludes, "One of our ambulances is missing since your man went A.W.O.L."

Two men who were unable to reach the F.S.S.F. in time for the invasion of France stowed away in an L.C.I. carrying engineers, hit the beach D-day, and worked with them until located by the Force. The engineers were very proud of them as they understood they were A.W.O.L. from the hospital.

The stay at the luxury resorts resulted in this particular phase of the Force's history earning the name "The Champagne Campaign." But the stories of those days all have a peculiarly *fin de siècle* feeling.

Conrad Legault became the Force's liaison officer with the French Forces of the Interior, Pat O'Neill, the redoubtable Irishman, became the Provost Marshal of Monte Carlo shortly before being recalled to the Far East command to become a member of the advance party going into Japan. All the other colorful figures continued being just as colorful . . . but with one major difference. They no longer merged their personalities into the Force. Their exploits and misdeeds had become individual stories.

Toward the end of November 1944, the 1st Airborne Task Force was dissolved. On November 22, Major General Frederick visited the Force headquarters at Menton in order to present awards and bid a final farewell to the men who were as dear to him as if they had been his brothers.

On November 28, the three regiments of the First Special Service Force were pulled back to Villeneuve-Loubet. The final days of the Force were now at hand.

The day of the need for a small, elite assault force had passed. Divisions, corps and armies were required for the final struggle with Germany and there was no longer any place for the handful of men who made up the First Special Service Force. There were no more contests for the next mountaintop.

The Force had rarely numbered more than 1,600 combat men at any one time. Yet, in its brief history, it had many times that number of casualties. Hundreds had died in battles; battles which are now only brief historical footnotes but which, at the time, represented major gains for the nations arrayed against the Axis.

On December 5, the call went out for the final parade. The Force gathered on the Loup River flats at Villeneuve-Loubet and heard their chaplains read a prayer for the men who had fallen from Hyères to Menton.

Then the flags moved forward . . . the colors of the United States, Canada and the Force's own slapped in the wind as the adjutant read the inactivation order.

The red Force flag with its black dagger on white shield was wound to its staff and the casing slipped over it. At a barked command, the Canadians withdrew from ranks and formed their own battalion which then marched, behind their own colors, past the United States contingent, still standing at attention in the just-broken ranks.

For a unit which had prided itself on its scorn for the dramatic gesture, the breakup of the Force became a surprisingly sentimental, even tear-stained occasion.

Although, as Colonel Akehurst admitted, most of the men realized that the Force's dissolution "was bound to come about sooner or later," the actual inactivation order represented the coming to pass of a dreaded event.

The men had become brothers. Wearing the same uniform, laughing at the same jokes and swearing at the same enemy, the lines between the soldiers of Canada and America had been totally erased. There was a general shock when a man was finally identified as a Yank and another as a Canadian. There had never been time during the vicious battles to establish national origin . . . it had been enough to know that in any tight spot one man could count on another.

This was a highly emotional moment. The tears that rolled down the cheeks of the men in the line and the men marching past them were duplicated by the tears in the eyes of wounded Forcemen in hospitals all over the European Theater of Operations when they heard of the loss of that identity which every one of them had cherished.

The Canadians, of course, had also prized the informality which characterized the comparatively easy discipline of the American Army and the liberal give-and-take which existed between its officers and enlisted men.

The feeling of the Americans equaled that of the Canadians in its intensity. As a matter of fact, to quote a typical reaction, "I suppose this was the saddest day ever as far as we were concerned. This was the day I saw some of the toughest S.O.B.'s ever break down in tears. As the Canadians pulled out, some of us Americans ran alongside and behind the trucks for a mile with tears in our eyes."

Another man said, "I was really badly broken up as the Force had been through so much together, the training, fighting and all the good times. The pride in each other will stay in my memories for the rest of my life. It was too bad it had to be broken up as it was the finest unit I have served in my twenty years of service. And I have been in the infantry until 1960 when I entered the support troops. We need a few outfits like this SSF today for some of the missions the Army is given."

A few took the breakup in a philosophical manner:

"We were of course shocked when the Force was disbanded, but it had served its purpose, and due to the severe losses that it had suffered, it was impossible to secure the type of replacements required. It was rapidly becoming an ordinary outfit. I feel that the disbandment was necessary and came at a most opportune time for all concerned."

"By the time the Force reached the point of breaking up, there had been about 600 per cent turnover in the troop strength. Some of us had witnessed our friends mangled and we had lost friends daily, so we had about come to the point where we were just hardened against anything; therefore the feeling that remained in us all at the breaking of the Force is really not to be described. Wasn't as bad on some as on others. When we first went to Europe I knew most every man's face in the Force. I had been in personal contact with him at one time or another in his training. But when the Force was disbanded there was not too many of those faces left."

Of course, some were bitter. Their reactions indicated frustration, a feeling of having been cheated, and anger. Surprisingly anger, because they seemed to have deliberately closed their eyes to the bald fact that the First Special Service Force was designed to be used in a manner that invited their deaths. The phrase "suicide outfit" is overworked in the military lexicon. But if any unit merited that description, it had to be the Force.

Remember, these men were realists. It is not possible to believe that they did not realize that, inherent in every new assignment given them, was the possibility that any or all of them would be killed. And they willingly followed, indeed idolized, the leader who sought out such assignments for them and then gave the orders for their participation. Obviously, the emotion they felt for their outfit and their leader was strong enough to overcome the normal human fear of death.

Perhaps one man spoke for them all when he said, in this final comment, "I hated to see the breakup happen as I had found a home."

It was the home that Geoffrey Pyke had envisioned and Robert Frederick had built.

Epilogue

Thus ended a remarkable international experiment. The mixed composition of the Force had not prevented it from attaining an extraordinary regimental spirit; perhaps, indeed, it was in great part responsible for that spirit. Canadians and Americans have never found it hard to co-operate, and in the First Special Force they worked and fought together in a relationship which helped to make the Force the splendid fighting unit it was.

—"The Canadian Army 1939-1945" *

After the breakup, the men of the First Special Service Force were scattered much as a wall, once crumbled to dust, can be blown to whatever corners of the earth the wind chooses to seek.

Edwin A. Walker, now a Brigadier General, took a nucleus of Force members with him into the 474th Infantry Regiment (Separate), a new organization formed from fragments of others which had been either decimated or inactivated. This regiment, under Walker's command, served briefly in Germany and then, in the weird completion of a cycle which Geoffrey Pyke might have appreciated, was sent

* Colonel C. P. Stacey, O.B.E., *The Canadian Army* (Ottawa, Edmond Cloutier, Kines Printers, 1948).

to Norway after the final Allied victory, to take part in the disarming and repatriating of the German Army in the Oslo zone.

The Canadians went back to serve in various units under their own flag.

On October 15, 1945, the 474th Regiment sailed for the United States. Only a handful of ex-Forcemen who had known each other in Helena were aboard the ship.

Viewed pragmatically, the military experiment known as the First Special Service Force was a complete failure. Although it gained every honor in battle, rarely took an unsuccessful step, and was recognized by many responsible observers as the best combat unit among the Allied forces in World War II (some have even described it as the best small combat unit that America has ever fielded), the fact remains that it was never used for the purpose of its original design.

"It was the misuse of an unparalleled weapon," said Sholto Watt, the highly respected wartime correspondent for the Canadian press. Watt spent much time with the Force and filed a series of reports from Europe's battlefields which are models of professional objectivity. But he found himself, finally, lamenting, "It is no less than tragic that this North American *corps d'elite* could not have been employed in the lightning, staggering blow for which it been trained."

Many agreed. Bill Mauldin, Ernie Pyle, Clark Lee, and dozens of other seasoned correspondents found themselves detailing the situational misdirections of the men of the Force in a way that almost approached emotional involvement. This cruel and reckless waste of good men is not a lightly evolved accusation. The profligate squandering is apparent to anyone who followed the Force from its beginning to its end.

The same note of regret is sounded by Col. Stanley W. Dziuban in his book, *U. S. Military Collaboration with Canada in World War II.* * Colonel Dziuban speaks of this misuse of superior men, material and equipment in dispassionate terms, but the inference that their accomplishments could have been so much more is clearly audible:

* Op. cit.

Throughout its history, the First Special Service Force never found employment of the highly specialized types for which it had been trained. Despite its special equipment and training the Force had never made a parachute assault or operated in snow country, and of its two amphibious operations, one was unopposed. Its greatest operational value had been in employment of its hand-picked, high-caliber volunteers in difficult assault and raiding operations. In such operations, the Force was remarkably effective, as its record and the numerous commendations received from higher echelon commanders testify. Nevertheless, the Force represented a costly expenditure of resources and a complex administrative effort, particularly to Canada because of the Force's habitual remoteness from Canadian Administrative machinery. Furthermore, the nature and status of the Force required repeated examination by the Combined Chiefs of Staff of proposals for employment of this body of less than 2,000 men, as well as diplomatic exchanges to obtain Canadian acceptance of the proposals, all-in-all an inordinate amount of high-level consideration in relation to the size of the Force.

From the point of view of Canadian-American relations, however, the unique experiment was a remarkable success. There were other benefits, too, not foreseen by the original proponents of the Force. During the postwar period, a number of proposals of various kinds have been advanced in the United Nations and elsewhere, for the establishment of a military force comprising nationals of many countries integrated in a manner similar to the First Special Service Force. Those who may be charged with the planning for, or establishment of, such a force will glean much from the experience of the Force, even despite its limited binational aspect and the very favorable circumstances of the administrative and operational problems involved.

Before discussing the conclusions yielded by an examination of the short life of the First Special Service Force, it is first necessary to glance briefly at the present-day unit which is officially considered its successor: The Special Forces.

This group, picked from among the most competent 10 per cent of the officers and enlisted men in the Army, is an elite force in every sense of the word. Its members wear a distinctive uniform, a green beret, and are more than expert in the technique of demolition, parachuting, and guerrilla warfare.

Their average age is thirty. Most of them are married. They place great stress on education and an imposing percentage of normally off-duty hours is spent in some kind of advanced study. Without exception, every man in the unit radiates an aura of self-confident ability. They are men who inspire respect.

President Kennedy's widow asked that a detachment from the Special Forces be included in her husband's funeral ceremonies and their employment in Viet Nam and in other parts of the world has consistently resulted in the reflection of further credit on the unit.

The link between this force and the hellions of the Devil's Brigade was made official at ceremonies held at Fort Bragg, North Carolina, in 1960, where "the Honor and the Heritage" of the First Special Service Force was presented to the Special Forces as the highlight of a two-day program. All the surviving members of the original group were invited to attend, and the guest of honor was Major General Robert Frederick (Ret.), who presented the original Forces colors to Colonel Edwards, then commander of the 7th Special Forces Group.

It was an impressive ceremony, but there was a certain amount of irony inherent in the scene. As the superbly schooled young Forcemen marched in precision ranks before the reviewing stand, the thought must have occurred to more than one old Forceman that he would never have been considered eligible to join this new outfit. Frederick had asked of his men only that they had gone as far as the third grade in school and closed his eyes to every other black mark on a soldier's record so long as it indicated that the man was basically a scrapper. Today's Force has a far more imposing list of entrance requirements.

But certain questions and comparisons are unavoidable.

Was the drinking and roistering and plundering of the old Force an inexcisable facet of the kind of soldier who is wise enough to know that he has been given a suicide mission, brave enough to shrug at it, and strong enough to pull it off?

The old Force never took a backward step. They prized, beyond any fear of death, the dignity which simply belonging to the Devil's Brigade gave to them. Today's Forcemen are not unimaginative. They have little need to find their self-respect in the massed personality of a unit because each of them is a superior man, chosen for superior qualities and within himself can recognize abundant sources of security even if he had never been tapped to wear the green beret. The cold courage of the dedicated professional marks their every move in combat, but it's hard to picture them swaggering around in a burlesque village behind enemy lines.

At times, perhaps now, we must consider the need for a certain number of wild and irresistible fighters who believe so deeply in a man or an idea that they advance to the stature of giants. In the case of the Force, youth and maximum personal utility came together with such impact that it proved capable of jarring an entire army, Clark's Fifth, loose from a shackling situation.

This is not a phenomenon to be disregarded. Treated as a "sport" it is meaningless. But carefully documented and studied, it becomes an important addition to basic military and even geopolitical knowledge.

The primary conclusion from the study of the activities of the First Special Service Force seems to consist of a caution to recognize, prize and make full use of a Frederick or a Pyke whenever they appear. Frederick's rare qualities of leadership and Pyke's almost superhuman ability to reduce a complex problem into a series of simple answers represent valuable assets, and no establishment, be it military, political, or social, should be permitted to become so bogged down in an observance of its own mores that its only reaction to a radical thinker is to attempt to sweep him hastily under the rug.

The field success of the men of the Force is a story of first-rate teamwork. The present, never officially recognized antipathy of Canadians for Americans, and the incessant patronizing of Canadians by Americans constitute sorry evidence that the skein of victories smoothly rolled up by the Canadians and Americans in the First Special Service Force is being completely ignored. The wartime activities of the Force should have taught us that the boundary between Canada and America is an artificial line and that excessive nationalism in North America is also excessive ignorance.

If the United Nations could ever be made to function with anything approaching efficiency . . . which is, of course, another way of saying that if a majority of the human beings in the world ever decide that they honestly want a true family of nations, its law enforcement arm would, inevitably, closely resemble the profile molded out of a massing of the men of the First Special Service Force.

The formation of such a law-keeping body would require a Pyke to solve the problems of nationalism and to serve as the gadfly who chivvies the constituent countries into more than lip service and, quite possibly, to indicate where another Frederick could be found.

The new Frederick would attract a mix of outcasts and idealists and transform them into a unit capable of enforcing order in any part of the globe. His men would inspire respect because of the ferocity of their blind acceptance of the proposition that if he believed in maintaining world order, they should lay down their lives to see it attained.

The idealists would find an expression of their faith in the person of another Frederick and the outcasts would find an affirmation of their right to dignity in his person and in his faith.

These would not be professional mercenaries. These would be fighters for a cause and a man. If that man were accurately selected, his Force would have a value to world peace beyond any price.

Index

Baldwin, Orval J., 48, 50, 75, 76, 89, 98
  description of, 46
  diary of, 103
  report to Frederick, 59
  request for supplies, 103
Bazooka rocket launcher, 89
Beckett, R. W., 69, 137
Belgium, 12, 55
Belts, at battle on Difensa, 130
Belvoir, Fort, 62
Bennett, of 2nd Regiment, 162
Bennett, W. R., 62, 208
Benning, Fort, 60, 61, 66, 82
Berets, of Force, 34, 248
Berlin, Pyke in, 5
Bernal, J. D., 3, 17, 45
Bernstein, in battle on Difensa, 129
Berry, Capt., 160
Biblowitz, Sol, 186
Black Devil's Brigade, 166, 176, 178, 179
Blackburn, Blackie, 60
Bolero Plan, 28
Border, Capt., 133
Boroditsky, Sam, 60
Bourne, John, 95, 232
  at Anzio, 185
  in battle on Difensa, 134
  in Operation Anvil, 225
  in Rome, 216
  ski training of, 83
Boyce, W. E., 143
Bradford, Camp, 91, 92
Bragg, Fort, 247
Brave Men, 134, 136
British Broadcasting Co., 4
Brown, Norm, 228
Buckner, Simon B., 91, 95
Bundel, in battle on Difensa, 137
Burhans, Robert D., 32, 131
  in battle on Difensa, 145

  revisiting France, 239
  telephone conversation with Frederick, 76
  as Intelligence officer, 46
  on Marshall's death, 213
  move to Montana, 58
  recommends O'Neill, 78
  meeting with Roll, 50, 51
  recommends Shinberger, 52
  describing Walkmeister, 231
Burlington, Vt., 93, 95, 111, 112
Bursey, Pvt., 162
Bush, Chief Warrant Officer, 149
Bush, Jonas, 62
Bush, Vannevar, 17, 45
Bylvabelle, France, 233

Calgary, Canada, 61
California National Guard, 24
Cambridge University, 5
Cameron, Arky, 194
Camino Mountain, 121, 144
Canada, 32, 33, 36, 37, 46, 88, 198
Canadian Army Chief of Staff, 33
Canadian General Staff, 34
Canadian National Research Council, 35
Canadians, in Force, 20, 21, 34, 35, 58, 60–65, 69, 70, 77, 198, 201, 242
  casualties of, 198
Capa, Robert, 149, 161, 163, 164
Cassino, battle of, 159
Casualties
  Canadian, 198
  in Force, 145, 148, 198, 240
Caucasus Mountains, 89
Cavalier Bar and Grill, Charlottesville, 81
CCC Camps, 52
Ceppagno, Italy, 153
Champagne Campaign, 226, 240

Quisling Cove, 103

Rachui, Bill, 21, 133, 213
Radcliffe, Taylor M., 160, 181, 182, 210
Radicosa Mountain, 153–155, 158, 174
Raincoat Operation, 119
Randall, Ralph, 188
Randle, Sgt., 145
Ranger battalions, 196, 197, 202, 209, 233
Rasconne, Jerry, 228
Rattlesnakes, 53, 55, 83
Reader's Digest, 156
Recreational unit, Force mistaken for, 57, 159, 220
Remetanea, battle of, 119–144, 149
Replacement Depot (Repple Depple), 118
Reuters, Copenhagen, 6
Riviera area, 226–227, 233
Robinson, W. J., 60
Rocca Massima, Italy, 205
Rodehayer, Gerald, 98
Rohaly, Butch, 237
Roll, Finn, 47, 50, 51, 107, 125, 131, 135, 163, 164
father murdered, 186
questioning prisoners, 180
Rome, battle for, 200–218
Roosevelt, Franklin D., 10, 15, 17, 42, 168
Rothlin, Capt., 129, 131
Ruhleben internment camp, 6, 7
Russia, battles in, 87, 89
Russian Embassy, 30
Ryan, James, 187, 204

Sabine, Sgt., 197
Salerno, Italy, 225
Sammucro Mountain, 145, 150, 151, 152, 153, 154

Sample, Clarence, 154
San Francisco, Calif., 23, 224
San Francisco Bay, 97, 98
San Pietro, Italy, 145
Sanders, Forceman, 203
Sandhurst, England, 5
Santa Maria, Italy, 118, 133, 148, 165, 225, 228
Sapienza, Italy, 210, 211, 218, 219
Savage, Lt., 149
Schaeffer, Harold, 66
Scott, Fort, 25
Sector, Jack, 60, 184, 201, 208
Sessuno, raid on, 183
Severeid, Eric, 216
Shafer, Robert K., 92, 137, 213
Shearer, Buck, 190
Sheldon, William G., 197, 201
Shell Petroleum, 8
Shelton, W. B., 66
Shinberger, John Baird, 48, 49, 51, 54, 57, 68, 98
Bible study of, 53
birth of, 52
and CCC camps, 52
death of, 55
joining Force, 47
promotion of, 58
rattlesnakes of, 53, 55, 83
receiving Distinguished Service Cross, 55
recruiting party led by, 82
in seminary, 55
training standards of, 56, 77
in West Point, 52
Sicily, 148
Simms, Sgt., 109
Skomski, Anthony, 66, 75, 80, 219, 220
Skripac, Anthony, 214, 237
Slatumas, Stan, 139
Slawson, Bill, 118

Robert H. Adleman

Born in 1919, Robert Adleman was a longtime inhabitant of the American newspaper world, having written for many papers and edited a chain of weeklies. A graduate of law school, he entered the Army as a private during World War II, and emerged as a much-decorated major in the Air Force.

Colonel George Walton

Born in 1904, Colonel George Walton (USAR, Ret.) was a veteran of World War II and an actual member, by attachment, of the Devil's Brigade, having served with the Force in Italy. Also a lawyer and a former statesman (he helped overthrow the notorious Hague machine in New Jersey), Colonel Walton is the author of the *The Wasted Generation*, a study of draft-age failures in the United States.